Midnight Sun

A Novel by Alexander Hunsucker

Adult/Young Adult

Literary Gothic

Published by Franklin Publishers

Printed in the United States of America

For permissions, inquiries, or additional copies, contact:

Franklin Publishers

www.franklinpublishers.com

MidnightSun

Our faith does
not lay in the
stars,
not in the human
genome,
nor any other
form of
determinism.
We become what
we chose to be."

- Rabbi Lord
Jonathan Sacks

DEDICATIONS

This book is dedicated to love and my wonderful husband

Gerardo Rojas

You are my heart. Through you I've found that conscious love I so desired my whole life.

This also goes out to my mother Priscilla

You were my first love and my first heartbreak.

I think about you every day.

Forward

What you are about to read is based on my real-life experiences, with real friends, family, and other worldly beings, all documented meticulously by a sixteen year old Alexander Hunsucker who crashed on his Nanna's couch in El Sereno (Or "Woodrow" as I've come to call it.), California in two-thousand-eighteen.

This is my version of those twisted and harrowing events.

This is my cursed videotape. And I hope you enjoy it. I had an interesting time writing it.

I would like to preface this by saying I did not write these things to tell anyone what to believe or to state firmly that my consciousness is based in some higher realm of existence, or that my internalizations of the life that I've lived is meant to be definitive for you or others who were along for the ride—For better or for worse.

I wrote this to turn super dark times into something poetic, raw, and reflective of what these people, those experiences, and those times mean to me now. And to encourage you, should you have the desire, to look in and ponder the very nature of your own life, and ask, "What am I, really?" Just as I had all those years ago.

Are you the perceptions you have of yourself? Are you others' perceptions of you? Are you a fluke in a vast indifferent universe? Or something more? Crafted by the divine?

I believe we exist in a kind of existential superposition. The self is a collage caught between states. Haunted by the ghosts of people and the ghosts of who we remember ourselves to be. I also believe we don't have to feel so low, and we don't have to aim so high to make any of this life make sense or feel worthwhile. The universe doesn't have to be so dark. We are what we create. And our creation is only as Good as our idea of the world around us. How sublime is that? That our collective human condition is dictated by each and every one of us? Our understanding of the world and ourselves are an amalgam of every Living, Conscious, perspective. That on its own is amazing and terrifying. Imagine what we could achieve if we loved each other as we were meant to.

My entire life I had to fight constantly against the perceptions of me, the reality of me, my potential and the conflict I had within myself. My entire life I just wanted to know,

"What am I, really?"

I never got an answer. Along the way, I lost my family, my home, and I lost myself. More than once. Following that, one of my dearest friends died, I ran away, I fell in love for the first time, had my first heartbreak, met the love of my life—and fell in love again. Slowly, I pieced together a better response to that question;

I am here now. One day I won't be. The only thing that matters is the choices I make right now—because, in the end, it is those choices that will become the definitive answer I seek.

If I'm remembered for anything, I want to be remembered for my heart. I am someone who strives to be a Good man. Good for my husband, good for my peers, and most importantly of all; Good for myself and Good for G-d, my beautiful, loving, creator.

I don't always hit, but I give every swing all I have.

Who are you?

TABLE OF CONTENTS

I had that nightmare again—a memory's afterimage.

Beneath a glimmering red star, its hatred searing through the thick grey sky like molten steel, I stand at the edge of a cliff, hovering just above my oblivion. The haze went on forever, blurring the line where the sky met the sea. And those treacherous, swirling waves above were indistinguishable from those below. I was here just a few months ago, and every night, I return to this cliff in my sleep. And it's the same every time. I toss myself below with my eyes wide open—my last attempt to snuff out the seemingly timeless agony of being unloved by you, Mother.

It is as if in some way I really did die in the water. My body was the only thing that survived the fall. What of the soul I once possessed? It has been left right there in the waves, suspended in that moment forever. I may take in breath, but I do not know what it means to be alive anymore. This dark, loveless, existence is beyond consciousness. I am only allowed these harrowing glimpses of the surface, of this perfectly curated Inferno filled with every kind of pain.

Mother, I'm so tired. I often wonder as I clutch my stomach against the pain, what if I devoured you? Bones and all? Would I then finally feel your love inside me?

Or would you rather continue devouring me instead? And cursing my body as you have in life, saying, *"This tastes Vile,"*

Oh, Mother, my act of love. I've lost all of me between your teeth. And I weep at the sight of it.

Chapter One

And as I rise, I sigh with so much sorrow. The melancholy of life's insignificance plays on my mind the moment I wake from sleep. It is a harsh fact that's haunted me for a while now, like death is a shadow always with me that I can never outrun. Ever since that night, I feel like death and me are walking hand in hand, chained by the wrist. Together forever. I feel its icy breath tickle the back of my neck like an unwanted kiss.

There are those who spout the passive truth that *"life can end at any moment,"* But I don't think that philosophy bears any tangible fruit unless you've experienced any sort of death firsthand. Only then can the sheer magnitude of your own mortality's grand implications change you. But I did not expect it to change me into this macabre, nihilistic parody of myself. I wasn't the slightest grateful to be alive when I finally washed up on shore, coughing up pints of saltwater through a tight and hoarse throat. The pain haunted me for days, a feeling of sandpaper rubbing against the walls of my esophagus. Every time I took in breath. A constant reminder. And I think the intense retching lowered the tone of my voice an octave or two. A once polite sound broken into a low and gruff harangue I did not recognize as my own. I wished I'd simply drowned instead of washing up on shore, transformed into this hideous thing with bruises that won't heal.

So much time has passed, and the emptiness has only expanded. That void housed in my chest could suck all the air from a zeppelin in a flash and still leave room for seconds, thirds, or, hell, even four-thousandths. A pain larger than my little ribs can handle. So much so that I wish I had died in the waters of my mother's womb instead, to spare me the cruelty of this waking life and the echoes of a promise that isn't kept: conscious love.

I sat alone in the darkness of the room I shared in shifts with my aunt Valene, wrapping my aching hand tight with boxer's tape I stole from her gym bag. And again I could feel that tug, that black hole drawing me in, that slipping further into my family's ways, becoming one with their bleak, frozen lives. All they are is all they'll ever be. And I fear that now I am the same. With every waking breath, my soul sinks deeper into whatever abyss holds theirs captive. I feel its hand beneath the floor, feeling me up as much as it can. It wants me forever.

We all live crammed together under one roof like some malformed coven of witches. I find it fitting, though, in a way only the damaged could find fitting. I can see us now, below, just as we are above, packed tightly in that spirit prison opposite Abraham's bosom. Paradise within a looking distance, but we'll never join them.

And... Oh, do I writhe over it. Feels like fourth-dimensional ants crawling all over me in every direction at once. And as they creep, they bite me, enjoying every tasty mouthful of this cursed skin. And it is a very real, non-metaphorical, generational curse seeping into every part of me. And I could trace it back to my mother, and her mother, and the mother before her mother—misshaping me into something else. Something likened to them. Miserable and cruel. All I have left that separates me from rest is the sheer indignance against this hopelessness. I have not yet resigned... and God knows I want to. It would be so much easier that way.

Today is Halloween, and yesterday I turned sixteen years old. I had that nightmare again—a memory's afterimage. I shook it away, only to meet sharp and cringe-inducing memories thereafter. Memories of the night before, tightening the muscles in my body like rubber bands on the verge to snap. It was starting up again, that same feverish anger that took hold before I lost it and plunged my fist into the drywall after last night's festivities

Despite everything that happened this summer, I still came back to this decrepit two-star town at the behest of her and the threat of police. It was one thing for her to lie—to report me as a runaway after she and her horde made me leave—tossing me out into the streets like trash! *But to throw me a birthday party and pretend that my suffering was nothing more than water under the bridge?* Like last summer was just some fit of mine and *she* were burying the hatchet? That was an offense I could not forgive. It makes me so angry that I could spit! It makes me want to— punch something.

I sighed. Because I came home and convinced myself that there was hope. That things would be different. But they were the same, and I spent the daylight hours of my birthday as I have every day since then, wasting in the dark by myself and eating old candy corn.

Tyler stopped by to wish me a Happy Birthday, the only soul on this wretched earth, apart from my brothers, whose words didn't make my blood curdle. I hadn't seen him since the night I returned. I couldn't face him after I came back to California. It's been too hard... But he was eager to see me again. And what better excuse to swing by unannounced than a birthday?

I wasn't angry, truly, I appreciate the effort. But it makes me hate myself for being unable to reciprocate... After he left, I slammed my head into the wall and made sure it hurt. *No good deed goes unpunished.*

Katie simply called, despite knowing well that I didn't want to hear it. I would have sent her to voicemail if I didn't feel so guilty about being cruel. She wished me good tidings, of course. She's been my best friend since middle school.

"Hey, I hope you have a good day today." A fruitless gesture for sure, anyone with more than two brain cells would see that any sort of happiness for The Great and Terribly Anguished Alexander Hunsucker would never manifest beyond the very idea of a wish. Her mother asked if there were any birthday plans at home, and I told her no. She wasn't entirely surprised. She doesn't hold my family in the highest regards, for good reason. Most people don't.

It wasn't until dusk when the loose candy in my room was no longer enough to satiate my body that I finally decided to drag myself from bed so I could eat something real. But as I laid there, staring into the faces the ceiling made in the dark, I wondered:

Is this really the human condition? Wake, piss, suffer, eat, shit, sleep, repeat?

I grimaced, all the muscles in my face twitching and morphing into man's hate as the burn of loathing flared in my chest like hot chains in Hell. My light—my potential—felt like a faint memory, almost gone. Like a story I had only heard once as a child and never again.

I tried to fight it, I reached down, deep inside of my spirit and reminded myself that this feeling isn't what it means to be human. This life, and their lives, are not the truth. To be human is to love and to care. It is the beauty in our finiteness. It's the art and music that we create. It is our connections and the cultures that we cultivate amongst each other. The vastness of our potential. Our incredible power to change. To evolve until we end.

But when I look into myself now, to find that true humanity, all I see is a pair of damned hollow eyes staring back—empty, black, and devoid of meaning, like some kind of Living Dead. And I start to think that perhaps I've just been in denial this whole time. Perhaps this *is* the human condition. To need love and care, but at the mercy of hate and bigotry. The tragedy of our finiteness. The dogma we invent to destroy each other. I gripped the door handle as if I could crush it, twisting it with defeat and muttering to myself,

"This isn't what I want to be."

The long, cavernous hallway stretched out before me, haunted by obscure shapes that lurched away from the thin beams of light that snuck in from the windows. I caught sight of a mysterious glow in the distance, something flickering just past the mouth of the hall. The orange hue of candlelight reflecting off the tile. I crept toward it quietly and beheld a secret gathering.

Had I stood in the room a little longer I would have been summoned to this display of ignorance by surprise. And that, I know, would have been worse for everyone. I was relieved that I caught it early. For my sake and theirs. I hate surprises. Although I was still undoubtedly stunned, at least I surprised them too. In a way we were even and that satisfied me.

They all stood promptly. Priscilla, my mother of sighs, hastily lit the last candle as I walked into the dining room. She seemed uncharacteristically nervous. My intense stare must have been lost on her, because she smiled at me as if I didn't happen upon this like a stag in headlights. And it was that same smile she's always had, the one that never met her eyes—but a smile nonetheless. Worn and true. It shook me up a bit to see. I had gotten so used to that permanent frown. The chains in my chest were doused and replaced this peculiar sense of shock and sadness. My little brothers, Tommy, Franky, and Jacob were all present beside her, seated impatiently but happy to see me. Their innocent faces unwound the tension in my eyes and my fists. Everyone was here—the aforementioned cursed-bloodline— The Hunsucker family: My Mother, my brothers, Nanna Irene, Great Aunt Val, Aunt Bonnie, Aunt Valene, and my cousins, Adriana, Stevie, and Max.

Was this by some cosmic fluke a sincere gesture? Or just cheaply made Hunsucker guilt? *"I hurt you, I give you something, it's all good now,"* Lava under the bridge.

I drew closer and they began to sing. A song sublime in its sorrow, a dirge disguised as celebration, their voices swelled across all tones, a haunting melody that made the hairs on my body stand on end. Before me was a homemade cake in the shape of a heart, multi-layered and asymmetrical, crowned with bright red candles and crushed Oreo bits.

And in my mother's distinct loopy script, the red frosting spelled out the hollow phrase:

Happy Birthday, Alexander. . .

One by one, I met each and every one of their eyes before bending over to blow out the flames, not bothering to be as puerile and sad as to make a wish. My dreams were snuffed out long before that cliff, the day my mother decided to homeschool me. I don't think they give scholarships to prestigious schools to homeschooled kids. And even if they did, the charm and prowess I once possessed are long gone. Take a look at me and these bruised eyes and grey skin, and see that I don't belong anywhere near the living. My brilliance and potential would be as lost on you as it is on my family and, now, me.

The darkness consumed everyone and everything the moment the candles died. I expected typical birthday charades to follow, vapid cheering and clapping after the candles were out—But it was just dead quiet all of a sudden. And it was so dark I could barely see my own hands before me. I took a moment to collect myself before I could even attempt to speak, but all I managed to choke out was the phrase,

"I don't know what to say." Which was the most honest thing I'd said in a long time.

I felt the ants crawling on my skin again. I didn't want to look any of them in the eyes again. I especially did not want to look at my mother, who lingered to the right of me, standing eerily still, like she wasn't even breathing. I knew I wouldn't be able to keep my head from spinning further off my neck much longer. I stared at the bloody wax seeping into the pores of the cake's white frosting and waited for something. Anything.

Then the room erupted into laughter and cackles like no silence had passed at all. The kitchen light appeared overhead, conjuring life back into the room. Valene, with her large, muscular arm, wrapped me in a playful squeeze and teased, *"Happy Birthday, Witch!"*

I guess they really are oblivious to the weight of my feelings, or else this party wouldn't be a thing right now. Either that or they know, and they don't care. Either way, my heart cracks another inch down the center. Before I could respond, a camera's flash blinded me, and I was pulled from my memory as the present spun back into view.

I winced, trembling hands before me. And the ache in my knuckles flared sharp and unforgiving. I pulled the tape tighter around my hand, but the frustration gnawed at me with jagged dog teeth, and with a long-drawn-out sob, I gave up, and let the shroud take me again. I threw myself back into the mattress and closed my eyes. The springs moaned beneath me like a wicked child's laughter. *EEEK—EEK—EEK—EEK!*

How my world has become alive with cruelty.

Sometime later, that time in between the day and the night arose, and I began to stir.

Typically, I grab a ball and toss it in the air, playing an aimless game of catch with myself until I get bore with that and open a book. I found myself picking at Natalie Babbit's *Tuck Everlasting* in episodes over the weekend, a brief tale of a young girl and a family of benign immortals that befriend her. It's a small, unassuming, little yellow book. Barely above a hundred pages long, but it's been shockingly hard to finish. I can't even bring myself to get to the end, and it's basically over now. I have yet to find out if she drinks from the jar of magic water the Tucks left her. I think the answer would spoil the experience. I prefer books with open endings, anyway.

I usually read more mature things. And there are a few things I read seasonally, like Shakespeare's *Hamlet* script and *New Moon* by Stephanie Meyer, madness and grief I find very relatable. My favorite book is *The Curious Incident of the Dog in the Night-time* by Mark Haddon.

I tossed Tuck Everlasting across the room, feeling more and more pathetic as I read on. I found it ridiculous how lost and gutted a story written for fifth graders was making me feel. I love to read. If nothing has changed about me since that cliff it's the fact that I'm a bookworm.

But reading this one brought me to tears.

The absurdity of it. My aching for another life—To be there, to be adored by the Tucks, a family cursed with eternal life but somehow untainted by its poison. Timeless, frozen people, but innocent. I imagined the joy of that life, of being loved by a family like that... and rubbed my eyes until they began to sting.

Whatever. I plan to do something other than reading today, and today's the best day for that, I think. Probably the only day I would, if I'm being entirely honest with myself. I think I'm gonna go outside and do Halloween.

I eased the door open, letting its hinges creak their protest. The sound bellowed throughout the house. And the hall was bathed in the purple glow of twilight. All the way down, through the punch-holes in the screen door, I saw Irene sitting alone on the porch, hunched over in a hand-held mirror and plucking her eyebrows.

I let out a sharp breath through my nose at the humor of the sight. Even in her sixties, the remnants of girlhood still shine through her. I could picture her in my mind, fifty years younger, still doing the same thing. On the rare occasion I ever visit her in her room, she's either doing that or something else small and repetitive, like putting on nail polish. And she's been that way as long as I can remember. All of the women in my household are like that, actually—girlie in the traditional sense. Pricey makeup, nice clothes, the whole deal. Even Valene, and she's a bodybuilder. I sucked in a heap of air and made my way toward her, dragging my feet the whole way.

She was startled by the metallic screech of the door when I swung it open, and she was even more surprised to see that it was *me* peeking over at her.

"*Oh,*" She cooed, too theatrically, clutching the mirror to her bosom, "*You're alive.*"

I tensed my jaw and forced myself not to overreact, especially when she began howling at her own remark with a playful smile. My face flushed all the way to my ears, not from her teasing but from the shame that crawled up my back for being offended by something so small. It humbled me enough to continue with a passive demeanor.

I forced a stiff chuckle to humor her, "Hah hah. Very funny." I let her finish giggling before I continued. "Hey, uh, do you think if I make plans to go out with a friend, you can drop me off?"

She blinked, surprised again.

"Well?" I blurted impatiently.

She took a second to gather herself in thought and hummed with obnoxious animation,

"Yeah, I can take you." But the tone of her voice was severely disinterested. She went back to plucking her eyebrows, "Have you told your mother about these plans?"

I rolled my eyes, "She doesn't even care enough to know whether or not I'm even alive. Of course I haven't."

She glared at me through her mirror, "Don't start that, Nunu, I don't wanna hear any of that!" She barked.

"Ugh, you know what I mean." I scoffed. "When have I ever ran anything by her that she didn't find some way to make into an issue? I have—" I stopped to correct myself.

"*I've had* the most benign interests and hobbies, and somehow, every time, she makes me out to be some troublemaker out to do no good! If I *did* ask her, she'd probably assume me and Katie are going out to shoot stray cats! Please!"

She leaned away, wide-eyed, looking at me with the same mix of bewilderment and disdain you reserve for an eleven-year-old throwing a tantrum. In that moment, I realized that I had just shouted at her.

"Okay—Okay—Just stop," She begged with her hands to ease me, incredulously. I swallowed the fire in my chest and let go of the signs of it in my face.

"Who are you going with, anyway?" She blurted. Before I could answer, she added, "If it's Katie, why can't she pick you up? She always does."

I dropped my head, *"I'm not going with Katie."* I muttered.

She went back to her eyebrows and her mirror. "Well, that's surprising. Who then? Your tall red-headed friend?—What's his name..... ? ... Dante?"

"I have two." I grumbled, "And, yes, Dante is one of them, but no. I think he and Jessie are going to some party, anyway. Or hanging out with their girlfriends. I don't know. I don't like parties." "Besides—I haven't exactly figured that out yet. I'll let you know—but—just—Can you take me or not? If not, I'll just take the bus or something."

She hummed, indifferent again. "Mmmn, no, I don't want you doing that on Halloween, it's dangerous. Whatever—Yeah, I can take you, but it won't be for a couple a' hours. I have an appointment at the Chevy dealership."

"H-Thank you." I said through a quick and sharp sigh. I disappeared as quickly as I came, letting the door slam shut behind me as a bit of harmless spite. She jumped in her seat and called after me.

I smiled, a small, wry, thing tugging at the edges of my lips, not quite meeting my eyes—from a flicker of excitement over escaping this shoe-house, however briefly.

I dropped onto Valene's worn white rug and surveyed the room in all its scattered pieces of identity; my many odd belongings littered about like mold consuming the surface of rotting fruit. Nestled with her various things were the little indicators of my presence too. Small crystals and geodes in varying size and color wedged and hidden amongst framed photos, stacks of novels and composition notebooks with dark little poems—tossed pantyhose and loose nail polish bottles among them. And that plush cat I gifted her before the summer, with its glow-in-the-dark eyes, on top of her dresser.

I think out of everyone in my family, aside from my brothers of course, Valene could be who I am most fond of. If 'fond' is what you can call a sufficient lack of disdain in comparison to everyone else. She's the only one who seems to have a life outside of this pale concrete house and that makes me respect her a whole lot more than the rest.

I looked around for something I could hack-up and sew into a last-minute costume. My gaze settled on a fresh linen sheet Valene had brought into the room earlier this morning, still neatly folded and bright white. What little part of that sensible, considerate, Alexander that remained thought I was insane for cutting up my aunt's sheets—But I began snipping away at it to make a sack-mask anyway.

The rest came quickly to mind as I worked. I thought of that man from *The Strangers*. I also thought of how chilling that movie was. There was an exchange between The Strangers and their victims at the end that just shook me up inside. When the married couple was tied up and confronted by their masked tormentors, the wife asked,

"Why us?"

And one of them responded very simply with the line, *"Because you were home."*

There was something I found so callous about the way it was said. As if it was quite literally because they were home. It could have been anyone, but to their dismay, it was them. Just like death, they reserved no bias. It was just their door which was knocked on. I've only seen it once because I watched it at a bad time. I think that movie really spoke to my fear that the universe is truly indifferent. She answered the question like it was not a problem for her. Violence for violence. The rule of beasts.

I wonder sometimes if I were pushed far enough off the edge... could that be me? I shivered. My eyes focused on an old framed photo of my family on the wall and I shook away the thought. Even if I don't agree with them, and they burn me, I don't think there's anything they could do that would turn me into someone like that. That being said, everyone was in the photo except Me.

I held up the face I'd cut out and peered through the eyeholes to make sure I had punched out the right shape. With an eyebrow pencil I swiped from Valene's vanity, I etched a crude smile onto it. Then, pulling a needle from the sock monkey I used as a pincushion, I began stitching the rest of the mask together by hand.

I have known how to sew since I was a young boy, about age ten. I remember once a teacher of mine had asked who taught me, and for whatever reason, I lied and said that my mother had. I was in the care of another family at the time, and I had been separated from my parents for about two years at that point.

Really I had just taken a spontaneous interest in something, as children often do. But I think that might have been the first lie that eventually got me to where I am now. It was around that age I began my years-long crusade to convince everyone I had the best mother in the world, so I could feel and look normal like all the other kids. So much so that I even convinced myself. And when she and I were finally reunited only a year ago, I learned very quickly that she wasn't the woman I made her out to be. And that truth turned out to be so very damaging. Bad for the soul. There was a reason we were taken from her and my father in the first place.

As much as I burn now, laid still on my back with flames wafting off my body, I know I'm the one to blame for all this calamity. I fought tooth and nail to summon her back into my life. Sure, I suffer and fight against this curse, but still I remain, paying recompense for that original sin—the sin of believing I could be loved the way I needed. And I hate myself for it.

I shook away the thought and kept on. When the mask was done I frayed all the edges and seams with the blade of my scissors to give it more of a ragged look. It fit well when I tried it on, not exactly screen accurate but enough for people who've seen the movie to point at me and say, *"OMG you're the guy from that one movie!"* And that was enough to satisfy me. All I'd need now is a dingy grey suit and a prop weapon of some sort. And perhaps a bit of dark eyeshadow. That, at least, would be just as easy. I have an old, ratty, blazer I picked up at a thrift store over the summer, and Valene wouldn't notice another bout of me snooping through her cosmetics. She still hasn't noticed her black nail polish missing, or the fact that I've been wearing it. The rest I could gather from my own wardrobe—white collar, slacks, and a necktie.

I've always dressed with a formality that's drawn in many comments from all sides. "Newsie," "missionary," "paralegal," and my favorite, though often dished out most acidically, "pretty boy." I take them as compliments most of the time, as condescending as they come off, though I've never fully understood why I favor this style. Most boys my age wear athletic gear basically all year round. My brother Tommy is a punk rocker type and Franky is still a child, so he wears shorts and graphic tees exclusively. California definitely has the weather for that. But not for jumpers and wool slacks. Because of it I stick out like a sore thumb amongst everyone else.

A stray teen called me "Boss Baby" last week for a laugh. And I could see it—short guy in a black and white suit. Hah hah. But I like looking nice. Perhaps it's some strange inheritance like the other invisible chains passed down between us. Irene, for instance, also keeps herself presentable at all times possible. What separates she and I, however, is our tastefulness. I find her a bit self-involved. I remember once Franky slashed his scalp open on one of the outside fence's sharp finials. He bled out all over himself and the porch. Irene took her sweet time to shower and blow dry her hair before taking him to the ER, all the while completely aware that poor Franky was about to pass out from shock and blood loss. She didn't even rush! I fumed at her audacity. I pressed a towel onto his head the whole while we waited for her to finish perfecting herself.

I find her ridiculous at times. I shudder when I catch echoes of it in me. And I pray that I never become so vain.

With my costume out of the way, all I needed was someone to go out with. I hopped in bed and let my head dangle off the edge of the mattress, hoping the headrush would help me think.

Katie was immediately out of the question. She may act tough with that BB gun of hers she keeps under her pillow, but when it comes to anything remotely scary she's a total wet blanket. I cherish her, she's one of my oldest friends second to Tyler, but I wouldn't waste a perfectly good Halloween on someone who'd rather watch romances indoors and eat burgers all night instead. Not that I don't miss those days, sometimes I do, but we can do that literally any other weekend of the year.

Tyler came to mind next. He's like the older brother I've always wanted. Reliable, kind of estranged. I appreciate him, even if his love pains me so much now. And I know for certain that he wouldn't mind chaperoning me anywhere, I can always rely on him. But as I said, he's an older boy, almost nineteen, and much cooler and freer than I am. And he isn't all that into Halloween, either, at least not in the way I am. For him, it's another one of those many times of year he can infiltrate the gay scene and **party hard**. I'm not really into all that, nor old enough anyway. I'm positive he would drop whatever plans he has tonight for me, but I don't wanna take him from his fun. He's had a hard life too and deserves every second of happiness he can afford.

And Dante is out partying as well, as I've stated previously. I prepared for the possibility that I may in fact have to go out alone, assuming my mother doesn't corner me before I even walk out the door and pick another fight with me.

I don't have many other options... I don't really see Nelson outside of his various soccer games that I attend, so asking him would be a little too ambitious given that he and I are really only acquaintances, and Olivia is most likely out already with her girlfriends who think I'm creepy, so, not her. Santos is hanging out with Richard, and I don't like Richard, and I definitely don't want to attend the local church's "Trunk Or Treat" with my family. Evangelical Christians make me uncomfortable—and as a young theologian I tend to pick fights with the under-read attendees who have big mouths and harmful takes. And unlike most other snarky mystics, I do not enjoy arguing with people of different faiths. It's not Good for the spirit, and I'm already under the floor, beyond rock bottom. Last thing I need is someone else threatening to "pray" for me.

I searched deeper, trying to think of literally anyone—then an old friend came to mind, a girl named Lilah King. She was always very kind to me, and my closest friend in school before Katie came along. She was also one of the few people who noticed when I disappeared last summer, and checked in on me a while after I came home. I still had her number saved on my phone.

I sat up quickly, my pulse ticking with a bit of eagerness and a little bit of dread, and pulled my phone from beneath the pillow to text her.

I pride myself on my cleverness when I can, but thanks to my mother's constant scrutiny, she has led me to employ that cleverness to conjure intricate defenses against her judgment. I've been conditioned to brace myself for interrogation, even if my words or intent are innocent, I must have a motive, as though everything must be justified or else it's suspect. With my mother, and I guess by extension the rest of this damned house, innocence is subjective unless they decree it so.

So, rather than just directly asking Lilah if she wanted to hang out like a normal person, I found myself typing and deleting and typing some more, only to eventually craft a message like this:

```
HEY LILAH! WANTED TO SAY HAPPY
BELATED BIRTHDAY. SORRY I HAVEN'T
REACHED OUT IN SO LONG, AND HAPPY
HALLOWEEN TOO =)
```

Her birthday had always been something I committed to memory since it falls exactly ten days before mine. Reasonable enough, I thought, to start the conversation with a simple birthday greeting after all this time. I intentionally avoided mentioning my birthday all together, I didn't want her to assume I was trying to make it all about me and risk her feeling obliged to wish me a 'happy birthday' as well. That would only make it look as if I'd used her birthday as an excuse to get attention, not at all resembling my true intent.

This tangled web of thoughts and justifications spun itself fast and instinctively, as though my mind had crafted it before I could even verbalize the words I wanted to say. And here I was, sending this message to Lilah as though she, too, would pick my words apart as my mother does. I felt like one of Pavlov's dogs, trained into this frenetic, needless anxiety—the bell tolling, and here I am, salivating with a motive in case I need it.

She replied a few seconds later.

```
ALEXANDER OMG @ THANK YOU! I'M LIKE
ALWAYS SHOCKED WHEN YOU REMEMBER.
HAVE YOU BEEN DOING OKAY? I HAVEN'T
HEARD FROM YOU IN A WHILE.
```

My eyes flickered a moment as I considered an appropriate response. A deep, aching part of me wanted to answer truthfully. I wasn't at all doing okay. I thought about my bruised knuckles and my perpetually disheveled hair. I thought back to when she and I were both younger and how I could confide in her about anything. I was never ashamed to tell the truth. I felt a bit helpless and betrayed by this sudden shame. But shame for what? My pain? I sighed.

HAHAH, YEAH. NO PROBLEM =) ITS NOT SOMETHING I WOULD FORGET. I'VE BEEN HANGING IN THERE, I HAVEN'T REALLY GONE OUTSIDE ALL THAT MUCH SINCE I'VE BEEN HOME.

I'M SORRY ABOUT THAT 💀 AND THANK YOU, YOU'RE SWEET. ARE YOU DOING ANYTHING FUN TONIGHT?

THAT'S ACTUALLY WHY I REACHED OUT, WOULD YOU BY ANY CHANCE WANT TO TAG ALONG WITH ME? IF YOU ALREADY HAVE PLANS THAT IS FINE :D

I'M DOWN! I DON'T HAVE ANY PLANS 💀 I WAS JUST GONNA STAY HOME TBH. WAITING FOR MY MOM TO COME BACK WITH SOME PIZZA. WANNA COME OVER?

WOW REALLY!? THANK YOU LILAH, THAT'S AWESOME. UH, MY NANNA IRENE CAN DROP ME OFF ACTUALLY BUT WE CAN DEFINITELY HEAD OUT FROM YOUR PLACE =)

WE MIGHT HAVE TO STOP BY PARTY CITY BEFORE BECAUSE I DONT HAVE A COSTUME MY BAD 💀💀 LMK AND I'LL TEXT YOU MY ADDRESS :)

The screen went black and I met face in its black glass—old joy tugging at my lips. But still, the little smile did not meet my eyes.

"I'm happy you're going out tonight..." A disembodied voice murmured behind me—every word excruciatingly clear as it conjured itself from thin air. The static waves of the presence made my skin run with goosebumps. My smile sank into my gut with my heart. I turned around slowly and met a pair of shining familiar eyes gazing coyly into mine.

"Jonah." I hissed through an exasperated breath. "I told you to go away!"

He hovered beside me, face flickering with shame and muttered, *"Alex, please...* I only came to check on you..." his voice as soft as a lone puff of smoke.

I swat a hand at him and watched the air contort where he stood. He reconfigured by the bedpost, before his impression in the room dissolved entirely and I could no longer see him. But I could still make out the shine of his eyes from behind the headboard. He kept staring, moping like a guilty dog, and whined my name,

"Alexander..." "Please, please—we can just talk? Can't we? I mean—I—"

I sighed and bit my cheek impatiently, "Jonah. Because of you my mother thinks I'm summoning demons and I haven't heard the end of it!"

He slithered further out of view, the outline of his form bent the darkness where he hid.

"I asked you to lay low and go haunt Twinkle for a while, but here you are again, pestering me! Just one week, Jonah—one! And you've stretched it out to the whole damn month!"

He scoffed and I felt him move closer, creeping his hands over my shoulders, ice-cold finger lips pressing into my skin. "She's an impossible woman, really..." He said, "Calling me a 'demon'... Perhaps she should look in a mirror some time."

"Hey!" I snapped, a half-hearted defense. "She's a wretch, but don't—" and I stopped with a hard breath. I had yet to break out of the habit of defending her. She does not deserve that from me of all people.

Nevermind. "Where's Twinkle?" I pressed.

"Back at his place. He sent me to check on you, you know... You've been ignoring his calls and he's worried sick.

"Wos quite touching, actually. He clasped his hands together in prayer and everything... He knows how your mother would react if she caught him knocking on your door again. So I came."

"I feel terrible." I muttered in a low growl. "She's been so hard on my back and out of nowhere she throws me a fucking birthday party, can you believe her? Total curveball to my face.

"He did stop by yesterday but Irene was on the porch so he barely stayed a minute. Said' he'd wait for my call, but I never called."

Jonah's face softened as it reappeared, and a deep, almost maternal sadness took in his eyes.

"I know..." He sighed, "I'm genuinely sorry that you're going through this, Alex—I mean it—And—I just—wish I knew the right way to be here for you."

He spoke with a sincerity that unraveled my frustration, even as he struggled to find the right words to say. Though, there are no right words. I pressed into my temples and pinched my eyes shut, trying hard to keep it all to myself.

"I just need things to die down, Jonah. I just can't afford another pointless tussle with her. I don't know how much more I can take.

"I just need you away long enough that she forgets about what happened and I can have you back here with me where you belong and everything can go back to normal."

He tilted his head and clasped my face gently, to bring me closer to him,

"And what about your friends, Alex? Will everything go back to normal with them?"

I said nothing.

"You mustn't hide from the ones who truly love you. You've been all the more alone because of it. Twinkle misses you. Katie misses you. It's all they talk about when they cross paths. And... I miss you too. There are people out there who need you—"

"But they can't save me, Jonah!" I shouted, desperation clawing at my throat, "It's too late! The damage is done!"

His pupils shrank in panic, "Shh—Alex! Keep your voice down!" He urged in a whisper.

The door flung open and my mother barged in.

"Who are you talking to!?" She blurted, her voice icy and harsh— somehow even louder than the thud of the doorknob against the wall. She glared thoroughly around the room like she knew he was there.

"No one!" I lied hastily, all traces of my anger violently replaced by panic—"I was reading something I wrote out loud! Honest!"

I gestured toward the open journal on my bed, hoping it would pass as proof. But it was apparent that she'd caught onto my quick lies.

Her eyes narrowed in on me and she pointed a mean finger, "You better not be talking to that *thing!*" the word dripped with disdain. "I told you to get rid of him!"

I groaned, *"I just told you I was reading, are you deaf!?"*

She took a hard step forward, and I flinched, bracing myself.

"Who the fuck do you think you are?" Her hand came fast and sharp, sending a hot sting across the side of my face. The force parted my hair the opposite way. *"Don't talk to me like that!"*

I shot to my feet, fists clenched, and I locked my gaze with hers. Even at my height, I towered over her, trembling with fury.

"Do not strike me again!" I warned, each word pulled slowly through my teeth. For the first time, I saw a hint of fear in those piercing green eyes of hers, and she took a step back.

Irene's voice cut through the tension as she appeared in the doorway, "What the hell is going on in here!?" looking between us with disgust.

"She just fucking smacked me over nothing!" I shouted, and my mother's face turned red, voice rising like with accusations about Jonah Irene had grown tired of. I looked around the room to see where he was hiding—but it was clear to me that was no longer there.

"Priscilla, leave him alone!" Irene snapped impatiently, "There's no demon in here—what are you crazy!?" She put herself between us, gripping my arm to pull me behind her. When she touched me I caught a hint of contempt directed more at my mother than sympathy for me.

"I wasn't talking to no demon!" I spit, "I was just reading out one of my poems!"

"Yeah?" My mother prompted with a sour face and bulging eyes—calling my bluff, "Let's see one of these "poems" go on!"

I shoved my hand into my hair in frustration.

"You're being erratic!" Irene continued with a nagging finger in my mother's face, her grip on my arm getting tighter. I tried to pull away, but her long mauve manicure dug deeper into my skin as I pulled away.

"You just threw him a birthday yesterday—have you lost it? What's the matter with you!?"

My mother's mouth twisted in anger.

"Exactly!" I added, feeling brave with Irene on my side.

"Shut up, Nunu!" Irene barked, dousing the little bit of safety I felt. "I told you, Pricilla, to not go over there and pick on that boy, come on man!?"

My jaw tightened. Beneath the heat of the moment, a twisted sense of gratitude came. I understood why my mother barged in so hot headed all of a sudden. Irene must have told her about my Halloween plans. This was bound to happen anyway, even if I had asked her first.

"You seriously couldn't confront me like a normal person? Instead, you come in here making up stories about demons!?" I shouted.

She glared at me, knowing well the tricks I'd played to my own defense before. I was gaslighting her, of course, a trick I learned from her. Pushing those into doubt they don't deserve. And she seemed peeved by Irene's unordinary protective stance. She knew she wasn't getting away with this one.

"Well then I'm not letting you go out with Katie." She said with her arms crossed and her nose in the air, shaking her head in disapproval like a mad woman, "If you are then no sir you're staying in this house!"

"Well good because I'm not!" I screamed, shoving past both of them and slamming the door behind me.

I collapsed onto the bed and pressed my face deep into the pillows to smother the echo of Irene berating my mother in the hallway. My body curled in on itself, knees to my nose as I clutched myself tighter. An anguished howl ripped from my throat, low and broken, before rising into a scream of raw agony, engulfed by the pillow and my own breathlessness.

I'm not going anywhere tonight. The thought hit me like a final, crushing blow.

Jonah's voice returned and drifted close. In a string of shameful whispers he said,

"No, Alex, No... Not Again—Alex, I'm sorry... I'm sorry..." again and again, lulling me away into another frigid, restless, sleep.

For the first time since that night I did not dream of the cliff. I found myself in some other place. A total darkness. No sense, No existence, just nothingness everywhere. An uncomfortable void much like the day's sky—but not familiar to me at all. And there was no air, nor the subtle tug of gravity beneath my feet. It was a dark soundless place, save for a faint, distant echo of some dripping. *Drip...* Each drop, which should have been barely audible, felt like a gong right in my ear. My sight remained fixed ahead. I couldn't even blink, as though I no longer had eyes to see. There was Nothing. Nothing to feel, Nothing to be, only nothing and that sound. *Drip...* like tears.

I opened my eyes to the static pitch black of the room. For a moment I thought I was still dreaming. Then, a pair of glowing green eyes beamed down on me—I flinched with a hitched breath—And then realized it was just the toy cat on the dresser. I sighed.

A sudden knock at the door cut through my half-conscious haze. I rose like a husk, feeling the fabric creases of the sheets etched painfully into my skin like shallow scars. The crush of dry tears matted the side of my face and I heard that sound again in my mind. *Drip. . .*

I opened the door and it was Irene.

"I want to talk to you." She said. The edge of her tone was soft, but still characteristically blunt. She seemed upset.

God... What now? I dragged my feet behind me as I followed her to her room, stepping around the shadows that repopulated the hall where moments ago the hope of a decent day was murdered violently. I had not one ember of rebellion left to flicker inside of me—just a gnawing emptiness where pain once burned, as if the fire hallowed me out like a burnt log. I didn't even think such a low could be possible—I am absolutely, already, irrefutably at rock fucking bottom. My will to live and fight another day had finally taken its last bow. Forfeit. I followed without question or care—I followed because it was easier to just take it like a lamb to slaughter.

In her room I was greeted first by the shrine adjacent to her door on the far end of the wall, dedicated to her only son, my late uncle Richard. Her eyes seemed to linger on his photo for a breath longer than she'd admit to herself. Irene sat delicately on her bed and pat the space beside her so I could sit.

I remained standing, unwilling to humor it any more than necessary, glaring at her through that hard Kubrick stare everyone hates. But she didn't waver to my awful face, she pressed her lips into a hard line and said,

"I'm sorry about your mother."

I recoiled. Irene had never, in all the years I'd known her, ever uttered the words *I'm sorry* to anyone in this house. And to apologize on the behalf of someone else? *What is happening to the world?*

"Okay." I shot with a shrug.

"Watch it!" She nagged, but the softness in her eyes remained, and it gave me pause. "I'm still going to take you out tonight. I know it's late, but I need you to get out of this house, away from all this noise."

"Why?" I croaked, "I don't even want to go anymore. It's useless."

Her eyes were downcast a moment before she sighed, "You *should, though*," "Maybe if you got out every now and then your mother wouldn't be making up stories about demons and witchcraft."

"Oh, so it's *my fault?* " I hissed, feeling the heat of my disdain return.

"I'm not saying that." She said, keeping her voice low and easy, almost polite. "Your mother—she's distressed, I don't know what's the matter with her right now, but whatever it is, it's not something I can help. All I can do is just pray for her.

"You're a good, smart, kid. I don't wanna see you wasting in the house all day. I have enough of that with Bonnie and Adriana."

I glanced down the hall, feeling the walls of the house closing in on me as she spoke.

A good kid? None of them have ever made me feel like that. To them I'm just my mother's dramatic gay son. Too emotional, too sensitive, too blasphemous. To them I'm just her devil-born curse, raised with caution. Once she'd gotten so drunk she called me "Rosemary's Baby." among other terrible things. It was a memory from a long time ago, but the conviction in which she claimed it was seared into my heart as clear as everything else.

I let out a hard sigh, eyebrows so crunched that I could feel the skin twisting in my forehead. *"None of you make me feel like a good kid, I feel like a fucking monster!"*

"Watch your mouth!" Her voice was even sharper now, but her face remained collected.

"How do I make you feel like a monster?" She asked with emphasis on every word, hands folded on her knee. A fair question, surely. Her eyes were unwavering. She expected an answer.

But I was thrown by the sudden prompt. I searched for the words, but nothing came to me. How could I describe the feeling of a thousand small, invisible barbs from every odd look and every sigh? It was just that—a feeling—a terrible sense that no matter what sense, reason, or Law—I'm wrong. Wrong, wrong, wrong! Everything about me wrong! Utterly, entirely wrong down to the atom!

I've tried so hard to tell myself that I'm not so unlike everyone else on the surface. I am a human being—with needs, agency, and meaning—And yet, time after time, it's been made so painfully aware that I'm a pariah amongst the worst of the worst.

I simply rolled my eyes and said nothing. A little defeated that I couldn't find the words to say.

"Look." She sighed after my silence gave her the wrong answer. "I'm not your enemy. And whatever you have going on with your mother I need it to stop. I'm not saying that you're responsible or that it's your fault–I'm just saying, as the head of this household, I need some peace here. Your little fights blow up the whole damn place, even if the rest of us aren't a part of it."

Little fights? That's her way of putting it? My mother treats me like an abomination, like I was some plague sent down on her. They all make me feel that way, in some form, but my mother is the worst of all; She believes in the worst of me, sees trouble in every corner, in every shadow

I cast. And she used these baseless, ignorant, heinous ideas as justification to destroy me!

Everyone enables her. I feel it every day, no matter how much they wash their hands of it. My blood is forever dripping off their fingertips—red and gleaming ruby insides.

"You don't understand." I muttered.

"You're right, I don't understand. Just—" She resigned with a breath. "Just avoid her for now, Nunu. Go hang out with a friend and come back when you've gotten it out of your system a bit."

She seemed so bored by my heartbreak and the idea was so crushing. Whatever had a hold of me released its grip and the tears came, silent, and unbidden. My shoulders trembled as I let them flow. A second later I found my face pressed into her shoulders as she wrapped me in an unexpected hug. I melted reluctantly into her embrace, letting the thickness of her coat envelop me.

She wiped a few tears from my face and seemed pained, as if the idea of soiling her good coat with my grief was as uncomfortable as my anguish. I wiped my runny nose, shaking off the last of this fit, not wanting to let myself surrender to the little bit of hope she'd stirred up in me.

"It's too late to go out now." I said, "It's almost eight."

"No, baby, it's not." She said, still holding me close. "Go get ready and I'll take you wherever you wanna go."

She caught my eyes again and I caught a glint of excitement sprinkling in hers. "Guess what?"

"What?"

"You get to be the first person to hitch a ride in my new car." She beamed, swinging her hips with a little playfulness.

"You already picked it up?" I asked, a little shaken that I missed the whole thing. She talked about it for days. She must've left right after the fight.

"Sure did. It's freakin' gorgeous. I *love* it!" She gave me a light smack on the behind, urging me forward. "Now, hurry up!"

I buttoned my trousers with fumbling fingers as I ran out the door to catch up with her, my unfastened tie lodged between my teeth. Irene waited impatiently in her new car, having already gotten bored of standing outside and taking photos for her Facebook while I washed up and put on my costume.

With hints of politeness lingering still in her otherwise stony demeanor, she called out to me from across the yard, "Hurry up, Nunu!"

I was rushing, but the house had this gravity to it that tugged at my ankles. I felt the chords that bound me to its shadows slow me down the further I stepped like a ball and chain. I stopped for just a second to look back and found myself transformed into a pillar of salt. My mother, suddenly on the porch smoking a cigarette, staring at me with a morose gaze. Our eyes met for just that one second, but it stretched far beyond a quick look. I swallowed the unease and turned back toward the car—but then it hit me—something I missed that made me jump. Her eyes were... glowing?

I turned back quickly to look again, but she wasn't there anymore. All that remained was a wisp of smoke that vanished into the air with a twirl. I flinched—what the fuck?

"*Nunu!*" Irene shouted again, the charity in her tone beginning to thin. I hurried to her, trying to suppress the growing pit in my gut. The car roared to life the second I threw myself beside her and fastened my seatbelt. She took a moment to adjust herself in the rear-view mirror and we were off.

I forced a smile as we drove off into the night and we made small talk, but my hands and my face were as clammy as a dead body. I watched our house shrink through the side view mirror until it was no longer there. The chords shared between us snapped like rubber bands.

Chapter Two

A group of children burst from the bushes beside us with wild shrieks, the echo of their laughter haunted the dimly lit sidewalk, a whirlwind of fragmented fall leaves and candy wrappers gust behind them in a hectic swirl. Their smiles were wound high in their precious, painted, little faces. I marveled at their joy and smiled too, trying hopelessly to remember anything light from that age as I watched them fade into the night.

Instead of sifting through those fuzzy memories, I imagined that perhaps in those earlier years I had a childhood much like theirs. Costumes, friends, and innocence — my mother a few yards away, watching me with a loving, careful, eye. I felt a rush of nostalgia for this unowned time, losing myself for a moment in the romance of such an idea. Normalcy. Although, I know my brief imaginings couldn't be any further from the real truth.

Lilah's mom took a candid photo of us and the flash pulled me away from my thoughts. Loud honking from impatient drivers that followed their kids unenthusiastically, a sea of voices that flooded every nook and cranny of my eardrums, and the incessant Halloween music shook the air. It reminded me again why I so often tune out the world and retreat into these private soliloquies. We lingered at the steps of the haunted house thrown every year here in Woodrow. A flashy display of skeletons, speakers, and flickering lights.

The night got to a late start. Lilah and I had a slice of pizza and exchanged pleasantries for a while at her apartment. The conversation was light. Easy. That, I appreciated. I liked listening to her speak. Her life seemed so mundane... I thought it a blessing. I always found her a beautiful soul, it pleased me to know she was doing fine. I hadn't seen her since Daniella's quinceañera in the spring and that was before... well, you know.

I still hadn't shaken the fight with my mother, and I made a great deal of effort to direct the conversation literally anywhere else. I wanted to keep that elephant hidden as long as I could. Despite all reason, I think a little bit of fun snuck in here and there. My favorite part of the night was our trip to Party City. Lilah threw together a last-minute seraphim, fuzzy halo, glittery eyes and all. Her smile cast sparks to the ash of my old, dead, joys. But even that echo of an echo of happiness was fleeting... by the time we made it to Collis... I was tired again.

It was a sensory assault the second we stepped inside in the house. Her grip on my arm tightened with every sudden scare as we made our way further inside. The air in the foyer was thick with the smell of cheap latex and glycerin. The speakers were so loud I could hardly tell what the audio was supposed to be. Disjointed shadows jerked and stretched along the walls as the strobe lights pulsed, each flash revealed costumed assailants lurking amongst the props. She clung to my sleeve with eyes half closed and giggled with a mix of fear and excitement. We stumbled into a repurposed dining room, fake corpse laid on the kitchen table with a prop cleaver lodged in the head. Lilah's laughter and gasps were a sharp contrast to the growing knot in my stomach. Despite the cheap presentation I had a very real sense of danger. Like I was being watched from afar the whole time. I was genuinely afraid—And what an intense feeling after months of blinding depression.

I kept imagining this dark presence the entire time. I felt like I was in the gaze of a horror's omniscient eyes. No matter where I stepped, looked, or hid, the feeling of being watched was ever present. I could feel it everywhere.

We turned the last corner and a man dressed like Michael Meyers popped out of a closet with an extremely realistic chainsaw and lunged toward us. She screamed again—this time with more terror than fun — and fled the opposite way. I reached for her hand to pull her forward, but in the chaos, we got separated by another blinding flash of the strobe light.

I called out, but my voice was drowned out by the screams and sound effects. I ran back down the hall after her, narrowly dodging a couple who mistook me for a part of the attraction and borrowed past me in a panic. I jumped out of their way and lost my footing. I slipped and my head struck the banister of the staircase with a nasty hard thud. I reached for her hazy white shape in the dark as it disappeared. I stumbled up as fast as I could, chest tight and bolted toward what looked like a kitchen—my heart pounding so hard I could feel it in my ears. I tore off my mask to catch my breath only to collide with a wall in the dark while I was distracted. I crumpled onto the hard-wood floor and hit my head a third time.

The pain was raw and Serious. A large lump swelled under my scalp. I laid on the ground and let the pain settle for a few moments before I dared to move another inch. My temples throbbed violently and my eyes struggled to find focus—every time the light flashed it split everything it touched into three.

Ugh. "Lilah?" I groaned in a weak voice that lingered after I spoke. My body dragged behind me as I sat up. I felt around beside me for my mask and shoved it in my coat pocket.

I staggered to my feet once more and stood, stumbling into a closed door and opening it with a faint grip. It was a large, vacant garage. The air felt heavier and colder all of a sudden. The uncanny valley took me in my disoriented state, and I could swear that I stared into an infinite space. I slammed the door and turned away, muttering curses under my breath—questioning why I had even done that in the first place. I was beginning to panic—Then I froze.

My eyesight returned with a rush of adrenaline when I caught someone watching me silently in the dark. In a doorway opposite to the one I stood in, there was the monstrous silhouette of a man, impossibly large and still. His broad and bare, hulking, frame seemed to drink up the scant light behind him. Just a ghoulish horned silhouette with a thin blue outline.

"Hey, man!" I croaked, holding up my shaky hands in surrender. The buzz of a dying fluorescent light somewhere was all that lingered in the air now. All other sound in the house had disappeared.

I kept my eyes pried open, too afraid to lose sight of him. Too afraid to blink like he'd rush toward me and do something to me. I pleaded,

"I hit my head really hard, can you take it easy on me, please?" and clasped my hand on the raw part of my scalp, unable to find his eyes. I could not even see a face.

I tried again and made a strong effort to project my voice as clear as possible across the kitchen and all the noise that returned with a vengeance. But the man didn't move or speak at all. He stood motionless. He didn't breathe. He didn't sway. He simply... was. I leaned in and stared harder, and the fear swept me up when I saw clearly that I had missed something; How impossible his size was. He was like a statue. A Very Big Statue. And I was certain it was a man. I felt the burn of his predatory eyes like a lion that vied the flesh of a gazelle. I kept my body facing him as I edged away slowly. When I was far enough I broke into a full sprint down the hall.

The more I misplaced myself in this house, the more surreal it all became. The settling concussion came and disturbed all of my senses. Buzzing in my ears gave way to a static hissing over the volume of the night. People ran and moved past me in a haze, their blurry shapes a few frames behind them every time. My vision dimmed until the strobe lights were barely visible, just a subtle shift in low light, and my body ran cold and sweaty all over. I tugged at the collar around my neck and loosened my tie but it was no help. I felt like I was suffocating.

I kept going, and finally I found the back door. I stumbled down the narrow hall and held my hands out, pressing them into the walls in an attempt to hold myself steady as I kept forward. My hands were so slick and sweaty I lost my grip on the wallpaper with a loud squeak and I fell over again, landing on one knee and heard a loud thump that sent it numb as my head. I got back up, walked and walked, but the hall stretched impossibly far, like every step forward added another foot to travel.

I started gasping for air, my heart struggling to keep up with the load of my heavy breaths. The feeling of being watched was no longer a feeling, but a truth as final as a death sentence. I stumbled faster, after what felt like forever of hobbling straight ahead, I met the chill of the open air and took in deep breath.

But the relief was short-lived. When my head stopped spinning just enough, and I could see again, the world outside was so wrong. The music was off. The streets were dead and the Halloween decorations were depowered and lifeless on the ground.

There were no people, not one person in sight. Like I was the only one left. Even the stars had gone missing. I whimpered and limped into the middle of the street.

I called her name out into the neighborhood.

Nothing. Not even an echo, or a draft.

The fall leaves sat grey on the pavement, and the moon sat solemnly in the sky as if it too were in mourning of the end. I walked down the road and it was the same.

A sudden flash of light erased everything. I looked above and felt my eyes burst to flames at the sight. Everything was white.

And then it transfigured.

Collapsed into three pure glowing white orbs that took a breath before taking a violent spin into a great ring of light. It shrieked, too loud for the human ear. Like an angel's song, its power shook everything. Spacetime bent and took impossible shapes around me. I pinched my eyes shut—*hard*—frantic for reprieve from the excruciating pain. But no matter how hard I clutched my eyes shut and pressed my fists into the sockets, it was a visage I could not unsee.

I fell to my knees and began to scream. I had been branded! All I could see was the ring. The pain didn't stop—it only grew stronger—I screamed louder—

And then,

as quickly as it happened,

It ceased with a sharp electric
snap!

Nothing.

A different kind of darkness settled into view. A state without form, like that of total blindness. I brought my limbs close, all paralyzing ambiguity biting me, and stood up from the ground I could feel but not see. My sense of gravity was completely askew, like the fabric of reality had been dented in random places. Its embrace, usually overlooked, suddenly so clear and so absent in my all my reflexes. Never once was I floating, but every other step my stomach would turn as if I were suspended in the air. Everything was wrong, wrong, wrong!

Existence itself seemed broken. Lights out. I wondered if it was now the apocalypse—maybe the big crunch happened sooner than scientists theorized, and I am one of the unfortunate few left behind.

Even as my sense of mind returned from the head trauma I could not make sense of what I was experiencing. This is not *darkness*. This is something else completely. Something vast and incomprehensible. Uncanny, but, for some reason, not so unfamiliar... like a cloudless blue sky.

My breaths thinned as I fell deeper in horror. *Certainly I'm still alive. I'm still breathing—I'm still thinking—Or at least... I'm trying to*. But I felt as good as Dead.

And how awful it was to know that even here in a death so final I still mourn my mother despite all she has done to me. Her face lingered beneath my vision. Absent. Disconnected. Awful. I hated myself for every piece of me I'd ever given her. How bleak—How fucking tragic, it is? That I find myself alone at the end of the world? All that's left of humankind is a boy who erased himself over a mother too broken to hold him close.

Then—

Drip. . .

I gasped and spun around in a panic to find the source of that sound. But it left not one echo in its wake. Quickly I wondered if I even heard it at all. It happened and it was gone. Like an intrusive thought.

I curled into my knees and let out the most soul crippling squeal. The sound, raw and helpless, sent me back to the eve of my eighth birthday. The night I met Jonah; A young mind shattered forever when he peered into the dark and saw something else staring back. I knew certainly that I was no longer alone. I became aware of another with me. The one that had been watching me the entire time.

"Hello?" I cried into the dark. Mewling. Broken. It tore from my throat into an afterthought. Like I had not spoken the word at all. Even sound seemed to refract incorrectly off this broken dimension I found myself in.

What followed was instantaneous—but horror elevated every wicked detail. My mother's voice swelled first, followed by my own, and then countless others all at once. They moaned and fused in pain, fused into a single, booming, monstrous voice. A voice built from the many distinct tones of everyone I'd ever met—and then some.

The darkness shifted on every syllable. The sound warped this senseless place even more.

Finally, I know for certain that I am as small as I've always believed. A little stain on a pale blue dot, engulfed by a cruel and indifferent cosmos. A little stain now under the foot of some vast intelligence.

OH, THE HORROR! THE WAVES OF ITS INFLUENCE RAVAGE MY MIND TO SPEAK!

"Hello?" it teased—mimicking my shrill voice through a low and sinister growl.

An awful sound followed. Intense, like being swept up in a tsunami. I clasped my hand over my throat, desperate, as the awful sound came upon me and stole the last of my breath. A frequency humans were never meant to perceive. The nothingness bent and snapped until the reeling stopped—settling with long drawn-out moans like floorboards in the cold. No matter how deep I gasped afterward, my lungs never caught enough.

Nothingness.

I waited, hung on a thread of sanity.

More and More silence.

Then I broke—

"WHAT IS THIS PLACE!?"

Nothing. No sense. No existence. Just nothingness... everywhere. Any attempt to *look* at all was futile. Horror fell into a greater pain. What a fitting penance for a boy who hollowed himself out for love. I stood completely empty. On the inside, and now, on the outside, too. I waited only a moment, but it felt like forever. Time was a smear just as it had been before the ring descended.

It spoke again. This time in a distinctly male voice.

"This is The Empty." He answered.

I struggled to keep myself from tipping over in the quake of his voice. The last syllable lingered in the darkness and morphed into a hypnotic buzz that faded, too. I opened my eyes sure and hopeful that what I was about to behold would strike me dead. I wanted it to—I wanted to be free of this terrible place.

I looked   And still I saw

nothing.

"Are you afraid?" He asked, nasty and amused, voice coming in from all directions. I fell dizzy. I clutched my throbbing head with both hands. Only then did it sink in: *This voice is sentient. This voice Real.* And whatever it is, it's speaking to *me*.

"O-o-f c-ourse I'm af-fraid." I stuttered, pathetic. Intuition, perhaps? Or wishful thinking?

"A-are you an A-angel. . ?" I asked, my voice clawing against me with so much terror that I answered my own question.

No.

"What a curious assumption..." He mused, quieter.

"Something like that."

"I am... The Wayback."

I peeked around the nothingness—still there was no one there. Would I soon be driven mad by this impossible task!? To grasp sight of anything in this untenable place!? Have my eyes been burned blind!? I let out a squeak and asked,

"Wh-h-h-hy are you called The Wayback?"

"No one calls me that. Just you."

Then he laughed. Not deep and villainous like his voice, nay, so much worse than that. So much worse than that. The sound made my insides turn to liquid. It was like a gaggle of cruel children painting fingers at me and giggling. Cruel school children pointing at my naked soul and laughing at all that I am.

"HAHAHAHAHAHAHAHAHAHA!"

His voice returned to that deep, ferocious growl once again. And he called my name through a long-drawn-out sigh like he, too, was bored of me.

"Alexander..."

My face twisted in a million different feelings a million different ways all at once.

"... d-do you know me. . ?"

"Oh intimately. I knew you before your mother stained the earth with that absolutely wretched spirit you hold."

"I know you more than you know yourself. And worst of all, I know what you are. And I like you. Very much so I like you, Alexander Hunsucker."

"I like your power."

I stopped trying to breathe.

"When you're looking for an excuse to burn it all down, I'll do you one even better...

"I'll look you in the eyes and tell you the truth. The truth about love, and God, and all the other things that ail you."

"And that will be more than enough."

Like a tidal wave, everything came crashing back in sharp images I couldn't even begin to make sense of. The force of it—of this suppressed memory being juxtaposed onto the fabric of my mind shoved me over and hard into the ground.

There was darkness. I heard the lionous roar of a wave and its succession back into itself, hundreds of little pebbles gurgling against the sea on some distant shore behind me. I looked up and it slammed into me again—throttling me into a large rock and knocking me out cold.

I felt the pressure of the ocean in my ears and the fizz of air being replaced by water in my lungs. My near-lifeless body suspended there in the cold, rigid, sea.

A large hand burst through the surface and snatched me up, palm rough and hot like summer pavement, reached into the water and yanked me by the arm, lugging me out of the sea as if I, with my heart as heavy as a collapsing star, were feather weight. I was thrown ashore without grace, love snuffed out by hate, like Samael being cast out of heaven's gate.

On the shore I stirred—shrieking in pain and horrified at the differences—like I was in some alternate version of the night that's haunted my dreams forever.

A quaking in the sky above me. Like the displaced air when an airplane flies overhead. Everything was shaking. The rings glinted, fiery in my eyes once more. *IT BURNS! IT BURNS!* I trashed around, free of these visions, bound to this Empty place.

Fallen to my hands and knees, I wept into the void, retching and coughing up bands of seaweed entwined with long ribbons of my mother's shiny blonde hair. I swung back and reached into my mouth in a frenzy, grabbing hold of one last lock lodged deep in my throat and pulled it out using both fists. I could feel my stomach bruising. When I was done, I cried out again, tears on blood stained blonde and toppled over onto my hands and knees a final time. That's when finally, *something* caught my gaze.

Ahead of me—watching—someone there in the dark.

I saw, far, far in the distance of this horrid place—

A face white and brittle like bone staring back at me. A twisted, gaping, smile, and black eyeless sockets. And in those sockets there were rings of light that looked exactly like the rings in mine.

"I wanna see what's really in you." He said.

My heart jerked to a stop. Like a fist had reached into me and crushed it. He vanished and sent me home with a wicked smile. One last image singed into my eyes.

Chapter Three

—giggles erupted beside me, sharp and sudden. A moment had not passed—Something that should be impossible—And yet—here I stand.

I flinched through the catatonia. Lilah's voice was bright. Innocent to the horror. I couldn't understand a word she was saying. The world returned with weak presence, like cosmic microwave background radiation.

She took a step forward, a light tug on my hand as though to lead me along. I was planted firmly where I stood. I didn't want to move. The light seemed so fragile all of a sudden—it's warmth so dire. I thought everything would shatter into nothing again if I dared to move. She noticed the look on my face and her smile faltered quickly. Her wide eyes taking me in at my worst—pale and hollow under a dying streetlight. She hesitated a moment before reaching out and asking,

"Is everything okay?"

Gently, she released my hand, the absence of that little embrace had broken me open again.

"Alexander?" Her voice was dainty and tremulous, hardly enough to cut through the fog. But I could feel the discomfort swell in her. Then... the worst happened.

"Alexander. . ?" I heard her say.

" ... you're scaring me . ."

Those words pierced my heart like a wooden stake. I was helpless—How had this night spiraled so out of control—this night—of all nights—Halloween night—How has everything spun so violently out of control? *What is happening. . ? What is happening... ?*

I fought hard to break free of whatever episode I was having—I shook within myself and brought my voice to a stammer, not yet able to form any coherent words. My teeth chattered—and I mumbled words that fell clumsily onto the floor.

I said, *"I don't want to scare you... I'm sorry... I think... . I think I'm just confused ... I hit my head too hard... a bunch of different places..."*

I brought forth shaky hands to my throbbing head and held myself with as much strength as I could muster. I could feel it—being moments away from collapse. I was in shock. She let out a soft gasp. The vacancy raw in my face. The tremor of every movement. She rushed to fill the space between us like a dam breaking. The neighborhood spun violently and all of a sudden, I could feel the eyes of passers-by, motionless and fixed on me as I buckled to the concrete sidewalk.

"Mom—" I managed to choke out, desperate, before my voice was crushed into a strained slur. She caught me in her arms—I felt her fingers brush against the massive knot in my scalp. I caught one last glimpse of her face before I was swallowed whole and I was gone.

The black spun into a dimly lit room and I had been returned to who I was before I ventured out into the night. Just a nihilist joke. As I stirred in bed I wondered. . .

Did any of that really happen? Or was it all just some horrific nightmare. . ?

My sense returned—had enough time to recuperate somewhat. I noticed the itchy badges wrapped tight around my head and palms. I jumped—That nasty sterile smell in the air was all too familiar in the worst way. My mother sat exacerbated across from me, anxiously tapping a lone heel on the tile under her foot. The incessant clicking grew louder, as the wires in my brain found their right places.

That pale droopy face of hers sank in—And the memory of pulling her hair out of my throat took me. I clasped my hands over my neck—feeling an echo of that pain and began to panic.

She lunged forward, the legs of her chair shifting on the floor with a nasty muffled scrape.

"Mmn Mmn! Don't move!" She whined brusquely, gently pressing my shoulders down into the bed. I groaned and slumped over.

"Lilah... Where's Lilah. . ?"

"Lilah your ass!" "What the fuck happened!?" She nagged, loud and frantic. *"**Nurse!** Someone—! He's awake!"*

I tried to swallow the hard lump in my throat and groaned again, feeling an icy pain shoot up my neck and into my brain.

"Mom..." I strained, *"There's a button on the wall for that... Don't be... rude..."* I reached over and pressed into it with two wobbly fingers. A soft bell began to toll, and the small blue light started blinking.

She sighed and shook her head, and took a long, cautious look into my eyes.

"Are you okay?" She asked, masking any concern with her stern, annoyed, intonation. But I caught her voice shake as she spoke, revealing some semblance of care in there. And it brought me the slightest relief, but even still, it was not enough. I felt like I had just survived a bombing.

I closed my eyes again. *"You should have asked that first, don't you think?"*

My Great Aunt Val laughed exaggeratedly at what I had said, to my mother's displeasure. *"Aye, Buddy, that mouth!"*

"It's always something with you!" My mother shouted.

"You could just let me die."

I winced. Perhaps karma for being so defiant—I felt the sharp tug of the IV lodged in my arm.

"Aye!" Val interjected, "Nobody's dying on my watch!"

I twitched—unsure of what could be so funny about me confused in a hospital bed. That being said, I found her carefree demeanor preferable to my mother's needless cold shoulder.

I sighed and looked to my aunt, "I'm assuming you brought us here, Val, thank you."

She smiled and said, "You're welcome." And then tapped my mother's knee, "Call Irene and tell her to get her ass over here,"

I shot up. "Absolutely not!" I blurted, "You being here is *enough!*"

"Don't be fucking rude!" My mother spat.

"You practically invented it, you hypocrite!"

The nurse walled in suddenly and ducked past the curtain with a small flashlight in hand. My eyes still locked to my mother's, I saw him walk in from my peripheral.

I wasn't sure if it was the fog of narcotics in my blood, but I was quickly distracted by him. When he approached I was unable to look directly into the light as he instructed—instead I gawked at his handsome face. It made me feel a bit better—like eye candy. And he was my favorite kind of man. Ethically ambiguous, tan, perfect teeth. Black and silver chest hair peeking from the low collar of his scrubs. So unbelievably sexy.

Then he hummed deep with concern as if taking my inattention as something else. Something serious.

"Does it hurt?" He asked. I blinked hard, somehow able to see the veins in my eyes when I did. I let out a chuckle and smiled,

"My bad—I can't think of anyone who wouldn't find staring directly into a light painful. But let me try again, I was distracted."

He laughed at the first part, that friendly, obligatory healthcare worker laugh, but seemed to miss the implication of the second part. My audacious attempt at flirting with a middle-aged man in front of my mother and aunt.

He leaned in closer and flashed the light in my eyes once more, instructing me to track his finger. I caught stray mutters under his breath—something was puzzling him. He made me go through it a few more times.

Now it's painful, I thought dryly. Eventually he gave up and said that I seemed fine, but mentioned "something weird" he "kept seeing." He asked my mother if I had any eye conditions, to which I said no. And I didn't think much of his question until my mother asked what he had seen. And he said,

"When I shine the light a certain way I can see this shiny, ring-like scar. It's on both eyes, too. I doubt it has anything to do with the concussion, but it's definitely something I'd get looked at if he has any eye problems. Looks like cataracts or something, maybe. I'm not sure."

"What? What do you mean?" My mother asked dramatically, scaring me. He continued.

"It's nothing to panic over, it's very faint, it just took me by surprise the first few times. It's just..."

His voice trailed off as I sank into myself in terror. The memories came back in sharp flashes, too fast for me to handle. *What am I seeing!?*—Bile shot up my esophagus as I hunched over and puked all over myself.

The room erupted in chaos and I closed my eyes to hide from my mother's face and the judgement of the hot physician.

Another round of vivid, invading, visions. The white face. Seaweed. Blonde hair. Darkness. I gasped and opened my eyes to see *what* exactly I had thrown up—but my mother was in front of me and covered my eyes with her hand, urging me not to look in a soft voice like silk, eyes still far away from me. She and the physician yanked all the blankets off me and threw them onto the ground.

Hours passed, and finally, I was approved for discharge. It was the break of dawn, November first. At some point, amidst the chaos, she moved her chair closer to my bed and remained by my side the rest of the night. My great aunt Val was asleep, cheek pressed into the wall, bound to leave a nude imprint behind from the heavy foundation she wore.

My mother turned away and let out a private sigh of relief when a nurse came in with the large packet and a prescription for God-knows-what. But I wasn't sure if it was relief for me or relief that it was finally over. I thought it the latter explanation.

I kept my eyes narrow, half awake, not wanting to be spoken to but unwilling to fall back asleep, afraid I would return to that empty place from my nightmare. When my mother went to the restroom I sat up and waved my hands in the air—enacting a miracle—wishing that Lilah would forget all about last night and never think of me again. My lip curled into a terrible frown.

My mother reached for my hand, only an inch, before pulling away and sighing. I stirred.

"Where's my phone?" I asked, snapping her from private thoughts. She did not look at me as she spoke. In a preoccupied string of words she said,

"You must've lost it because if you don't know, and I don't know..." finishing off with a vacant shrug.

"Why are you talking to me like this?" I hissed.

She didn't even flinch. Instead, her face sprung right back to life—annoyed, on her last nerve, exhausted, eyes popped,

"What happened out there?" her voice barely breaking an intimate whisper.

"I hit my head, obviously!"

Again, words pulled carefully through a whisper, *"Keep your voice down, you're going to make a scene."* She warned—as if she was going to do something if I did.

I let out a sharp, dry chuckle and shouted,

"That's rich! I'm always just causing a scene, there's never *any* reason for it, yes!?—"

She cupped her hand over my mouth and silenced me. I stared at her in shock. In the audacity of it. Before I could yank her hand and pry it away, this look in her eyes stopped me dead in my tracks.

Fear... but not the same kind from earlier. A different kind of fear... worry. Her lip was shaking.

"I don't want to argue, Son. Please. I want you to tell me what happened, everything that happened. Now." She removed her hand carefully and placed them back on her knee.

Jonah's right. She is an impossible woman. I rolled my eyes and turned away, stung when my gaze landed on a poster of an eagle that said, *"Make it a great day, or not, the choice is yours." - Ralph Waldo Emerson.*

I cringed. *"What a shitty sign to hang in an emergency room..."* I said.

My mother stood silent. And that silence simmered and boiled over inside of me. I turned to her, betrayed, and asked,

"Why are there daggers and knives between us all the time? When there should be love?" Ready to lay it out on the table.

She ignored me with a look of disbelief. It angered me—Am I not worth a conversation of substance? Or raw truth? Am I not a person anymore? Is this what I deserve? To be condemned after wishing I could be strong enough to lift the both of us?

I wanted a moment more. Nothing. Heart fracturing another inch down the center. I made a final attempt to reach her.

"Remember the last time I was here?" I asked, smiling for her. Trying not to be so hollowed out. She let out an abrupt chuckle, one that betrayed her broody attitude. She shook her head and covered a smile that fought her lips. I felt tears swell in my eyes.

"Yeah." She blurted through a breath. "You got crazy glue in your eye... How the fuck does that even happen?"

She sighed, glanced away and muttered, *"Only you..."* woefully under her breath. But that smile lingered and graced her eyes for once. And I hoped the woe her voice was tinged with love.

The memory was funny. She was so scared. I recalled that face she made as she began to hyperventilate over me, begging me to stay calm. And I laughed at the thought. I should have been the one freaking out, but it was her. And when we got to the hospital she was just as angry. Hard, annoyed face. Tapping her heel.

She laughed with me. Her strained voice and the passage of time swept me up... I began to cry. Now I'm laying here desperate for even morsels of concern.

She stopped laughing.

"Mom, I'm scared." I sobbed, trying to keep her gaze as she peeked away. I choked.

"What's wrong with me?" I begged. And I wasn't asking about my condition—I wanted to know, badly, what is so wrong with me? Fervent and convicted—I would fix it. I would change. I would change for her right now. Despite everything, I love my mother. Despite everything, at the end of the world, I want my mother's embrace.

I just want my mom.

She sniffed and wiped my eyes with her sleeve. A wave of relief washed over me. And that relief, like sunbeams, vanished when she still said nothing.

I began sobbing even harder, every hiccup begging her to say *something*. Anything. But still. Nothing.

Then a nurse walked in and said we were good to go. His chipper voice sliced me in half. My mother stood promptly and shook Val's knee to wake her. My heart was eviscerated. I closed my eyes and bit into my lip until it bruised.

I just want to sleep.

new years 2018

NEW YEARS 2018

—HAPPY FUCKING NEW YEAR!" Tyler shouted in my ear, unleashing a full breath into his kazoo. The sound shrill in my ears, I groaned and plugged them with my fingers. *"Ugh!"*

He laughed. Impervious to my shitty attitude. I had absolutely nothing to celebrate. Time means nothing at all to me now, after everything that has happened. Every day is just a repeat of the last. The only thing that changes is the feeling... . That emptiness feels even greater. It should be impossible and yet... it breaks me down every time. As I rise I sigh with so much sorrow. Every day will stay exactly the same—and defy me by feeling even worse every time.

I sighed, letting the sound spell out my disdain. "Alright, it's midnight. Can I go now?"

Tyler's face softened and he gave me that look—the one that makes me feel like an angsty little man. Shame upon me. It disarms my defenses every time. Without a word, he slung his arm around my shoulder and pulled me into a suffocating hug. The sheerness of his physicality enveloped me. I could feel the reverb of the laughter deep in his chest as it erupted from him.

I broke free for a second and he whined with a wavering enthusiasm, *"Come on, don't be like that, King,"* The months of apathy must finally be wearing him out. Ugh. He swayed us gently, forcing us into a makeshift dance. I was stiff and uncooperative in his arms. I tried to squirm away but he clasped my neck and shoved my face back into his chest.

"New year, new you, buddy! We're leaving that tortured brunette energy in twenty-seventeen, aight!?"

Katie chimed in behind him, hollering "Yeah!" as she joined in on the hug. That meant something, at least. I could appreciate the love. Katie isn't a hugger.

I broke free, disheveled. They both laughed endearingly as I ran frantic hands to fix my hair.

Tyler cooed, "Aww, I'm sorry buddy." and blew into his kazoo again, wrapping up twenty-seventeen with a final war cry that split the air.

I threw myself onto the couch next to Jonah. He was quiet for a moment, looking at me with those piercing neon green eyes. At least they were easier on me tonight. He shifted closer, a little inch, and whispered, *"Happy New Year, Alexander."*

I peeked over at him, tortured. And he smiled for me, soft as it crept over his freckles. He seemed content. My gaze wavered and I glanced away, unable to bear it any longer. It hurt too much to see. That a ghost was somehow more alive than *me*. And even so... I was not bitter. I wouldn't wish this feeling on my own worst enemy. And I am my own worst enemy. What a fucking crime...

Katie approached me, "Alex—" and grabbed my hand to drag me up. "Come on, we have to par-tay! Ocean's eight is coming out THIS year!"

"Is that really the only thing you have to say about the new year?" I asked dryly. She smacked her lips, brushing off my cynicism like dust and thrust her nearly empty glass of wine toward me.

"Have some?" She asked, hopeful that I'd accept.

"Katie, I'm not old enough to drink." I chided, "And neither are you!"

Tyler snatched the glass from her hand and downed the last of it with a smile.

Katie giggled. "You gonna tell on me again?" She teased in a voice. I sighed and slumped into her shoulder. Katie picked at my hair absentmindedly as she and Tyler resumed their conversation. The same three artists looped on Katie's Bluetooth speaker. *Kylie Minogue, Phantogram,* and *Daughter.* It was good music. I tried hard to pay attention but the weight of the past few months was even catchier.

Life following my concussion has been bleak. I lost my phone and Lilah's number with it. And in a way I lost a potential friend. I never found out what happened that night from her perspective. According to Katie, Lilah didn't seem to recall a thing about the haunted house incident when they ran into each other a few weeks later. It wasn't until recently that I've accepted it was all in my head somehow.

At least... that's what I choose to believe now. I thought it would help me find some semblance of closure, but it doesn't. I still wonder when *he'll* visit me again. Even if that's in vain.

And I stopped having that dream. Not once have I dreamt of the cliff. Instead, I have crude nightmares that leave me waking disturbed. Sometimes I'm not sure whether or not I'm awake or still sleeping. The terror of not knowing spirals quickly into paranoia. I stare at the world through a pinhole most days. . .

"Alright, alright, alright! Top three baddies of twenty-seventeen—Go!" Tyler shouted suddenly. The absurd prompt snapped me out of my thoughts. Katie leaned over and took a swig of a miscellaneous soda can before nominating the following three in this exact order; Cate Blanchett, Katie McGrath and Rachel Weisz. She was so affirmative. I couldn't help but chuckle a little.

Her smile and her shiny black hair framed her face so beautifully. I looked to Tyler, with his thick red stubble over his huge smiley lips and wondered how, despite their own struggles, they managed to be so light. And despite how draining it must be to keep me around, they host me. I sighed and sank into something outside of myself. That long-buried

Alexander they still remember, and I allowed myself to believe that there's still hope that this will all somehow get better. That I'll change, and they'll lift me up, and I'll be happy again. "In time." Another one of my many lies.

They are a gift to me. I wished that I could be easier on them. I always feel so ashamed, believing their eyes for me are undeserved, for I am so deeply unappreciative. All they have to offer that gaping hole inside my heart, they give to me. And the taste is not enough. This suffering has such a lust. It consumes me.

Tyler snapped his fingers and leapt to his toes with excitement. "Yes! Love Rachel Weisz! Remember when she tongue-kissed Rachel McAdams in that one movie?"

Katie squealed. "AAAAAA. DISOBEDIENCE!?"

Quickly my musings felt a bit overstated. They went back and forth, Tyler nominating "Wolf of Wallstreet" *Margot Robbie, Natasha Lyonne,* but the 'current-milfy-version' And *Rachel Weisz.* I felt wildly inappropriate for even listening. But I suppose that is the teenage spirit. Sometimes I'm just a prude.

When I was asked, I uttered an uncertain, *"Elizabeth Olsen. . ?"*

They exchanged a look, *"Girl..." "Be so serious."* And burst out into laughter after a pause. I sighed. They were making me play along.

"Okay but don't judge me!" I nagged with a finger in the air. Katie crossed her arms.

"Uh—*Henry Cavill,* obviously. *Daniel Radcliffe*—but, like, him now as an adult. And my number one every year; Cornell University Ivy League Wrestler *Yianni Diakomihalis.*"

They cheered, *"AAAAYYYYYEEEE—!"* beaming at my effort to power through the fog. Little did they know it was only for them. Everyone gets the shell. Especially me.

My gaze landed on Jonah and I smiled at him. He was peeking at me through the crack in Katie's closet door, his visage soft in the shadow.

Are you okay? I asked him in thought.

He smiled. *"Yes, I am. Have fun, Alex. You don't have to be so serious all the time."*

I sighed.

Tyler and I stood at the foot of her front door. The crickets behind us played a loud symphony in celebration of the new year.

"Are you sure you don't want to sleep over?" Katie asked.

"I can't." I said. Which was a lie. I simply did not want to. I'm partied out. And last time I slept over Katie kept me up all night playing telephone with Jonah. I couldn't endure it a third time.

"Aww, okay." She said, "Tell Jonah I said Goodnight." waving her fingers adieu as she shut the door.

We began walking into the open street. Our footsteps bellowed eerily throughout the neighborhood.

"Where's all the noise?" The people of Los Angeles are notorious for being obnoxious with their fireworks every holiday. But not tonight. And it couldn't have been the weather. That never stops them.

"Um, don't get 'em started. These bitches'll get it jumping like Iraq out here if you ask."

I laughed. "I hate it so much. Like... what's the point?"

We headed toward the Metrolink Station on 151st Ave. When it's late you can hitch a ride without the ticket man on duty to validate your fare. It's honor code past midnight. Around these parts that has no meaning.

I felt guilty at first. As I always try to be a law-abiding citizen at the very least. But I've been doing this so long now I guess I can make exceptions for myself when it's convenient. First it's free train rides then it's domestic terrorism. I shiver.

Tyler wasn't incredibly chatty the entire way. He kept ahead and gawked at old houses. Every now and then he would make a comment about the smell of the rain.

I tried to impart some knowledge and tell him that there was a word for that smell—Petrichor. But he laughed instead and started teasing me.

"Dude, your vocabulary is crazy. I can barely understand you."

I let out a breath. "Ugh, how is that? We talk all the time!?"

He was gentle suddenly, "I don't mean it like that, bro, I'm just, like, always surprised by the words you come up with." His little shrug made me settle. I hate that I'm so high strung.

"I guess." I muttered.

"Remember that time you said *Acquiesce* instead of, like, literally any other word? Girl..." He cackled. "Bazinga! Bazinga! Hah hah hah. What's that muthafucka's name? Sh-Sheldon—what?"

"Sheldon Cooper."

"Sheldon Cooper!" *"Hah Hah!"* "You're crazy."

I grimace at the comparison. It didn't even make sense! "I said that because it was the word that most accurately conveyed what I meant to communicate! Hello!"

"There you go again! *Convey...* Crazy."

"Nevermind, Twinkle. Nevermind."

He stopped under the streetlight and looked at me, his hands shoved into his pockets. And stared at me before letting out a kind breath.

"What?" I prompted.

"Do you wanna sleep over at my place?" He asked.

I paused. I'd never been to his apartment before. And I always wanted to ask if I could, but I knew my mother would never let me. She has her conspiracies about him that complicate our friendship.

"I don't know, man, my mom wouldn't let me." I said disappointedly. "I already texted and told her I'm on my way home. *She replied with the letter K in all caps and a period.* She's not in the mood for any funny business tonight."

"Then just say nevermind—Say that you changed your mind and Katie asked if you could stay the night. You do that a lot, right?"

"Oh! Lying to my mother? I couldn't."

"You literally lie to her all the time."

"Okay but that's to my own defense, never to blatantly deceive her."

He let out a sharp breath, blowing a band of hair out of his face. *"Wow."* "No shade, but she has you by the throat, Alexander. You don't owe her any explanations anyway."

I sighed. "I can't say I disagree with you."

"Okay—Well, what are you supposed to do? Take it on your back? Rebel a little. You're doomed anyway, let's face it."

I scoffed—He smiled and got closer. Still teasing me. *You're doomed anyway, let's face it.* If only he knew.

"Okay fine." I blurted. "But I'm not texting her a thing. See if she'll notice."

He beamed as we kept forward.

The caboose groaned and clattered beneath us. The wobbling rattled my stomach faint. Rain streaked against the windows in jagged, uneven, lashes. Everything past us was smeared into lights and shadows behind the graffiti etched into the glass. On the pane behind Tyler, in tiny, inconspicuous letters, the phrase ABRACADABRA had been scratched into the surface. I couldn't help but feel like it was an omen of some kind.

Tyler sat on the opposite side of the aisle in an obnoxious man-spread that took up two seats. A thought occurred to me then.

"Don't you have work tomorrow?"

He sucked in a breath through his teeth. I tilted my head, already skeptical of what he was gonna tell me this time. I waited.

"Okay, hear me out—" He began, already argumentative. "I was pushing some old lady down the hall in her wheelchair, right? And she coughed—But like, she's old, and sometimes old ladies pee themselves when they cough.

"Anyway, she coughs, right? Like, I'm talking tuberculosis type beat—And this bitch pees herself crazy and gets it all over my shoes!"

// ११ //

I covered my mouth.

"So, anyway, I'm like, ya know, fuck it we ball. It happens," "But she looked *so* embarrassed. So I panicked—I panicked and like—I thought it would be so funny if I said, "Bitch! COPD? More like CO-Pee-on-me!" "HAHAHAHAHAHA!!!"

The train jerked suddenly. He laughed for only a few moments and cut himself with a sigh,

"I got fired cuz I actually said it." His voice was lower, now tinged with a self-deprecating edge. "She didn't even have COPD... Sad story..."

"Twinkle..." I said, feeling sorry for him. "You were hardly there a month!"

He nodded. "No. That was two weeks ago..." But he smiled again, "But don't spaz, I got something lined up at Baskin Robbins!"

I blinked at him and sighed in relief. Stunned to silence for a moment too. Sad story indeed. But I admired how quickly he conjured a sense of optimism. It was like a spell I couldn't dream of mastering. I made an effort to be supportive. When I was a dreamer that's all I ever needed.

"That's great." I said, reaching over to give him a playful nudge. "I know this one'll work out."

He winked at me.

The dark, rattling train felt less unpleasant then. We sat in silence the rest of the way with our heads against the windows and stared at the ceiling.

When we made it to the steps of his apartment complex he held a finger to his lips and whispered,

"I'm not allowed to have people over at night, so, I like, need you to walk in like you have business here."

"Oh, okay. Um—what does that mean?"

He grabbed me by the shoulders. "Let me impart some wisdom onto you. If you ever find yourself somewhere you aren't supposed to be, always *act* like you're supposed to be there. If you're all meek and suspicious, people are gonna notice. You feel me?"

"Er... that's, like, really scummy. But, in a way, clever. I mean—why are you telling me this?"

"I live in a group home type-situation." He blurted, before clasping his mouth with theatrical gasp.

"Twinkle why didn't you tell me this! Can you even have people over!?"

"I just said no. But, dude, my dormie brings girls over all the time, trust me, I'm not the only one who bends the rules here. Besides, who is anyone to tell me I can't have friends over? Bitch I'm depressed."

"I—" "The people who house you certainly can... can't they?"

"No." "They only have those rules because some idiots fucked it up for the rest of us.

"I think this one guy had his girlfriend living with him and the church was not down to pay for that. So now there's a rule. But people pass in and out of here so much that nobody's gonna question you unless you bring attention to yourself."

I hummed in thought before agreeing with a nod. He smiled and unlocked the gate.

"So, do they like, charge you to live here or it is free?" I asked. He fought to find the right key on his chain before unlocking the door and holding it open for me. I walked in and lugged my backpack on the coatrack against the wall—the entire thing toppled over from the weight and made a loud clang against the hardwood floor.

I gasped, *"It was an accident!"*

Tyler shut the door and started laughing to himself as he put the coat rack back in place, my bag slugged over his shoulder. He tossed himself onto his bed that was a few steps from the door.

"What did I just say, bro!? Hahah!"

It really was just a room. No kitchen, no living room. Just an open floor, a bathroom, and a closet. Despite its bare bones he had a crazy set up. Fairy lights hung from the ceiling, and all the details highlighted were so intimate. His walls were plastered in layers of posters, sticky notes, and drawings that overlapped each other. He had a dartboard with all the darts lodged into it, and an old jumper nailed barbarically into the wall.

"Wow..." I said. In awe and envy. "This is so awesome. You have so much stuff!"

"Thanks." He said. "I've been here a long time. I think Johnny and I are the only two who have been here from the jump. Everyone else is new."

"Who's Johnny?" I asked.

He leaned back and kicked off his shoes. "Ah, he's this little guy down the hall. Sometimes we're cool, sometimes we're not. He's, like, going through a phase right now. He's been on about some reality shift."

"Reality shift?"

He sat up and began to whisper. I got closer.

"Johnny, like, thinks things. But not real things. He says he's some 'rewritten' demon-possessed-space-terrorist from another reality. It's his most intense delusion yet. *Dude swears on his life.* He's usually really funny, but I've learned to keep my distance when he gets like that. He can get a little scary."

"Oh! Fun! How far down the hall?" I asked through a squeak.

"Mmmmm, like three doors down. Don't worry, he's not gonna get cha. He hardly leaves his room these days. I only ever see him when I'm taking out the trash. Weird dude, I'm serious."

I nodded. "So is everyone here, like, you know," I then swirled my finger in the air. He laughed.

"No. Just Johnny and I. Probably why we've never moved on elsewhere. No matter what we throw at the wall. Sucks."

I frowned, troubled by the idea he sees himself that negatively.

"Twinkle, you're not crazy." I said. "You're just having experiences that most people don't understand. I'm sorry if you truly feel that way— that you're here because you're crazy. I promise you that isn't the case."

He smiled again, but lacked the white glint in his navy-blue eyes. They seemed as black as pearls.

"Thanks."

We both instinctively looked out the window as a sudden flash of light lit up the room. It began to storm outside.

"Welp." He said through a breath as he stood. "I'll take the floor, you can have my bed. I washed my sheets last night, so it's not gross, I swear."

"Thank you." And I sat timidly. "Uh, do you have any pajamas I can borrow?"

"My clothes will swallow you whole. Just sleep in your undies, I won't molest you." He said, and then winked. *"Or will I? Bum Bum Bum!"*

"Twinkle, please, that's not funny."

He seemed frustrated with himself for a brief moment and blinked. "Fuck—I'm sorry. Sometimes I just say stuff."

I untucked my collar and began to undo the buttons.

"No, No!" I said, "I'm just serious all the time—I'm sorry. I make everything awkward."

"Nah, that wasn't cool. I forget you're so much younger than me sometimes." He trailed off.

I cleared my throat and placed my shirt beside me after folding it.

I stared anxiously at his ceiling after we exchanged goodnight's. I took in a deep breath and braced myself for another nightmare as I closed my eyes.

In the darkness, a cherub emerged in the form of an infant, illuminated by a halo of neon blue light.

It stopped inches from my face, sniffing not at my body but something intangible within me. The sensation was unnerving, as if all thoughts had been laid out bare for him to see. Then, without a sound, he turned away and vanished into the abyss.

I blinked and suddenly I was on Diamond Avenue in Pasadena. The air was thick with the tang of wet asphalt and rotting leaves. And I stood alone under the light of a midnight sun. Its golden beams broke through the trees in uneven shapes and danced in the fog that twisted like tendrils. I let out a breath and released everything that bound me. The wind blew and I heard the sheer of the leaves succeed like pebbles on the shore. The light was so beautiful. And I was at peace.

A loud, anguished moan erupted behind me. I turned to see a soldier stumble out of the shadows, with wild, bloodshot eyes. He yanked me by the arm with a desperate grip, his trembling hands streaked with dirt and blood. The man's face was censored by shadows, as if he wore a glamor to conceal his identity.

"Is it true!?" He screamed—voice breaking. Betrayed.

I jerked back, breaking free of his grip, and gave him a cold shoulder. As I walked away he crumpled to the ground like his heart and stopped beating suddenly. I turned and saw his hand lift to cast a bizarre sigil on the wall beside him. I would never forget it. A bunch of perfect squares in a broken ring, drawn with a lone bloody finger.

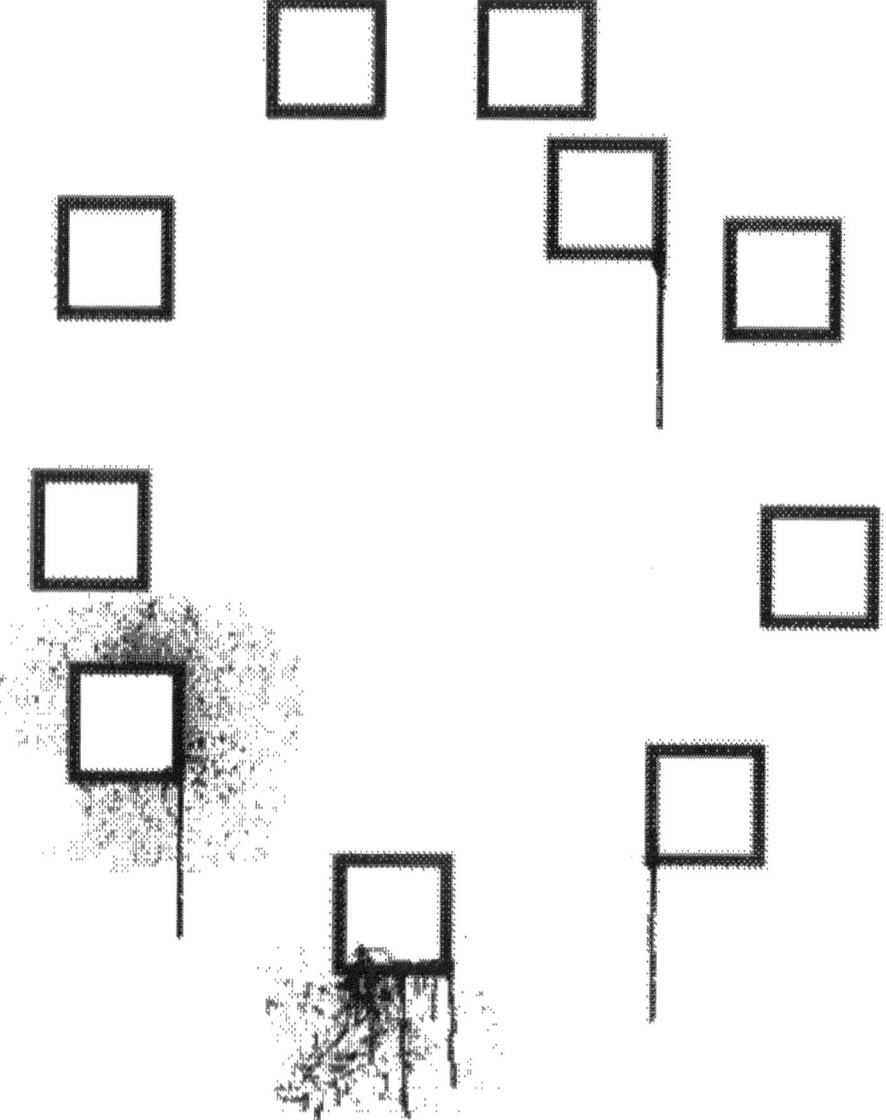

He dropped dead. A crowd of people gathered behind his body, their faces drawn down in despair. A woman shouted that the moon was falling. I looked—And saw it bright and crimson, menacing, swelling in size as it descended upon us.

It is the apocalypse.

Despite the impending doom, no one screamed. They all just wept into their palms.

Men in blue cloaks raised their hands to the sky, casting frantic, invisible spells that shimmered and dissolved into the air like whispers. Their efforts only drew curses. The people damned them, begging God to strike them down. I kept onward.

I noticed a warehouse in the distance, its heavy metal door slightly ajar. The dancing candlelight seeping out from the gap beckoned me closer. I entered without a thought about it. There, a bishop stood on a chair in the middle of the room, preaching while he waved an athame in the air. Everyone turned to face me. The bishop smiled and pointed at me, calling me a name I couldn't repeat as two men reached out to grab me.

A sudden hand yanked at mine from outside and dragged me into the street before the men got close enough. It was Leonel, and he was urging me to run.

I fled after him, the streets blurring around us until we reached a random house on the outskirts of Woodrow.

A black house, old and weathered, overrun with ivy and moss. A witch stood in the doorway, her long tangled hair spilled over her shoulders and onto the floor by her bare feet. She whispered to me as I passed, repeating the dead soldier's plea,

"Is it true?"

Leonel pulled me further inside. The house was cluttered with twigs, crystals, and handmade things that hung from the ceiling. He led me to a hidden room in the hallway.

Inside, the room was barren. Its white tile walls and floors were blunt and cold. The entire room smelled of bleach. He sat us down on the floor, his breaths slow and careful. His shirt hung open, his tie was undone, revealing beautiful smooth tan skin. I stared, gaze caught in a strange dance between indifference and arousal. He met my eyes, his expression hard yet pleading, as though seeking permission. I leaned in and I kissed him, my hands gracing the tender parts of his body. I undressed him, tracing the curve of his back with my fingers as I slid my hand beneath him to pull his body under me.

The air was light. It was suddenly easier to breathe. We locked eyes as I found myself inside him, and we made love right there.

A deafening boom shattered the moment. The ground trembled violently. The lights flickered out and extinguished.

In the darkness I saw that white face that smiled at me in The Empty, its eyes gleaming with neon blue rings.

"I KNOW WHO I AM!" a voice screamed with shredding conviction—The words blared in my ears like a church bell. I woke up with a sharp gasp, my heart pounding hard in my chest, hand clutched over it.

The clock read 3:12 A.M.

"What the fuck!?" Another voice shouted. I jumped out of bed in a panic—it was Tyler.

"You havin' night terrors!?" I could feel his heart pounding in tandem with mine. His face hardly visible before me, the blinds sliced the space between us into uneven bands of red streetlight and shadow.

I raised my hands to keep him at a distance, "I'm okay——" the words clipped and dry in my throat.

"*Are* you okay?"

I didn't know what to say, I was so embarrassed. He folded his arms and I watched his brows knit as a stress took hold of him.

"How long has this been happening?" He asked, firm, like an older brother asking for truth. And, afraid. But for what?

I tensed up, thankful for the shadows that obscured my face. He moved closer and placed his hands carefully upon me, his fingers crept closer and closer until the very tips graced my collarbone.

"You really worry me, Alex. I'm scared for you."

He paused, leaning in slightly as if to emphasize his plea. His concern for me is unbearable. I feel it rip at my chest like cat talons. Thin stinging lashes all over me.

"I, uh..." My voice wavered and I swallowed hard, "I've been having night terrors for a while..." I admitted, each word dragging out of me.

"And I can't sleep a wink these nights. I wake up at the same time, every night, and I can't go back to sleep until sunrise——"

His eyes darted to the digital clock on his nightstand. The glowing red numbers confirmed the time.

"——It's been going on for months."

He let out a heavy, lamented, sigh. His eyes were sorrowful. So much blue sympathy.

"That's fucked. Why?" He said.

I unraveled with an equal breath and leaned into my knees, shoving each and every one of my stressed fingers into my hair and confessed, *"Friend, I haven't the slightest idea what's happening to me."*

He was at my side in an instant, urgent. "Tell me what it is—Tell me something—anything about it. So I can help you—"

I spun away and curled into a ball at the foot of his bed.

"You couldn't understand it. I promise you. I shouldn't even invoke such things by speaking of them. Please, Twinkle, please let us nevermind this. Just go back to sleep—I'll leave before you wake."

"What?" He blurted. "Alex—" and sat down beside me, "Calm down—I want to know. Swallow your shame for, like, a second and just say something that's been on your mind—anything."

I went mute again.

He tilted his head. *"Dude."*

I met his marble eyes once more in the dark. A waxy ultramarine gaze. I sank into the carpet and let my hands drag down my face. And I kept them there until I was ready to speak.

"What do you know about quantum mechanics?" I asked—the silence between every word vast and booming. The prompt felt like the moment before a first kiss. Not butterflies, but moths in my stomach. Fluttering in the empty space where my lungs once slept and crashing into my ribcage.

"What?"

"I promise this is related."

"Okay..." He seemed stressed. "I've only heard people say it, I think. Can you explain?"

"Well, there's this thing called *observer effect*. A theory based on observed phenomena. When scientists observe electrons, those teeny units of energy that orbit our atoms, they behave differently. As if somehow our consciousness... our ability to *perceive* reality... influences it on a quantum level."

He chuckled—involuntarily—and blurted another joke despite him. "Hah—You got the whole homeschool-thing on lock, don't you?"

His eyes were still weary. He bit his lip. "Sorry—"

"Yeah—I know, it's okay." I hissed, already frustrated with myself. "Sorry." You're not an expert on anything unless you can explain it in layman's terms. Good thing I'm not an expert. Just a victim.

"Basically, everything you can see—me, you, everything—And even the things you can't see—like the air, or Wi-Fi, or the quarks in our atoms—these things are a tangible part of our existence. These things are what we consider reality. Every wavelength of every thing—and it all interacts. It's all connected."

"To observe something is to alter it forever." I muttered to myself woefully.

I continued, "The observer effect suggests the ability to manipulate reality just by using our eyes to see it and our minds to conceptualize it. Small scale probability manipulation.

"The lapses in how space-time is understood could drive someone mad if they think about it too long. But, maybe, we aren't the only ones here to see it—I mean—there are cosmic laws that create this order we try so hard to know. Think of gravitational laws and their precision to even allow matter to exist as it does. One number off the mark and... you get nothing. No existence. Only nothingness... everywhere.

"Isn't that terrifying? To think it all hangs on a decimal? *Everything?*

"It's like... there is some intelligence, if not intelligences... somewhere beyond what we can see. The way the universe interacts is so sentient... And intentional. Maybe even built."

He stopped me. "Woah—Alex, hold up. *This* is what keeps you up at night? Alexander—" He let out a sharp exhale, "You gotta get your head out of the Neil deGrasse Tyson and pull it together."

He was being sincere. He looked so worried. "Please." He added.

"It's not that, Twinkle." I droned, like a mad man. Trembling. About to say it. "My whole life I've felt my waves of influence bleed into everything.

"My words and thoughts alter reality in deviously indirect ways. Every manipulation is small. Pervasive. Only known to me and no one else.

"A quick lie conveniently no longer being a lie. Careless words wreak havoc like a spell—

"I think something out there knows.

"I think he knows I cause things and something—I don't know what—But something I did got his attention—"

Tyler's face turned white. Toes curled in, arms tightening around his legs. "Alex, w-wait—Calm down—" He urged.

"I know you see ghosts and stuff—But—what? What are you saying?"

"I promise you I'm telling you the truth—!" I shouted—on the verge of tears.

He put his hands on me again—gentle. "Alex—I believe you."

The words silenced me. And he said it again so I understood. "I believe you." "This is just really fucked up. Like—what? Can you take it from the top? I'm kinda shitting myself right now—"

I cut him off with a sharp breath. And I took in another.

"Sometimes I lose myself in it." I admitted. "I meander between the idea that I'm just predicting things or *making* them happen. Remember when the dog died?"

He nodded. Eyes heavy.

"I had made a joke about pranking Irene and telling her the dog didn't make it after me and Adriana dropped her off at the vet. Lily was only in there for a spaying. That would have been absurd. No harm, I thought."

"She died on the table inexplicably."

In the silence that built up between us I could make out the buzzing of the neon sign outside his window. I went on, even though I really, really didn't want to.

"The doctor said she'd probably gotten hit by a car a few weeks before and the procedure was too much on her body. But she was an inside dog. You remember. So how do you explain that?"

I sighed again. "I waved my hands and hoped everyone would forget what I had said because I was so guilty I might've caused it.

"Never a word about it. No one remembers.

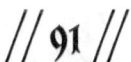

"From then on it seemed the more afraid I was of that power the more it happened. The more bad things I caused.

"And my mom knows I can cause things... I have been since I was a little boy. That's why I think she hates me. She knows I caused her into my life. But no one would believe her."

He got up and stood, pacing around the room with his hands in his hair. I guess I had finally done it.

I stood, "Twinkle—I'm sorry. Are you afraid?" I couldn't see him anymore.

"Alex I'm scared *for* you! What the f—" He sighed, stepping back into the light. "You're just... so... paranormal."

I was hurt. "What do you mean?"

He laughed—exasperated. Compassion in his sigh that followed.

"What do you mean, what do I mean? Y-Y—hahah—you're so fucking paranormal! I'm sorry if I sound fucked up, I swear—I swear I'm here for you—I'll fucking shoot the ghosts, I don't care—but Alex—!

"I'm scared. I'm scared... How can I help you? This is all so... much."

He was at my side, hands on me again. "Are you. . ? Are you scared. . ?"

I glanced elsewhere. I couldn't look at him.

"No, I'm not afraid. I'm not *scared*—I'm *terrified*, waiting for him to return."

"Who?"

"The Wayback." I whispered as quietly as I could—this being only the third time I'd said his name out loud since I saw him. And saying the name drained me of all energy.

He asked again, "What?"

"Nevermind, Tyler. Just forget it."

He unraveled, all the breath he held in burst out of his nostrils as he fell back into the mattress. I panicked. I'd said too much. I forced a smile and tried to make light of everything.

"I-It's a mystical situation... don't you think?" But it sounded so false. I brought loose fingers to my adams apple—and realized that it was my own voice that had awoken us moments ago. It was I who screamed. The thought made my skin start to tingle.

He sat up, face smeared in several emotions with his jaw hung loose.

I continued. "Everything intersects... it's f-fascinating."

"What is?"

I chuckled despite myself. A sign that I'm surely going mad. "Hahah—Just—Life. Just life... Existence as we are here to experience it and is indeed paranormal activity."

His breaths seemed to even out. An unseen hand clasped my shoulder—in the dark I knew it was his.

He muttered somberly beside me, "Sometimes bumps are bumps, I tell myself. But I know there are things that exist like me and you do... I just think we live on separate planes for a reason.

"But you, Alexander... It can't *really* be something you've done, right? Like... why? What have you done?"

He pulled me in closer, his body like a stiff mattress against me. The question tore me apart.

Why *is* this happening to me? What am I, really?

"It's because I'm a manipulator, Twinkle. I manipulate things. Indirectly... most of the time."

"Oh Alexander, manipulator is crazy! You gotta think of yourself as someone better than that—I mean—you said it, right? *To observe something is to alter it forever?* I—I—" He tripped over his point and took a second to collect himself.

"Is it true?" He asked. The question snapped me out of the agony and into the thick of my life's greatest suspense. I got goosebumps.

"... Is *what* true. . ?"

He shrugged. "You know. That stuff about the observer effect?"

I let out a breath. I misunderstood him. But I knew deep down, somehow, I caused him to ask me this question. What are the odds of such an insidious coincidence? My hands were stinging.

"Oh." I muttered. Swallowing it before it could sweep me up yet again. "Yes. It is a real thing that has been observed by scientists."

He cursed under his breath. *"Fuck."* I brought my hands up my arms and held myself tight by the shoulders. Tyler got closer.

"What else have you caused?"

My eyes shot to his. *"I don't know."* I muttered quickly. A lie. Defeated as dozens of events flashed through my mind. Horrors I shouldered all alone. But I couldn't bear to keep scaring him. And I didn't want to scare myself any more than he and I already had.

I felt... truly sad for the first time in a while. Not deep, vicious, agony. Not woe. Just sadness. In that moment I imagined him and I from above us as we were; two young men sat beside each other on shaggy carpet, sharing a moment of their cosmically fleeting lives.

And there were countless others, conscious just like us, everywhere, all over a gargantuan world we'll never ever leave. And that world, all those people, all that grief, love and hate—that whole entire world is but a pale blue dot in a stunning, endless, universe we'll never really know. An endlessness we'll never behold.

And yet, despite how small and finite our lives are in the grand scheme of everything, we create entire realities in our minds that can become so vast we're killing each other over made-up lines in the dirt. It is a mystical thing that we happened at all, only to end up with so much hubris in our little selves.

Homo effectus est divinorum operum contemplator. As if my very existence is a symbol no one asked for, I was made a nexus of tragedy and metaphor.

Every act of love is a miracle in this superposition. Every shared bed, every nudge, every smile, is a flash of light in the empty. All we have to offer each other is love.

He wrapped his arm around me.

It's not enough.

Chapter Four

A ballet of dust particles waltzed through the beams with grace. The sunlight that snuck into the room was soft like platinum, caressed me like a loving hand. It was the first thing I saw when I opened my eyes. And what a difference it makes to wake and see light instead of darkness.

For the first time in what felt like a lifetime of nightmares and insomnia, I was rested. What a nice surprise—that I had somehow fallen asleep in the night. I stirred in Tyler's arms, his steady warmth still lingering where he'd held me. No darkness. No creeping shadows in my periphery. I let it settle into my bones like a hot bath. It had been so long since I'd had that... .

I turned and caught sight of him, already awake, looking at me with careful eyes. I sat up, slipping politely out of his embrace as though afraid to disturb the peace. A vision struck me—his hands shimmering like diamonds, pressing into my ice-cold skin.

"You okay?" He asked.

"I fell back asleep." I muttered in a daze. "What time is it?"

He jumped, "You got somewhere to be?—I—" and tripped on the quilt he covered himself with. As he steadied himself, I glanced at the clock. It pulsed in four red zeros, like it had been unplugged in the night.

"No—No. I didn't mean to startle you, sorry—"

He brought his hands to his hips and smiled. "Nah, it's okay—I thought, maybe your mom called or—you *sensed* her or something."

"'Sensed?'"

He flushed and shook his head, red curls bobbing as he moved. "I was being sincere." and chuckled to nevermind, "You fell asleep right in the middle of talking. You told me you never get any sleep, I didn't wanna wake you."

I let out a breath of gratitude. Happy that finally I had a clear mind to say to him what I had been denying my friends for so long.

"Hey, I love you, buddy." I said in a quick string of words, unable to really look him in the eye as I did. It made my face go numb but I meant it. "Thank you—for having me over." "It was nice."

His face didn't change. In a good way. He came up to me and brought me into a hug saying, "I love you, too, Alex."

After that I walked home and everything was the same. Two whole weeks passed away into nothing. Unnoticed time lost in pavement cracks. Before I knew it, I found myself in the middle of January. Nothing out of the dreadful ordinary. I was beginning to think my Hunsucker petrification was complete. Until I saw *him* again. In another nightmare. A white smear sinking into nothingness, slow and fading like a dead man toward the bottom of the sea. Ringed eyes gleaming like the sun.

The sound of a text notification pulled me out of sleep. I had forgotten all but the last scene when I opened my eyes. I clenched my fists.

"They're only bad dreams..." I whispered to myself as confidently as possible. I sat up, his face still clear in my mind. A face white and of old bone. A skull flayed by someone unknown, with little nips of cartilage and flesh in the tight spaces. Teeth to mock me, silver fillings and a crooked left incisor just like mine. And his eyes I thought were empty sockets— Were fixed with some kind of black glass. Shiny and deep like the thick screen of an old television. I began to shake as if I were really seeing him—really staring into those eyes. I could feel the rings in mine begin to sting.

I yanked my phone out from beneath my pillow to free myself. It was Tyler.

What else have you caused?

What? I tapped the notification. When my lock screen vanished, so too did the message. I glanced around the room. The shadows were too thick for the hour. I started typing faster.

What buddy? Did you unsend your message?

He didn't reply. I cursed under my breath when I noticed the time and jumped out of bed—I'm gonna be late! I sped down the hall with my clothes bunched haphazardly in my arms. In the rush I slammed right into my mother who was already storming toward me with that name-brand exhaustion of hers. My foot slipped out from under me, the collision sent my clothes scattering all over, I tripped and hit the floor square on my tailbone.

"Nunu!" She barked, fingers kneading the air in frustration. "Why did Mrs.Blanco call me and say you missed your test again?"

"I slept in—"

She cut me off, "How the fuck are you always tired but always waking up late? Are you dead?" With a swat she wacked my shoulder, "You're gonna get kicked out of that school if you don't haul ass over there and take that test!"

I blinked. Incredulous. "You can't get kicked out of home school— How does that even work?"

Her hands flew to her temples. "Why do you *always* talk back? It's independent study! You still have to do your state tests!"

I scoffed. If only she cared about my life as much as she cared about my attendance.

"Get up!" She napped, holding out her hand to lift me up. I hesitated, then took it. She yanked me to my feet with enough force to make me flinch. "Go get dressed and get your ass on that bus before I give you a reason to flinch."

I stared at the tile, my jaw tight. I felt her eyes pinning me down like a moth under a thumb.

"Fine—" I hissed. "I swear, I set an alarm. I didn't *mean* to oversleep—I assure you, it was hardly an indulgence. I'm still tired."

She sighed. It shook me up like a cold draft crawling up my boxers.

"Yeah I bet you are. Just hurry up. And don't—" she pointed a finger "—*Don't* wander around the school when you're done. Come straight home. I get enough complaints about you trespassing. You know you can get a ticket for that?"

"Okay, I understand, Mother!" I sang as I bent down to gather my things. She snatched my shirt right out of my hands and walked off with it, like a petty act of punishment. And what kind of punishment is that? I watched her disappear into the kitchen bewildered. I was sure she meant to iron it for me, but her face was more in-line with a woman about to set it ablaze.

I rushed to the bathroom and turned on the shower. The cold water hit me like a crisp slap, exactly what I needed after that fiasco in the hallway. *Why must everything be so difficult with her?* That look in her eye makes me feel like *I'm* the one who jammed that stick up her ass. Whatever.

An abrupt sigh snapped me awake from the nagging thoughts. Take away all the bitterness, that look in her eyes when it's just she and I alone make me think she'd have been better off had I simply never been born at all. And instead of feeling defiance against that thought, I agree with it wholeheartedly.

When I began showering cold a few months ago I did it as a fucked-up form of self-punishment. But slowly I grew to enjoy the feeling. It's one of my few pleasures left. Being near her feels like rubbing sandpaper on my chest every time she speaks. Cold showers soothe the bloody scrapes on my skin. Either that or I'm a budding masochist. Can't imagine they had good childhoods either. *They look so pleased in the porns...* I thought. Perhaps not. But wouldn't that be a fun life?

As I was drying myself I caught the hum of arguing beyond the wall. A common occurrence in this hell house. I pressed my ear against the door and listened closely. It was my mother and Irene. I cracked open the door as carefully as I could manage, but of course the hinges squealed out into the hallway. Luckily for me the sound went unheard—they kept at it, viciously. I shook my head and closed the door.

When I was finished I ventured out into the hall with dread, knowing full well I would have to approach my mother to retrieve my shirt. I'm already late as-is. I considered swiping a different one and sneaking out of the house to avoid getting swept up in the fight, but I had a feeling she'd flip if she'd actually taken the time to press my shirt and I simply left without a care. I bit my nail and marched toward them.

"—YOU'RE JUST GONNA HAVE TO DEAL WITH THE CONCEQUENCES, PRSICILLA!" Irene screamed. They argued through the open door of her room—basked in the sunlight that poured in from the open window. What a perversion of such nice weather. It disgusted me. I lingered just a few feet away from them, by the china cabinet, hoping my intrusion would halt the fight, if only a moment. My mother stood there clutching an immaculately pressed shirt. *My shirt.* I sighed.

A bitter, defiant giggle erupted from my mother. It sent a shiver through me.

"I'm not asking for permission, mom! I'm telling you that I don't know what to do!" Her voice was raw. Shredding. Every word came out desperate for understanding. I tensed. She sounded exactly like me.

Irene caught sight of me in her peripheral but didn't stop. She put a hand in my mother's face.

"I don't give a crap, Priscilla! You're not getting a damn abortion! I won't allow it."

I gasped, both hands clasped over my mouth. The words struck me with the shock of watching a cartel beheading the internet. Their eyes shot in my direction simultaneously. Irene looked disappointed. My mother looked furious. They let a nasty silence bubble up as they waited for me to say something.

This terrible awful feeling choked me up.

"Mom." I croaked. *"You're pregnant?"*

She glanced at Irene and her face grown harder. She flung my shirt at me, *"Go to school, Alex!"* She snapped, voice final, *"And stay out of adult conversations!"*

I caught it, reflexes high in the adrenaline spike of her sudden movement.

"Wait!" I choked—desperate. Shirt clutched in a trembling fist. "Mom, we should talk about this—I mean, from what it sounds like—"

"We?" She interrupted, laced with disdain. "You're so fucking—Fuck it. Nevermind! Get your ass to school and get the fuck—"

She stormed toward me, her movements sharp and deliberate, " — OUT! This is a A and B conversation!"

She shoved me away and I stumbled back—funny bone slamming into the blunt edge of the china cabinet. Everything pulsed in and out of black. Irene's voice rose again, furious, but I couldn't understand her in the midst of hypotension.

"—it's too far into the pregnancy! You should have thought of that when you found out!"

The implication hurt even more than the physical pain.

"You've known this whole time!?" I shouted as I scrambled back up. She stood there completely unmoved by the distress that bled out of my voice like a bullet wound.

"Are you retarded? Of course I've known! I haven't had a period in two months, what else am I gonna think!"

"Well—How can this be?"

"It's not Jesus!" She hissed through her teeth. Eyes telling. Oh. My jaw dropped. I stopped breathing. I covered my face again.

Irene cast a bomb into an already raging inferno with eight words I'd rather not repeat here. My mother started screaming profanities at her that I hadn't even heard of. My ears started to ring as I broke down into another dissociative fit. Riiiiiiiiiiiiiiiiiiiiiiiiiiiiiiiiiiiiiiing turned everything into a low render that made hardly any sense. I felt so unbearably small. It was like being in The Empty again. I saw my soul engulfed by that great nothingness, face just as twisted and pathetic as mine. Times like these I find myself no longer afraid of my power. Times like these make me loath it. To see myself among them, a man just as they. Conscious. Feening for true love. A right owed to us by existence, given to us in highs and punished for being addicted. If it is true, if I am a monster, I still love.

I still love. Even with a heart so irrevocably burdened, dangerous, and broken. I still love. I don't have anything else to say except sorry. We just want love. And I know that to be true. So... what really makes me so fucking different? What makes me the exception to her warmth?

"MOM!" I cried. The walls snapped as if in response. She turned to me.

"Why didn't you tell me?" I asked. Defeated. Desperate for something. Anything to make sense of her cruelty.

And she answered with a question that shattered me.

Existence tilted. I stood there, blank and hollow as if to fall over and cease to be.

Who are you to me? It's worse than I ever imagined. Worse than all my fears and all my doubts. I always wondered—always seethed—always second-guessing myself—grasping at straws—hoping I was wrong about everything. But now I know. Oh my God. *Now I know.* It flew off the tongue like it cost her nothing to erase me from existence.

I don't mean anything to her. I'm just here. I'm just in the way. My lip trembled as I met her eyes one last time. She waited, face sharp, expectant, as though she wanted me to lash out. To fight back. Or say something provocative. But I didn't. I couldn't.

I nodded once, turned away, and left.

The bus sprung to life with a violent jolt. I was catatonic. Eyes blank—they might as well have shut, all other senses sharper to make up for the lack. I felt the sky darken as a storm descended. My ears twitched as rain poured down in sharp bursts from all directions. I had more of an awareness of the stiff, embalmed plush of the bus seat than my own body.

A sound swept me up then. Something that screeched to life like an old radar tower. Unrelenting, agonizing, the sound's slow ascent into harmony that should have been holy in its beauty—but it was so invasive. It worsened that emptiness. Like rocks tied to my feet, dragging me even further into it.

Before I knew it, I was soaking wet at the steps of the high school. I stood as stiff as stone, no desire to remain in this body, yet I slid gracefully inside like a rook across the board. The halls dimmed to an unnatural shade of blue when I entered the building.

I barged into Mrs.Blanco's office and took the lone chair across from her. She jumped and uttered my name in surprise before fixing her posture and putting on a kind face.

"Alexander! I'm glad you're here but you should have called." voice stern but well meaning, "You can't just barge in here, Alexander, I don't appreciate that."

Suddenly her eyes flashed to the desk lamp beside me, brows creased in surprise as the light dimmed to static and died in the bulb with a low sizzle. The shadows around us devoured the empty space. It startled her, but her reflex was quick. A flick of the wrist and the room was bathed in fluorescent light. The shadows grow thicker despite her efforts. Her finger was still glued to the light switch.

"My mother told you I was coming, did she not?" I asked curtly. She turned to me, in shock at my tone. Mind still buzzing about the lamp.

"W-Yes, but she didn't say when. She said she would call me back after she talked to you. But she never did."

The realization made my stomach sink. I had to turn away a moment and fix my face. But before I could, I caught sight of Jonah's reflection in the glass of a framed poster beside her. He stood behind me, face twisted with concern. Eyes shimming off it like laser points. My jaw clenched.

"Helloooo?" She sang.

I met her eyes. "Honestly, I fly through these little tests. And I only need you for that." I blurted. "There's no consequences or stakes that make me care enough about any of it to be prompt. Nothing matters. I'm just, like, being really honest with you. Nothing matters. Especially the easy stuff. Can I just cut to the test and be done with it?"

Her face threw me. She seemed hurt. Which was a sadness to me. I know she *likes* me—our small talk and shared interests made it seem like we had a bond. But in the grand scheme of everything she did not matter. Hell—there is no grand scheme. Just a joke at my expense. I huffed in my seat and—suddenly so terribly angry.

"Alexander!" She snapped. Appalled. "That isn't the way the world works. People have lives and schedules and we organize things so everything is fair. I was sure *you* understood that—"

She scoffed theatrically. "I—Is everything alright? You're so... unlike you right now." Her voice was as icy as my mother's, but her eyes conveyed a different temperament. She seemed genuinely worried about me.

A cruel smirk crept onto my face, I fought against it with every muscle. But it was to no avail, the words just tumbled out of my mouth like hot coals.

"No, I'm exactly like me right now."

I laughed in disbelief of myself and felt static electricity snap in my hair from the subtle movement. I glanced at Jonah and freed her from my dreadful gaze a moment. She was unnerved.

The horror of my careless words tugged at my lips. I sighed and rolled my eyes to fight back a frown. Name-brand shame peeking through, chirping at me like cuckoos.

"Nevermind." I spat. Eyes back to her. "Just—Just let me take the test, please." The chair moaned beneath me as I leaned forward, my leaky sleeves pressed a wet outline onto the desk. She watched in disbelief.

"—I'll just do that and be out of your hair. I'm sorry."

She blinked and continued without a word, lost in a storm of private thoughts, and handed me a scantron.

"They'll give you your login and password in the library... Tell the nice lady that you're from City of Angels and you're here to take the CAASPP."

I wasn't listening anymore. I already had what I needed.

I think they say anger is really just sadness. I wonder what stage of grief this is, then? Or am I right back at the start?

The light returned. I sighed and stormed out of the room.

On my way to the library someone yanked my hand from behind. My shoes skid on the abrupt stop—I almost fell over.

"*Alex!*" Jonah nagged. I turned—eyes wide in shock at his strength. He continued, "Whut was that, Alex? You were being saur rude to that lady," and crossed his arms.

I took a quick look around to make sure no one was nearby so I could speak freely with him. Outside, lightning flashed and lit up the whole corridor a blinding white for a second. It swallowed everything except Jonah's piercing neon eyes.

"I can't do this right now, Jonah, okay? If anybody finds me talking to the damn air they're gonna think I'm nuts! What do you want?"

He lurched away a little, overwhelmed by a sudden shift in the air. I felt it too. He gawked at the space around me with weary eyes, as if he could *see* something I could not, and lifted a finger to point at what I could feel but not see. Some kind of static electricity that flooded out of me in waves.

"Whot is *that. . ?*" He asked. I felt him make an attempt to snoop around my mind for answers—but he couldn't pierce through the radiation.

"Leave my head alone!" I barked. He softened and stopped with clasped hands, like a child caught stealing.

"Alex, we're friends..." He whined, pouty eyed as he got closer. His form was immediately disrupted by the waves, but still, he trudged, reaching toward me with a slow creeping hand.

His palm graced my cheek and the waves subsided in an instant. Poof. Gone. And so did the blue light disappear.

My chest tightened. "How did you do that?"

Jonah pressed his lips into a kind smile and dimmed his eyes so that I could meet them.

"I have lots of tricks up my sleeve." He shrugged, a bit teasing, but preoccupied by his speculative thoughts. "Let's go somewhere private so we can talk, Alex, please,"

He removed his hand from my cheek and I was assaulted by all the harsh words I had said. I felt sick. Every letter stabbed at my eyes with toothpicks. I winced and stepped back to put some space between us.

"I have to take that stupid test. I can't."

I guess it was a nonissue. He nodded in understanding. "Okay, then, I can wait."

I hesitated a moment before pulling him into a hug. I hadn't seen him in days.

"My mom—" I croaked, fighting back a fit of tears, "She—She—"

He wrapped his arms around me. *"I know... I know."* voice muffled in my shoulder. A tinge of anger on the last word. It all relayed painfully in my head as he took in the weight of my pain. He was reading my mind again.

Jonah attacked my mother a few weeks before my birthday.

It was the first—and only—time he revealed himself to her.

I've known Jonah as far back as I can remember. He appeared to me when I was a child. Before my father was arrested and my mother took to hard liquor. Back then, Jonah was my only friend in a house full of dancing shadows and disembodied voices. From the night we met he was fiercely loyal to me, though I never came to understand why. Maybe he thought I was worth protecting. Or maybe, just like me, he was lonely.

My father, despite his intrigue in armchair occultism, never believed Jonah was real. He'd shrug him off as an "imaginary friend" that I invented. My mother believed otherwise.

It was just the four of us then. My parents, me, and baby Tommy—but in truth it was never just the four of us. My mother saw many things and refused to admit it until it got too dire. She claimed she once saw the devil in our kitchen.

It terrified her.

Lightbulbs would burn out days after installing them, her favorite rings and necklaces would vanish and turn up odd places by the time they were replaced. Once she woke up with teeth marks and bruises on her arms and legs. I remember crouching behind the couch, trembling, while she sobbed into the phone about it. I never found out who she called that morning. And I never asked.

I saw a lot of things in that house, too. Not just ghosts. Once my mother and father got into a fight so bad she was holding a knife to her throat by the end of it. I remember being eight years old, crying my eyes out on the other side of the bathroom door—praying to God that I wouldn't find her bloody all over the floor.

You can imagine why I'm so messed up now.

In October my godmother Rosalie threw a family party. Something nondescript and sprung on me. I was still raw from the summer, barely able to utter a few words to anyone—let alone knowing faces I hadn't seen in years. The attempt on my life haunted every waking thought. I didn't want to go, but my mother insisted. She framed it as an opportunity to reconnect with my cousins. I wasn't sure why she cared so much but it seemed to me like she was trying, earnestly, for once. When I was gone she fell back into the bottle with abandon. I blamed myself even though I knew that it was absurd. Her guilt was my guilt. My mother has been an alcoholic for as long as I've understood the word. By the time of the party she'd been sober for five weeks. Vulnerable as I was, I went. For her. I had to.

The air between us was still thick with unspoken things, but at least it wasn't soaked in Zyr. After a few hours I allowed myself to feel hopeful. She followed me around the party and reintroduced me to a few people. Once, we sat alone together and she shared stories about her and Rosalie when they were my age. It was... nice. I felt like her son again—her number one. Just like when I was a kid. Every now and then, wherever she was, her beautiful sage eyes would glance around to find mine. The gaze between us was fleeting... but there was love there.

Then disaster struck. I caught her peeking at an open ice chest packed with seltzers and Four Lokos. Everyone else was sipping on something except her. Instead of condemning her for being human, I was simply heartbroken. I knew that look in her eyes all too well. Something was nipping at her with rat teeth. A silent torment. Panic surged through me. *Don't do it, Mom, please,* I thought desperately over and over. The volume of my thoughts must have summoned Jonah's attention... because he appeared suddenly at the edge of the yard with his eyes fixed onto me. I excused myself to the restroom and he followed. His presence confirmed my worst fear. That I would leave this place in tears.

"Are you okay?" He asked, his voice quiet but urgent.

"I'm fine." I said dismissively, my mother's face in my mind's eye. "You should go home."

"I have a bad feeling." He said. "Let me stay just in case." I didn't argue. I had a bad feeling too. A creeping awful dreadful feeling. When I returned to the yard I saw her—my mother—with an open can in her hand mid-sip. And she saw me too, a shattered face. Her eyes shifted just a little, but she glanced away as if nothing had happened and went back to laughing with her friends. Something inside me snapped. I ran over and swiped the can from her hand.

"Mom, no!" I cried. Everything stopped and fell silent. Everyone was looking at us. And the clouds rolled over the sun.

"What are you doing!?" She hissed through her teeth as she reached for the can, but I held it out of reach.

"You can't!" "You can't, you have a problem!"

Her cousin Darlene tried to intervene, murmuring something placating but I wasn't having it. In a fit of rage I glanced at her with the evil eye to shut her up. I continued, voice cracking with desperation for everyone to see.

"Mom, please. Please."

She yanked me by the ear, pinching hard, and dragged me inside the house. Jonah ran after us, shouting, *"No! No! Alex!"*

"What the fuck are you doing!?" She yelled, grabbing at her drink again to take it from me. "You're making a scene! I'm just having a drink, now everyone—"

She cut herself off with a heavy sigh. Her eyes red with frustration. "Call my mom and tell them to take you the fuck home—I can't with you right now. I can't with you. You're too much."

My pupils shrank. *"Me!?"*

Jonah was tense, standing there trembling beside me. Hands gripped so hard on my sleeve that I could see the dent in the fabric.

I'm too much? I locked eyes with her and tipped the can upside down—spilling it all over the floor. Her eyes popped and she sent the back of her hand flying toward me—but to my horror a voice not my own came shredding from my mouth.

"I'VE HAD ENOUGH!" Jonah screamed, loud and inhuman. He caught her wrist mid-swing with the grip of an industrial clamp. He was in control of my body—I sank helplessly to some other place, trying to squirm free in vain. According to my mother the walls quaked and the lights flickered.

"LEAVE HIM ALONE!" He roared.

And then, just as suddenly as it happened, he was gone. I wrestled control of my body back and sent him flying into the wall.

My head spun so long I started to see stars. But my mother started screaming about the lights flickering and Jonah's voice—I couldn't risk anyone else finding out about Jonah. The stress of everything brought me to manic tears—and in an attempt to discredit her claims I lied and said,

"She told me that I wasn't her son anymore!"

I wasn't thinking. It was just careless and off the dome. Sure, that's how I felt on the inside but it was a big fat lie. I regret it every single day.

The words silenced everything. My mother's fury turned into betrayal. Her voice broke as she screamed,

"Why are you lying!? I would never say that to you! Never!"

But no one believed her. Her reputation had condemned her enough. Everyone believed me. And it shattered my heart once again. *I would never say that to you.* No! Fuck—God no!

In all the chaos Jonah stood there shaken, hands clasped over his mouth, invisible to everyone except my mother and I. And she kept screaming and pointing at him saying,

"It's right there! It's right there!"

But to everyone else it was thin air. They thought she was having some kind of episode.

My blatant manipulation drove another splintered wedge between us. Sometimes when I'm at my lowest of lows I tell myself that if I didn't deserve her hatred back then I sure as hell deserve it now.

I never talked to Jonah about what happened. Because I didn't want to admit for a while that I was afraid of him. But he's still here. And he still cares.

And as I followed him to the abandoned bungalows behind the football field, I knew that today would be the day we finally try to hash it out. And he couldn't have picked a worse day for that.

Thunder rolled in the sky.

He sat pensive, rubbing his hands. For once his eyes weren't on me, instead downtrodden, tracking raindrops that hit the pavement.

"Alex... what's happening to you?" He asked through a breath.

I crouched beside him, his face turned just slightly away. I put a hand on his shoulder hoping he would meet my eyes, but he did not.

His cluelessness terrified me. Jonah's always doubled as my pocket psychic. But until very recently, he's been reduced to nibbling on secondhand thoughts. Unpermitted to swallow unless I say so. I was grateful to have a secret for once, even if it had to be a secret pain. Throughout my life with him I've learned one thing to be law; You can never keep a secret from Jonah Mason. *He knows.* And if he doesn't... he will. There's no use to lying. But he doesn't know about Halloween night. Or anything else that has happened since then. Just the external stuff... and... . I really really prefer it that way. If things were the same—if things were like how they were before... Jonah would be terrified of me too.

A beast that weeps is still a beast. No matter how fucked up I am my guilt will not purify me. I have still sinned. Inherited or not, there's blood on my hands.

What's happening to him? He thought, with so much heartbreak.

I guess I have a way of disrupting lives—even the life of a dead boy. He's been so guilty about what happened. If only he knew.

"My mom basically said I'm not worth shit to her. I guess my ultimate lie came true, just like the rest of them. And I don't know, I think I've just finally snapped. . .

"When I got on the bus I heard this noise and suddenly I was so rageful. And so empty. I-If you hadn't done what you did to turn it off..." I trailed off and bit my lip as punishment. I felt like a maniac.

"If. . ?" He asked, glassy eyed as he turned to me. I pinched mine shut to send away the thought.

"I'm so sorry, Alex." He blurted with a shame that seethed him. His pain made my stomach upset, but I kept my expression indifferent, eyes lingering out in the football field where teens began to amass.

"I blame myself for all that, Jonah. I don't want you to be sorry. And I promise you... I'm past it. I have to be. I have much worse things going on right now."

"Alex—No, I'm telling you I crossed a line I didn't even know was there—I've been in turmoil over how I violated you. I made everything at home so much worse... I don't have anything else to say except sorry."

My eyes flew to his. He was crying. It made my lip curl in just a little. What a fucking tragedy to see that he and I live in completely different worlds now. I brought my knees in and shifted closer to him, feeling my slacks stain under the chalky wet gravel.

"I have more control over things than I'm consciously aware of, Jonah. And sometimes more than I want to admit.

"Jonah—I blame myself because I *let* you take over my body. To be honest—some part of me, this darkness deep inside, was grateful that you scared her the way you did. I wanted her to know that she shouldn't be so ruthless with me—that she should be so lucky—that after everything she put me through, I still had love to give her.

"And isn't that a sick thought? Is my love transactional or in vain? Either way..... every part of me I've given and she's taken... becomes darkness.

"I am nothing now. She was the last one to take. And I'm just..." I sighed. "I don't know."

His face shattered into an expression I couldn't read. He looked just like me. Traumatized. The light in his eyes cut off and he went back to staring at the floor saying nothing. I put my arm around him and brought him close, he laid his head on my shoulder.

"When I'm mean, Jonah, I'm not mean because I blame you. I'm mean because you love me and that makes the entire world feel wrong.

"My mother hates me, my best friend is a ghost and I'm a monster. That's my life. But you love me... and it makes me want to believe that it's possible others can love me just as much as you do.

But it's not true. And it never will be. The world is as it is. It's fuck up and I can't fix it. So... I just keep away. Sometimes it's too much... sometimes it's too real."

"Alex..." "It doesn't have to be this way." "How can we make this better? I miss you. My whole life you've never been so far away."

My heart wrenched. I pinched my eyes shut and fought to take in breath.

"I miss you too, buddy. But did you ever think once that I was gonna get older? And change. I'll never be the same as I was Jonah. I lied when I said I needed you away until things went back to normal."

His breath hitched.

"I was hoping it would kill me by the end of the month."

And I guess, in a way, it did. But not in the way I wanted. This is so much worse.

"Don't ever think this is your fault—or your responsibility. The living failed me. Not the dead."

I brought him back into my embrace. He shut his eyes and I let out a cold breath and as I ran my fingers through his rough sandy blond hair.

The rain picked up again. I watched the students scatter to get away from it.

When the fog lifted I could see the skyline of Los Angeles in the distance. The high school sat at the very top of the Ascott hills where Jonah and I hid. We remained there, watching the clouds shake off every shade of grey until the final bell rang and the rain stopped. It was beautiful. I felt Jonah fade in my arms as the sunlight broke. His spirit passed blissfully away wherever it is he goes when he's not around. And the light wasn't so beautiful anymore.

I stood, dusted myself off, and marched toward the crowd.

I like taking the bus with the high school kids. Not many of them speak to me, but the possibility gives me a thrill every now and then. I've made a few odd pals throughout my various cameos amongst their student body. I ran up the steps of the stadium and bumped into one of them, a nice curly haired boy named Nelson.

"Hey what's up, Alexander?" He said handsomely.

I shook his hand. "Oh, hey, how are ya?"

He nodded, seeming pleased with his disposition, "Life's good. I'm playing Volleyball right now, we got a tournament coming up on Thursday, hosting here, you should come support."

"Yeah sure—I mean—Er—Where do you play, exactly?"

He raised an eyebrow, "Here. On the basketball court. We set up the nets and everything it's dope." And laughed, a playful tap on my shoulder with his fist.

What a stupid question I asked. I appreciated that his answer was amicable. It made me crack a little smile—not much but I found it so sweet. I often tell Tyler how much I wish Nelson and I could be friends. His world seems so boyish and easy. I could never fare in it but I loved to dream. Loved... past tense. Now I just feel like a loser for being so coy.

"Oh. Hahah. That makes sense." "Yeah, man—Uh, count me in."

I smiled. It didn't meet my eyes. I knew it the moment his shifted in response.

"Are you alright these d—" The chime of my phone cut him off mid-sentence.

I held up a finger to stop him from saying another word. "Oh hey, I got a—" and flashed my screen. He saw that I had a text.

"Haha, alright, good seeing you," He nodded goodbye and smiled at me before walking away.

It was Tyler.

What is you tallum bout!? ☐☐ What message ? LMAO

A shrill of screechy violins erupted as my gut sank to my feet. I had forgotten about what I had seen this morning. I let out an unnerved breath.

Just waking up buddy?

Nah I lost my phone last night it was so fucking weird. Just found it RN right where I left it!!!! What the fuckkkkkk It just vanished from my desk I was late to work this morn cuz I couldn't find it. Also I got fired ☐☐not cuz I was late tho don't kill me king I swearrr I'll tell you wha happen later………………..

I clenched my teeth. There was a story in that long hectic string of words...

I lost my phone last night — Just found it RN right where I left it — vanished from my desk — I couldn't find it.

It could have very easily been a half-asleep hallucination. Or a technological error. I'm an insomniac and I pirate so much shit my phone's bound to get hacked by someone. It just seemed too intentional to be real. I saw The Wayback in my dreams this morning after weeks without it.

What else have you caused?

Twinkle I got a really weird text from you this morning. Did you really not send it?

Yo what? Wym? Yah I swear I haven't had my phone since last night. Are you okay?

Yeah I'm okay, just a little rattled. I got a text from you saying "What else have you caused?" and when I clicked on the notification it wasn't there. It just disappeared.

Speaking generally on it like that made me really start to think I had just imagined the entire thing. Maybe it was just part of the dream.

Actually nevermind it was probably just a dream haha. Now that I think about it.

God I'm such a fucking mess. I shoved my phone into my back pocket and let out a stressed sigh that rolled into a manic chuckle. I saw The Wayback's face again. A white skull that barely broke darkness—smiling at me. I then thought of my episode on the bus—it all sank in. A moment of clarity.

Holy shit. *Am* I crazy?

Four massive drops of water burst on my head. I looked at the sky, storm clouds gurgling above again. I tightened the straps on my backpack and as I ran inside, away from the storm that roared to life out of nowhere.

It was chaos in the hallway. Everyone seemed in a rush, shoving and slithering between each other. I walked in the opposite direction. Halfway down I ran into Antoine and his friend Karen. Her jaw dropped when she saw me, and she looked immediately at Antoine who seemed beguiled that I was there.

He marched right up to me. "Don't tell me you're back."

I went bashful against my will and fought back an embarrassed frown.

"Antoine. . !" I sang in a high pitch that gave me away. *"Hey buddy."*

"What are you doing here?"

I tried to be charming and tossed a hand into the air. "Uh—You know me, I'm like, the alumni who just can't stay away. Hahah."

"Aren't you, like, behind for our grade?" He asked dryly.

I coughed. "Uh—No, actually, I'm very ahead. I *was* behind but I'm doing so much better now."

I flashed him a smile and leaned against the locker as I twirled a piece of my hair. He looked me up and down before erupting into laughter.

"You're insane."

I cackled for him. But deep inside I was burning.

"I know it."

He got closer and slouched against the locker with me, friendly now. Karen passed him and shot a glance I did not know the meaning of. He ignored her and stood with me. And that surprised me. Antoine and I have an odd history.

I met him around the time I met Leonel. The spring before my life ended and this half-life began. I was just a young man curious about other boys... but I ended up really hurting his feelings. I was his boyfriend for about a week before breaking up with him over text... on KIK messenger.

His newfound kindness to me was a huge relief when it began. I often wonder if it had anything to do with the fact that I went missing and tried to kill myself.

"I don't see you post on your instagram anymore. Do you have any new art or writing?"

"Oh!" I blurted. "Oh—! Um, yeah, I do actually. But it's all super scary and fucked up, I've been having hella nightmares since... I came back."

He laughed again and shook his head. "God Alexander when you did get so fucking awkward? I miss when you were a robot."

"Haha... we don't talk about that." A film of sadness took to my face then. He saw it on my face.

"Hey, well, it's good seeing you." He said. "You look good."

I was touched by his kindness. Especially after I broke his heart. No goodness at all came from my mother's ruining of me, but if I had to find something silver in that hole, it would be that I did gain a better understanding of what it is to hurt over someone.

I genuinely don't remember how exactly Antoine and I met. Just when. But I do remember the way he cried after I rejected him. He was sullen for weeks. He even cut his long, frivolous, afro short. I remember, back then I couldn't understand why on earth he was so upset over *me*. My logic and pragmatism made me so rigid.

As I stared into his eyes I wished that I could apologize to him for what I had done. Being rejected by my mother made me feel the truest, deepest, most visceral kind of heartache. She denied me so hard it turned me into this... I wouldn't wish it on my own worst enemy. And I especially wouldn't wish it on a nice boy who just wanted to be my friend more than anything else.

I was honest enough today. I can't bring myself to tell him how I feel now. Instead I took in his smile. His eyes. He seemed happy again.

"Thanks, Antoine, that's really kind of you." I muttered, eyes to his Vans. "H-How've you been? Are you still in Music History?"

"God no! That was like a thousand years ago." He took a beat to smile some more and made an effort to keep my gaze. Shyly, he asked,

"So... are you back? Or are you breaking and entering like usual?"

This time my smile was sincere. But from his point of view my lips had barely moved a centimeter off a hard line. "I had to take some state test or else my ass was grass. It was lame. Took forever." I lied about the last part to seem more relatable.

"So, like, how does homeschooling even work? If you have to keep showing up here?"

"You know what, that's a fair question." "I don't know. I think it's not technically homeschooling although it is."

"That literally made no sense."

"Uh—allow me to reiterate. I'm, like, doing school at home but it's not homeschool—like my mom doesn't teach me shit, it's all me and a textbook."

"Oh wow, I could never." "I mean—Hey at least on the bright side you have the whole day to yourself."

I was taken by a flash of myself rotting in bed, fighting with my mother, and crying on the floor still shaking after a cold shower.

"Totally."

He nodded and caught sight of someone down the hall.

"I gotta go—see you later." He said, and brushed my arm gently with a lingering hand as he parted. I turned away and watched him disappear from my peripheral, feeling somber. My phone chimed again.

Girl whatttt are you sure???? That sounds freaky ASL lmk!!! please!!!

I sighed and kept down the hall, narrowly avoiding Leonel and his friends on my way out. I think he saw me, but I had spoken to enough old flings for one day. I covered my face with my hands until I made it outside the building.

Things were surprisingly uneventful when I returned home. I did not see my mother not once and Irene had some kind of church ordeal. Tommy was at the skatepark till streetlight and Franky was plugged into his *Grand Theft Auto V*. Jake was at the mall with Adriana and Bonnie, and the twins took Stevie and Max to the beach.

I had the house to myself for the first time ever. What a rarity. I took the private time to experiment with vintage pornography on my laptop but I couldn't bring myself out of the mute agony of what my mother had said earlier.

No matter what I couldn't pull myself out of the funk. It was all I could think about between the silences. I saw the words in my mind, bold letters, over and over again.

Who are you to me?

Who are you to me?

Who are you to me?

I buried myself in coffee rings, textbooks, and old candy corn as I sat alone in the kitchen plowing through my assignments. I left my laptop idle, glancing up at the screen with far too many tabs open every now and then when I was interrupted by a cryptic email.

It was from a name I did not recognize.

☐ **Adrian Lazo**   **Re: [deleted]** - Alexander Hunsucker...

I hesitated. A bad sign. Usually I jump at the prospect of talking to strangers online. But with everything else going on I wondered... is this another incursion?

I opened it.

Reply: [deleted6n16S75....]

Adrian Lazo <incdrXML.187D54E6AF7.kjev@instamail.com>
to me(444dreamcowboy@instamail.com)

Alexander Hunsucker   Is it cool to be gay?

"What the fuck?" At first I wasn't sure what to make of it. I don't know anyone named *Adrian Lazo.* But I'm not slow—there's no way in hell I plan on humoring such a weirdly invasive spam email.

Delete.

Hours continued to pass. I grew so bored of dissociating through tedium. I chewed on my pen so hard it popped and spilt black ink all over my lips.

I jumped and grimaced, *"OH! BLEGH!"* smudging it all over my face—the legs of my chair shredding throughout the house like Gabriel's trumpet. I sprinted across the kitchen into the hall.

When I saw my reflection in the mirror I noticed the smudge looked like an exaggerated frown on my face. Like sad clown makeup. I shriveled up, fists balled in spite of myself. I felt so fucking small. I scoffed and ran the sink.

My mother told me stories about "cancer from pen ink" as a kid. And although Google said otherwise, my ability to conjure abstract ideas into reality made me extra careful. I made sure to take my time getting all the ink off, and I felt crazy for it. My aggressive attempt to get it off me fueled by the anxiety of what if? I certainly don't want cancer. I scrubbed my skin so hard it turned pink. As I did, I wondered how the doctors would explain away the bad luck. *Cancer from pen ink.* Little do they know...

The sink was a mess of murky water and soap. My shirt was ruined. I tore it off and balled it my fist as I made my way for another one.

Then my ear twitched. I heard the familiar buzz of my phone vibrating against the hard wood table.

It stopped me mid-step.

My heart sank. I brought a hand, slowly, down into my back pocket and there it was—my phone. So what was *that?*

I stood on the heels of my feet and spun around. "Hello?" I called down the hall.

Nothing.

The air got heavier with every step I took toward the kitchen where the noise came from. When I turned the corner I almost shit myself.

My lost Nokia sat innocently beside my empty mug of coffee.

I rubbed my eyes—I thought I was seeing things—but when I uncovered them it was still there. Adrenaline flooded my veins and I started to tremble. I stood and stared for a while, rocking back and forth in the uncanny valley. I didn't know what to do. And Jonah, who had a knack for appearing at the worst times, was nowhere in sight. I tore off the bandaid, stomped over to the table with a heavy breath and snatched it.

I double clicked the enter key and the screen lit up an eerie blue. It had all the scrapes and tattered from all the times I'd dropped it. I knew then it was definitely mine and it was definitely *real*. My grip etched the blunt edge of buttons into my thumb. I wanted the screen shatter in my hand. I no longer felt alone, but the house was completely empty.

My vision spun out of nowhere—like there were black and white swirls in my eyes as some invisible force crushed me. I lost my mind and fell to my knees, screaming so loud I felt a tear my throat.

"WHAT DO YOU WANT!!!!!??????" I dropped to my knees and let mt forehead press into the cold tile.

I freaked—screaming like a maniac and chucked the phone across the room—my heart jerked in my chest, I lost my breath, as the sound of glass shattering snapped me out of the fit.

I gasped. Through the hole punched out of the window a black cat stared back at me, back hunched and tail frayed. His eyes, impossibly blue and wide, held mine until he lept out of view suddenly, over the fence and out of sight.

I sank onto the ground in a squat, arms pressed into my head like a monkey that had just been struck with consciousness as a cruel joke. Tears gushed out of my eyes in waves, each one more ravenous than the last until my lips dried and I passed out right there.

It must have been hours. It should have been dawn. I woke up dizzy and parched on the kitchen floor. How had I laid on the ground for hours and not one person tried to wake me? What the fuck? I pushed myself up off the floor, weak, and cried into the dark,

"Hello. . ? Everybody. . ?"

It didn't even echo. I tried to turn on the light but the switch didn't work. I glanced over at the clock on the wall but it was too dark to tell the hands and the numbers apart. A gust of air passed over my shoulder like the unwanted touch of a predator. It was so cold it made my bones ache. A fit of goosebumps so intense it hurt. My skin, worn and thin, looked like a featherless bird. It made me feel so deeply disgusted. Disgusted by everything. My fucked up little body, my frail state of mind and this fucked up house.

"WHERE IS EVERYONE!?"

The clock ticked—I jumped. When I saw it again the numbers were gone... it was just the hands. The light that crept in from the broken window made it clear as day. My eyes adjusted and the state of the house made my knees buckle in—a panoramic image of incomprehensible destruction. The couch torn to shreds with massive lashes. Like a monster had taken to it. Glass shattered everywhere. Picture frames, light bulbs, mugs, and plates. All destroyed.

I shot a glance at the ceiling light—instant understanding. *This is why the lights wouldn't turn on.* I was horrified that I even tried—another attempt to save myself, futile, damning—and it was in vain. Always in the dark. Always... alone.

"GUYS!?"

I stumbled back, breathless, blind panic, and kept stumbling back until the shattered window bit into my bare skin. I turned—only for it to burst—glass shards flying into the air, lashes all over my face—a pair of arms sprung through to snatch me up. Vile, unnaturally long, red and green striped sleeves, they coiled around me with an iron grip.

I tried to scream—but the sound lodged in my throat—useless. I was wretched through the window and gone in an instant. Swallowed whole by the night.

I awoke with a sharp gasp, the stench of my drool was blunt and toxic. I opened my eyes and my laptop was the first thing I saw—window open to the email thought I deleted.

I let out what might have been a breath of relief, only for the fact that none of it was real. Other than that I was disturbed. I brought my arms in to hold myself, my heart twitched—hands gracing my cold bare skin. I wiped my hand on my chest and felt around for my shirt—it was gone. I saw it then—that my hands were still stained in black ink. And I could still taste it in my mouth. The stench was trapped in my spit. And yet, my pen sat right there in front of me. Unbroken, unbitten. Cartridge full of ink like I had just filled it.

I broke. "Hahah! HAHAHAHA—"

I don't know what's real anymore.

The clock ticked. I looked. Nine o' clock on the dot. Eyes shot to the screen—to the time stamp on the email. Received at 6:37PM. *This is getting ridiculous.* I surrendered to this long, fucked-up day and went to bed. Valene is out for the night. Likely at one of her boyfriends, leaving the room to me.

Maybe, just maybe, since I had one nightmare I wouldn't have another. With every bit of control I could muster over my power, which, truthfully, is hardly any at all, I *willed* myself not to dream. I pinched my eyes shut and kept them there until I got to the door, repeating the intention that it should happen:

I will not dream tonight. I will not dream tonight. I will not dream tonight.

Anything, anything, anything would be better than another godforsaken nightmare. I'd rather be shot dead in my sleep than endure another fucking nightmare. I paused at the edge of the bed, my legs suddenly too heavy to lift. An ache tremoring through me, one that I tried to swallow as I swallow everything else. But I couldn't keep fighting. I fell to my knees.

"I can't live like this anymore." I sobbed. *If this keeps up, I fear that I might—*

No. I already went that route. Even if I did... My mother wouldn't care. Clearly I was wrong. Lucky to have survived, even. Lucky that I got the truth straight from the camel's mouth instead of soaking wet in a body bag. And what a bitter taste the truth is. Like coins, like blood I swallowed without wanting to.

I broke down onto the edge of the mattress and clasped my hands in prayer. As if it were instinct rather than a desperate cry for help. The corners of my lips twitched before I broke down into tears and whispered into the empty room broken prayers. To whom exactly, I don't know. Maybe God. Maybe my mother.

"I don't even know if you're there. Or if you're listening. But I can't do this anymore. I can't do any of this anymore. You've won. I'm broken."

The air was too thin. Too still. My chest burned.

"Darkness comes upon me, His embrace as sublime as thee, The Lord himself.

"Come to me, my father. Come down from above, and save me from this darkness.

"May your love come upon me. May your embrace be sublime. And stay long enough to hold the whole of me.

"Bury me, my father, as if laying me to sleep.

"And save me from this darkness. This darkness... that comes down from above.

"May your arms be my refuge. May your grace silence this wretchedness that grips my spirit.

"Though it is my greatest suspense. My deepest fear, that I'll find your embrace just as cold—"

" —grrhn—"

I gasped. I wiped my eyes—half expecting something—an answer, a gust of wind—or even a silence separate from the one that was killing me.

But there was nothing. Just me, stagnant air and my broken heart. I held my hands tighter.

"Lord God... it's all useless."

I sank onto the bed and curled to my side.

No dreams, I told myself one last time. No dreams. The sound of my mother's voice snuck through the tear in my brain. Agony ripped through me with the visage of her face in the hallway.

Who are you to me? She asked.

I'm not your son anymore.

What else have I caused?

Chapter Five

Hey

I know about your little move on Leonel And I
know about your brujaria too. Faggot.

I slammed my laptop shut and forced myself not to care. Being cyber-bullied is by far the least of my concerns. I peeked over at Jonah, who stared at me from beneath the kitchen table while I sat on the couch and waited for Katie to arrive. She's throwing her big Mario Kart party this afternoon.

I told him to stay home or else. Or else what, I'm not sure, but definitely something. Maybe I'll trap him in an oil lamp and throw him in Valene's lingerie trunk. Come to think of it... I wonder why I haven't considered that before. I tried hard to ignore him, as I have been since my mother... *said what she said.* The last few days have been rough, and Jonah the friendly ghost is worried about me. Has been pestering me since, constantly trying to console me, picking at my brain, monitoring my thoughts—terrified I might try and kill myself again. If anything he's been making me feel worse.

And I'm so fucking sleepy I can hardly think! Most days I'm waking up by the time others go to sleep. But on days like today, where I'm obliged to be out in the world amongst the living, I don't sleep at all. I stood up all night thinking of the past and writing poems. Took a twenty-minute nap under the running shower before I got dressed. Woke up this morning feeling watched. *More so than usual.*

Although Jonah seems like the obvious culprit of this haunting feeling, I don't think it's him. I can detect Jonah's gaze like I have a seventh sense for it. So I know with certainty that this feeling is something else entirely. Not prying eyes, but some... omniscience.

Maybe it's nothing. Maybe it isn't even an *it.* Maybe I'm just having a nervous breakdown. I find myself staring at random spots in the room, as if there's someone there I cannot see. Maybe it's just the cabin-fever settling in. I've been on thin ice for a few days now. I fear that today is the day that ice finally fractures beneath my feet. And what a perfect day for that to happen.

Today is my mother's birthday.

"Hey did you tell your mom I said Happy Birthday?" Katie asked, a little too friendly. I sighed, honestly unable to look anywhere else but past the rear window of her aunt's car.

Birthdays are the worst. As much as I can't stand to be around my mother right now, I feel terrible ditching her on today of all days. I dread her reaction once she figures out that I've taken a leave from the house specifically to miss it. But I can't risk another episode. *Not even for the sake of my mental health...* I pictured my blond ghost friend's face... *For the sake of my patience!*

At the stoplight I noticed an Animal Hospital on the corner and considered turning myself in to be euthanized. It would definitely spare me a ton of guilt.

"Yeah, she said thanks." I lied robotically.

I don't like mob mentality. I don't believe that kind of thinking makes for a decent society. That being said, Katie is, and has always been, fairly chummy with my family. And that was all fine and dandy when we were in middle school and their abuse was a lot more subtle. But after everything I'd at least expect her to have a *little* blind loyalty. She definitely demands it of me. So, no, I did not wish my mother a *Happy Birthday* on her behalf.

She peeked at me through the gap in the headrest with a smile. It stung a little. I guess I'm just sensitive. She seemed oblivious to my long face, perhaps a bit caught up in her delight to notice the rain cloud above my head.

"You think you can convince Twinkle to come? Everybody wants to meet him."

I snorted under my breath. "He asked who all was gonna be there, and when I said that it was your summer school buddies he said hard pass."

She seemed disappointed, pressed her lips into a hard line and said, "That's fair."

Her friends Damian and Luis were already there waiting for us to arrive, sprawled out in the grass of her lawn basked in sunlight. They seemed lax despite her arriving late to her own party. I find that about Katie charming, genuinely. She may not be so confident on the inside but she walks through the world like there's an explosion behind her— like those men in the action films. Completely unrealistic but everybody buys her swagger.

While I helped her aunt unload all the goodies from Costco she went out into the yard and made nice. I watched and listened from my peripheral while I loaded several grocery bags onto my arm. Everyone had eyes on her. She seemed happy. There was one additional teen in the lawn, lingering a bit off to the side, to her dismay. Damian had brought a plus one, a cute friend named Caesar who Katie's tried and tried again to 'forbid' me from flirting with.

She won't have to worry about that today. Seeing him there was to my dismay as well—I love to talk to him, so I'm sure he expects that of me. And I plan on coasting through yes and no's as much as I can. I trudged through her open door, both arms stacked with plastic bags and jugs of lemonade in both fists for good measure, and made sure not to make eye contact with him.

The rest of her friends arrived shortly after, Sunshine, Raf, and Ari. Danny showed up late with her sleeves pulled over her hands and walked in without as much as a greeting. She took a seat on the floor in the corner of the room in a squat. Her long, faded-blue hair covered her face and she just seemed out of place in a room full of geeks.

Katie watched her lurch from the front door to the far side of the living room, then glanced at me and mouthed,

"What the fuck?"

I shrugged. Danny's invitation puzzled me given that Katie did not want her here and it's her party. I chose not to question her or point this out, however. I've known her forever and learned that sometimes her motivations are beyond my comprehension. Her mother would say the same but for what I'd consider less-than-valid reasons.

Sunshine took a seat beside me after much deliberation, given that I was the only one in the room she kinda-knew apart from Katie.

"Hello, Alexander," She said in a singsong that was almost teasing, tossing one high-heeled leg over the other.

I raised my eyebrow. "Sunshine. I'm surprised to see you here. How have you been? How's school?"

She sighed. "A drag. But, what else is new? How's homeschool?"

I chuckled darkly. "Ditto."

She laughed and inched a little closer to me.

"So," She whispered, "What's the gossip on everybody here?"

I whispered back to her but made sure to stare at the wall as I spoke so no one could tell I was talking about them.

"Uh—the girl in the corner is Danny, she has a crush on Katie but Katie doesn't like her back. I think she's, like, a part of her whole friend group. Or at least friends with one of them.

"The tall one is Raf, he's—" I paused. "Actually, this is my first time meeting him, but the others I've met before.

"I like Damian over there, on the far end of the couch. He's the coolest. Super into legos.

"And the one with the long hair is Luis, he also has a crush on Katie. The girl next to him on her phone is Ari, she draws, I think. Or she likes anime, I dunno. Something like that.

"And the cute nerd in the trenchcoat is Caesar."

The bright red lipstick she wore accentuated her lips, she hummed with a puckered smile.

"Mmn. Hot Gossip. Who's the blonde?"

I whipped my head around the room full of brunettes.

"What blond?"

She glanced back into the dining room and got goosebumps. No one was there. She shoved her hands in her lap, eyes on Katie now, but she wasn't smiling anymore.

"Nevermind—" She spat quickly.

Katie stepped in front of the TV and began announcing herself to get the party started. Everyone started cheering. I clapped and howled with vacant eyes as I scanned the room again, a bit irked. Still, all I saw was a party of brunettes. Then, from just beyond my vision, something moved in the hallway— a shimmery smear that vanished over the corner. I stood and angrily marched toward it in the middle of Katie's speech.

"Where are you going?" Katie called after me, tone chipper but her eyes told a different story.

"Bathroom."

In the hall, I spun around three times and glanced around the corners. Nothing. And I didn't feel Jonah, either. I didn't feel anything, in fact. I was puzzled.

What had I just seen? Katie's house is far from haunted—I glanced at her grandmother's ornate crucifix hung above the doorway of her bedroom and pinched my forehead. I went into the bathroom to wash my hands— making absolutely as much noise as possible. Katie's the kind of person who would notice that I did not, in fact, use the bathroom. She'd probably think I'd gone off snooping, if anything. Which, to be fair I'm known to snoop but never maliciously. Tender items like years-old sticky notes and faded trinkets can tell you so much about a person.

Out in the hallway Sunshine waited for me, arms crossed, leaning against the wall.

"Oh dear—!" I flinched, hands clasped over my chest. "You scared me."

She got close, hush-hush, and pulled me in.

"You saw that too?"

I glanced around, uncomfortable, but playing stupid. "What are you talking about?"

"You know what I'm talking about—!"

Katie approached with her arms out. "Hello? What's going on here?"

"Er—Just gossip." I lied quickly, throwing in a casual nod to sell it. "We were talking about Danny."

Katie rolled her eyes to the name. "Ugh, I know right? So Pathetic. . Well hurry up, Luis is playing against like five japanese-users, he's about to eat shit!"

When Katie was away Sunshine flashed me a glance.

"You're scary." She said after a beat, and smirked.

I scratched my ear. "How so?"

"You're a liar."

I shrunk. "Honestly I wish I hadn't said that. Katie can be a little mean spirited."

She took the opportunity to call me out. *"Don't act like I've forgotten about the 'Edgar-allen-hoe' comment you made about me last year."*

I went pale. She pointed at me and squinted her eyes before marching off behind Katie. I hunched and followed her into the living room.

We played in a circle, curated by Katie, of course. Katie to start, then Raf, then Luis, then Damian, then Ari, then Caesar, then Danny, and last, Me.

Sunshine opted out despite Katie's protest like a badass and just watched, half-amused, half bored. I wondered why, when, and how Katie invited her. And I was even more curious as to why Sunshine showed up. Definitely not her scene. But she seemed to be enjoying herself in her own way. I thought it'd be better to mind my business.

"Can I smoke in here?" She asked, cigarette already in hand. Katie politely denied her, so Sunshine just kept it between her fingers and didn't light it. She sat like that the entire time.

Every now and then we'd all trade spots on the couch or linger in the kitchen where all the food was. Despite the terrible funk I was in, I found myself snacking quite often. If it wasn't my turn I was popping concord grapes and pretzels in my mouth. Which I found weird given that I lose my appetite whenever I'm in a particularly bad mood. You'd think after this past week I'd've lost ten pounds. And maybe I had, but the last hour certainly made up for the lack. Twice I heard my guts moan.

I decided to just grab a paper plate and pick conservative amounts of everything. Katie and I have always had the same taste in food so there wasn't anything on the table I didn't like. Caesar followed me every trip to the table but didn't say a word to me until the fifth or sixth visit, and we had a nice interaction while standing over the brownies.

"Hey Alexander..." He said coyly, practically gliding over to me. His hand lingered on the arm of the chair we stood beside, his unkept nail tracing the little scuffs in wood.

I smiled despite myself. Torn between impatience and my lustful curiosity about him. I still have yet to figure out if he's just a fellow intellectual or if he's interested in me.

"Uh, hey, Caesar. How have you been?"

He nodded, neither of us really looking at each other.

"I'm great, yeah, I'm great. . ." He muttered. He glanced at me for just a moment and then away as he asked. "Can I tell you something?"

I shifted a little. "Sure."

He smiled, and tucked his finger under his lip. "Well, first of all, let me ask—Do you think there's other elements out there in space? I was arguing with a friend of mine about this."

"How do you mean?"

He tittered. "You know, like, here on earth everything we know is on the periodic table. We have oxygen, hydrogen, strontnium, etcetera, etcetera."

"Oh. Okay I understand that, yes. Erm—as for there being other elements in space..." I shrugged. "I mean, I wouldn't be surprised if there was. Maybe Mars has metals we don't have here on earth.

"We can't possibly have discovered everything there is. The universe is too vast for that.

"As for *elements* ... I think after a while they all become unstable. Some on the table aren't even naturally occurring, I believe."

He was beaming. "I agree. The *true mystery* is how the elements interact. Think there's amino acids on Mars? Imagine what. Mars has and we don't. It's crazy."

He then sighed with great joy. "I've been so curious about the universe lately. I gotta tell ya, it's a wonderful feeling to follow curiosity!"

I looked at him. "Wow. Yeah it is. What has you on about all this?"

Caesar laughed innocently. "Uh—I don't know, hahah. I've just been going down an astronomy rabbit hole. I guess space is my thing right now. Earth is so massive, yet so small. I wonder what else is out there..." He trailed off and laughed again, a bit flushed.

I liked the way his nose scrunched up under his glasses, but I was sad. I noticed a stray curl in his face and fixed it while I tried to recall the last time I sat and pondered anything else besides my pain. I held in a sigh.

He turned to me. "Oh—Hahah." And put it right back. "I did that on purpose. Kinda going for a Clark Kent thing."

I furrowed my brow and half smiled at him. "Hah. Okay, Cesar."

Katie shouted across the room for me.

I stammered. "Ah... Hold on. Katie needs me."

He seemed a bit disappointed, but smiled me off. I sped toward her.

"What's up?"

She glanced at Caesar disapprovingly. "Don't start." She warned.

I sighed a bit aggressively—and I only knew it so because her face twisted in shock.

"I—I wasn't even—"

Her face grew meaner.

I resigned, stung again, and sat back down on the couch.

I crossed my arms and spiraled into a sudden episode of prickly thoughts. *I'm starting to see just how tired I am of her policing.* Even if I was flirting with Caesar, why is it a concern of hers? Does she not want me to be happy?

Sunshine seemed to pick up on the subtle tension and took a sip of her coke with an entertained look.

She whispered to me, *"Hey. You should do your thing."* And kicked back, leg tossed over the other and sneakily pointed at Katie.

"What thing?"

"You know..." She then flicked her hand and made a whooshing sound. *"The thing. Katie says you "cause" things. You should make her lose. Get back at her for being a cockblocker."*

My face turned white. Sunshine chuckled a little, perhaps playfully suggesting, maybe even making fun—completely unaware of how serious and how capable I am doing such a thing.

"I don't know what you're talking about." I droned.

I looked then to Katie, who stood mid-bragging about her winning streak as she prepared for her turn, thumbs flicking buttons quickly as she assembled a vehicle for Walugi.

Katie! Katie, Katie, Katie! I recalled that vicious email I had received this morning. *Who else have you told?*

I nodded and filled my chest with fiery air.

"Yeah. You know what, I think I just might." I hissed under my breath.

Everyone went silent, eyes on the screen. Invested.

3. ! 2. ! 1. ! GO! And she was off, thumbs pressed hard into the joy-con as if that gave her a speed boost. I hid my hand behind my back and jinxed her,

Katie will not place first, Katie will not place first, Katie will not place first.

Sunshine cringed my peripheral but I ignored her—I had to focus all my consciousness onto Katie. A few players passed her, nothing out of the ordinary. She snickered gleefully as she slugged three green-shells at her opponents and hit every single one of them. She was in the lead for the first two laps, but I didn't give up. I thought perhaps I wasn't being firm enough.

That smug look on her face unlocked some kind of resentment I didn't realize was long buried within me. I decided to channel all of that spite into my next attempt. I brought my hand out from behind me and flicked my wrist at the screen—entangling myself with all the microwaves of reality—and Katie was struck with a blue shell out of nowhere that knocked her right off the ramp.

"What the f–uck!? Where did that come from!?" She whined, stressed as Lakitu lagged in place took too long to set her back down onto the racetrack. While she was in the air four racers sped past her, boosted by mushrooms and gold stars—*"FUCK! FUCK!"*

As soon as she hit the track she did everything possible to catch up. Taking all the speed ramps and boosts she could, she managed to climb back up to third place—finish line just ahead—even at this point she seemed confident she would recover and win. She's saved worse rounds. The other two racers were just barely past her.

I did it again, *flick!* Only, she saw me do it this time and her eyes popped. Her kart was struck with a lightning bolt. Sunshine gasped and laughed, pointing a finger at Katie and the screen. Yoshi and Peach burrowed past her the moment she spun out of the way and finished third and fourth.

Katie tittered, shook her head in disbelief, and finished in fifth place. Her broken streak brought more fire into the room than any of her wins had. Sunshine practically fell off the couch laughing at her. Even Luis, who'd lick mud off the bottom of her shoes pointed at her and cackled.

Katie smiled, almost bashful, like she was in on the joke. Sunshine put her hands on my shoulders and shook me, mouth curled, saying, *"Oh my God—Yes!"*

Katie spun around and waited for me to answer.

I shrugged and smirked at her—but played dumb.

"Of course not. Fifth place requires real skill that only Katie has." I began to clap, "Speed-Racer!" I cheered. "Speed-racer!"

A few of them joined in, Danny included. *"Speed-Racer!"*

Katie, still grinning, slipped out of the room suddenly. While we waited for her to come back, everyone began to chatter about her being "dethroned". Not in a mocking way, but with good sportsmanship and fun. She was hosting some kind of competition after all.

I laughed—laughter that came easy, for once. I let myself sink into it and examined my hands.

I caused something. On purpo—

There was a soft click, barely audible over the menu screen music that chirped through the speakers.

POP.   A wasp-sting of pain struck my chest—and for a second I didn't even register what it was. Just the impact. I clutched my hand over the pain and a second one followed.

PAP!   right into the back of my hand. Just a scratch, but still, the little yellow bead drew blood.

Everyone gasped.

Katie stood in the dining room, BB gun clutched in her hand—still aimed right at me. The room went cold. And her mean face over chiptunes was actually terrifying. I didn't know what to do.

Her body was still, completely drained of humor. No trembling, no words, no nothing. Just a sharp merciless stare that hurt more than the little plastic beads she shot me with.

*"Don't you **ever** do your little warps on me again. **Never me.**"* She said, her voice high and awful. She shot me again—**POP**—it hit me in the shoulder this time—I threw myself back and yelped—my head slammed into Raf's stomach. He screamed.

Everyone looked at me—waiting for me to say something while my head began to spin, ears hotter than a clothing iron set to high.

The warmth that had accumulated in the room bled out like someone slit its throat. Caesar looked horrified, cowering in the dining room with crumbs all over his shirt. Sunshine curled into a ball on the couch—probably terrified that Katie would shoot her, too, for giving me the idea. Danny pressed her back into the wall to be as far away from her as possible. Damian looked pallid, he and Ari practically clung to each other. And worst of all... Jonah stood in the mouth of the hallway, with his jaw dropped, eyes wide, and a hand in his hair.

I groaned—Raf slid out from beneath me and joined Damian's huddle.

Katie shoved her hands through her hair and sighed, pressed her eyes shut in silent thought as she took in a new breath, and went back to her room to put the gun away. She walked right through Jonah and he broke out into static and white noise. The walls snapped.

The party ended after that.

One after the next someone had an excuse to go home early. Sunshine was the first to leave—she just got up and sped out the door, purse clutched over her bosom. Caesar "felt sick" and Damian took it as an opportunity to insist on "walking him home."

She never came back.

Danny, Luis, and Raf stayed—mostly accepting Katie's explanation that "our relationship is just like that" but none of them dared to ask me what I thought about it. I went mute until they were all gone.

When Katie closed the door behind Raf she turned to me and said, after a fit of stutters,

"What the fuck is wrong with you?"

I looked around. *"Me?"*

"Yes you, are you serious? You fucking embarrass me at my own party? Bitch you didn't think you'd get shot?"

I was speechless.

I've known Katie to be a little unstable. She's a teen bipolar. She's never officially told me, but I'm well aware of the lithium her grandma makes her take in the middle of the night. Once while I was snooping I saw a bottle with her name on it in the bathroom cabinet. Sometimes she's mean to me in the morning or she neurotically gatekeeps everything. Other times we take the metro to the beach and go halves for the cashier at the boba shop. I'm there through her lows and highs, and I ride with her because I love her.

But this... is an escalation.

And I'm starting to believe that I am not capable of humoring it anymore. I shuttered. She threw out her arm and smacked her leg, hair bobbing all over while she shook her head at me and grimaced.

"What was *that* for!?"

I told half-truth. "You always win. I guess I just wanted to see you lose, for once." *You have everything. You're so lucky and you're such a brat.*

I thought about all my clothes she had stolen, despite having a father and mother who give her everything she wants—even if it's not enough to fill the hole of her broken family—they still attend to her. I thought about all the times I let her boss me around like I'm a pussy. All the times she told me how I was supoosed to feel, or that I couldn't be bisexual because it "isn't real."

Just a few weeks ago I found out she was logged onto my Instagram on her phone and when I got mad at her for invading my privacy she said I was being stupid. And got even angier when I told her mom and she sided with me.

I crossed my arms—for the first time in my life very angry with her.

She scoffed at me. "You're insane." And just walked away and left me by the door.

I dropped my arms and rocked a little, hands snapping into fists.

She's like family to me. Exactly... like family to me. I spat out the thought and rubbed it into the carpet with the back of my shoe.

I decided to stay quiet and not make a scene. The rest of the night was business as usual. By twilight she and I were on her bedroom floor eating popcorn and watching Devil Wears Prada. She rightfully identified as Miranda Priestly. But perhaps she was just attracted to Meryl Streep. Little does she know how fitting it is.

Irene texted, asking,   *Where are you?*

I did not reply, but I stood, "Irene needs me home."

She paused the movie. "What?"

I shoved my phone in my pocket and felt around for my coins. "I have to go, today's my mom's birthday."

"You already missed it."

"Well, I can't argue with a command, right Katie? I have to go or else."

She tilted her head and bit her lip but didn't respond to my jab. "Okay, then. Do we need to give you a ride?"

"No. I'm gonna take the metro."

Despite the tension she saw me off as she always does. I lingered at her doorstep as we exchanged Goodbyes. Her mother came out of her bedroom where she'd been cooped up all day and gave Katie a good lecture for having the audacity to shoot me. She seemed annoyed again and waved me off with a false smile. I left, telling myself that we'd forget and everything would go back to normal. But I believe that will only end up being true for her.

I glanced over my shoulder as I walked away and saw Jonah a yard down the sidewalk, hovering just an inch off the ground with the tips of his oxfords dragging on the concrete as he followed me. I felt extremely betrayed. Once we were far enough I stopped in the middle of the street and spun around with my arms in the air to confront him.

"I TOLD YOU TO STAY HOME, JONAH! WHAT THE FUCK!"

He teleported a few inches from my face. The force of his sudden movement sent my hair flying out of my face. He seemed hurt.

"Alex... I—"

I threw a pinched hand in his face.

"NO, THIS IS WHERE YOU ZIP IT, OKAY!? I'm not Katie! I'm not trying to boss you around! I asked you to stay home because I haven't had it easy lately, Jonah, Goddammit! And your hovering is *killing* me! Don't you understand!? YOU CAN READ MINDS BUT YOU CAN'T READ THE ROOM!?"

He slithered away a foot, head low, he peeked at me through his fringe, eyes burning bright.

"Alex, Katie shot you—I love you, I just wanted to make sure you were okay—"

I huffed and crossed my arms. "Oh don't give me that bullshit Jonah, you were there before that happened—Sunshine saw you! I-I don't even know how that's possible!"

He looked up—the light in his eyes vanished—he was utterly sincere when he said,

"Alex I was home I swear it! Who's Sunshine?"

That omniscience watching over me became even more pronounced. My eyes were drawn to a random spot down the street and felt the hair on the back of my neck stand on end. Jonah turned, seeing nothing there, and looked back to me.

"Someone saw *me?"* He asked.

I met his eyes again. "Jonah... when exactly did you show up?"

"The moment that pellet hit yew. I wos asleep... the—*situation*—had stirred up my presence. I promise yew, Alexander, I wos giving yew space. I knaur I've been a bit much lately... I'm sorry."

I glanced at the floor and recalled what I saw in the hallway. I shared the image with Jonah through telepathy.

"I promise yew that wasn't me."

I believed him. And felt shame for becoming so cross. I bit my lip and rolled my eyes. Frustrated at too many things all at once.

"I'm sorry, Jonah. I'm just a dick. Forgive me."

He got close again, and reached out to touch me—but he didn't, aware that I did not want to be touched.

"Naur, I understand. I'm sorry."

I scoffed. "Don't—*ugh*... Stop apologizing to me. We're equals. Sometimes we misunderstand each other. It's. . fine..."

He still seemed troubled. He clutched his wrist with the opposite hand and brought his arms over his chest, eyes glowing again with pain and green light. "I just thought things were getting better between us, but everything I do seems to be the incorrect response."

I walked over to him and gave him a hug.

We held hands the rest of the way home and said nothing else to each other. Every now and then he'd squeeze mine to keep me from dozing off of spacing out. He meant well, but I wish he would've just let me drift away. Jonah vanished when I made it onto Morant Boulevard.

I stumbled past the gate in a drunken state, twenty-four hours to the decimal since I'd last slept. My mother sat on the porch and greeted me with an uncharacteristic interest.

"Hey, Nunu." She puckered her lips and took a drag of her cigarette. "Did you have fun partying?" asked with a bitter edge. Blueish grey smoke filled the space between us like a thick oppressive fog.

I was appalled that she was smoking, given her *predicament*. Yet I bit my tongue.

"You knew where I was?"

She exhaled, smoke obscuring her face. "I'm your mother. I know you like the back of my hand."

"No you don't." I spat.

She tossed her hand. "Whatever." and stood up, yanking the handle of the screen door and holding it open. I didn't react—or move—or do anything. I just stood there like a husk and stared.

She glanced around, incredulous. "Are you even alive?" She then asked.

I snapped to attention. "Huh?"

She shook her head and shot me a look, hand still on the doorknob.

Oh.

I walked inside and she shut it behind us. I sighed, so tired. So drowsy. *Did she even miss me? Did she think about me at her dinner? God I'm so desperate.*

"Mom?" I said in a slur. It sounded more like "*Mum.*"

"Yes, son?" She replied, exacerbated.

I realized how unhinged that question was and shook away the thought. "Nevermind. I forgot."

She recoiled. "How's that?" She then squinted her eyes at me, "Were you drinking?"

I laughed. *"That's rich coming from the recovering alcoholic!"*

Her face turned red but she bit her tongue and grabbed my face, eyes carefully examining me like she was searching for evidence to support her assumption. As audacious as it was... I ate up every second she looked me in the eyes. Though, I no longer felt her crying soul in her stare. It was more like staring into a photo of her rather than the real thing.

I tanked away from her. "Hey. I wasn't drinking—I'm just tired. I've never had alcohol in my life—and I don't plan to!"

"You had wine at her confirmation!" She nagged. "Remember that? I was there."

"It's catholic church!? And I spit it back into the chalice!? A-And—no you weren't!?"

She kept at it, connecting dots that weren't there. "Let's not go over this again, I don't believe you!"

I shouted over her, *"SOMEHOW, I MANAGE TO FIND MYSELF STILL DISAPPOINTED BY YOU, MOTHER! FOR GODS SAKE!"*

She let out a dry chuckle and wiped the sweat off her brow, seeming stressed suddenly.

"You always disappoint me, so I guess we're even." She said, and took in another rip. My silence was so stark I could hear the embers at the tip singe and hiss as she took in breath. I felt like I had been punched in the mouth. I just stood there, jaw loose and aching, completely, utterly wounded.

She didn't say anything else. She just stared at me with that fucking face on her face. That face I could now accurately name *disappointment.*

I turned away.

"Release his spirit. It doesn't belong to you." She growled in a strange, frightening tone.

I spun around. *"What* did you say!?"

With two fingers she swiped the cigarette from her lips.

"I didn't say anything."

I shivered in frustration. "I heard you say something, I know you did! What did you say!?"

She pressed the cigarette back between her lips,

"I didn't say anything!" She shouted, shooing me away with an annoyed hand, "Fuck off!"

"Valene's home tonight, I'm sleeping in the living room!" I spat.

She glanced at the couch then dismissively she shrugged and said,

"Fine then, I'll go."

She swung the door back open and slammed it behind her with the force of a powerful hand. Too much force. Far beyond the natural strength of any human, let alone a small woman like herself. ***THOOM!*** The windows rattled and cast this heavy, blanketing, dread all over the house. I hesitated a moment and twiddled my fingers before loosening my tie and throwing myself on the couch.

I brought out my hands and buried my face in them, letting out a long breath and feeling the lull of sleep begin to steal me away.

I heard the door to Irene's room swing open. I did not move, but waited, and listened to the angry footsteps barging toward me. I wondered if she'd believe that it was my mother who slammed the door and not me—I was too tired to argue. I thought to myself if I couldn't convince her then I would take the blame. It'd be easier that way. I'm too tired for shouting. . .

Then to my horror, *"Nunu! Are you slamming doors!?"* My mother screamed.

I snapped up and met her gaze in an instant, buzzing, that feeling of dread spilling over into full blown horror. Slowly I turned to look at the door—and through the stained-glass window I could make out the silhouette of *someone* just out of view, obscuring the light that broke in from the street. I rubbed my eyes and that figure had suddenly grown by three sizes—blocking out all the light then.

She sighed and pinched the space between her eyes. "Not tonight, Alex. I'm not doing this with you tonight." She then proceeded to head towards the front door, pulling a fresh pack of L&M's out of her zipper hoodie pocket.

I jumped up from the couch, knees buckling under the weight of what I had yet to comprehend.

"No. Don't." I uttered gravely.

She kept walking. "Don't what?"

I threw myself in front of her, tears in my eyes. *"Don't go outside."* I whispered, shaky. Her agitation rolled into something else. Suddenly unnerved.

"What's outside?" She asked through a tight breath.

"I don't know."

In tandem we both shot a glance at the window. There seemed to be nothing there. She pressed her palm into my shoulder to keep me still and went for it, swinging the door open to take a look.

No one.

She let out a breath of relief.

And then turned to look at me, a grimace taking to her face. "What is it now, Alex!? Why do you look like that?"

"L-like wh-hat?"

"Like you've seen a damn ghost!"

I shivered and felt myself nodding off despite the fear pulsing through me. I fought to stay awake. She walked over to me, door still open. But when she met my gaze she frowned and cut herself off from saying whatever it is she was going to say. She just glanced to the side and brushed past me and walked out the door. The soft click of the knob that followed broke me down to tears. I waded over to the couch and wondered if I had finally gone mad.

Then, with Jonah's hands on my side, shaking me gently to attention, I saw that perhaps I've always been mad.

If the lord is with me, why, then? Has this all happened?

"Go away." I croaked into the cushion. Silently, he persisted. I turned to face him, with a runny nose and crusted eyes—and SCREAMED.

Jonah's face! Completely disfigured!

Dead. Dead. Dead!

His skin was sallow and bruised like a rotting apple, and his eyes had sunken so deep into his face the sockets were a black crust!

He jumped back, cowering beneath the TV stand with a fearful gaze and asked,

"Alex what's the matter!?"

As if it hadn't happened at all, his face was suddenly as I've always known it to be. No disfigurement. No rot. Just the pale skin of a sweet boy lost to time and life. But still, I could not unsee it. That face! My head began to spin and in an instant I fell with a fever, hand clasped over my forehead.

He called to me again, "Alex? Alex, what's wrong? Alex??"

On the porch was one of my mother's cigarettes, haphazardly stomped out and still dying. She bent down and picked it up, scratching her head as she did. She opened the pack to see if all were accounted for, and they were. So, where did this one come from?

A creeping sense of doom grew even stronger. She dropped it on the ground in horror, wondering what I had conjured up this time. The thought sent a fury up my spine, like a flash of red light had overtaken all my systems. Though she and I were separated by miles of the heart and a concrete wall, I said to her,

"Nay, Mother. What have you conjured up in *me!*"

Jonah crept out from beneath the TV, ears twitching like a weary dog, shoulders hunched and tense.

"Alex. . ?"

The red light vanished and finally I collapsed into a dreamless sleep.

Chapter Six

A sharp metallic hiss snapped me awake. I opened my eyes to be assaulted by the sunlight that seized the living room. Irene stood an arm's length away from me, having torn the curtains all the way open.

"Nunu!" She shouted, snapping her fingers. I could feel a vein wag in my forehead. I kept my eyes closed and hissed under a breath.

"I need your help today, buddy," She said, suddenly playful, taking a little twirl and a hip sway toward me. Another rhythmic snap of the fingers.

"With what. ?" I groaned, my arm clasped over my eyes. The room was so bright the space behind my eyelids were bright red. I could make out the pattern of my veins from the inside.

"I want you to come with me, today's my first day doing Lyft."

I sat up and met her unusually lax face with a harsh look.

"... Lyft?"

She swayed again, dancing to a song in her head that I couldn't hear and snapped another finger. It was nice to see her so light. Only for the fact that there's less conflict in my face when she's in a good mood. I found the swaying and smiling to be some kind of attempt to charm me.

I didn't give. *That may work on all these sycophants here but not me!*

Sensing that dark shroud over my face, she gave up and put a hand on her hip, tried another method.

Bribery. "Come on, I'll buy you one of those tchotchkes."

I checked my math and realized... I haven't bought any since I'd come back 'home'. I felt that vein start to twitch again and scoffed like she'd spat in my face.

"Nanna, I don't collect Transformers anymore. I haven't bought a new one in months."

"Since when? You have a million of them in your drawer,"

"I don't care about some trinket, I don't want to go."

She smacked her lips, all lightness fled back to wherever she managed to conjure it up from. She put her palm in my face and sassed me,

"I want you to come with me, *puh-lease!* I'm *old!* I don't feel comfortable being alone yet."

I broke the staring contest I had with my reflection in her shiny black pumps and shot her an empty look.

Oh you're only 'old' when it's convenient. "I understand but why *me* of all people? Do you really wanna be stuck in a car with me for five hours?"

I watched her jaw slide back and fourth, like she was chewing on her own irritation. That scowl exaggerated all the little tired lines in her skin. Crows feet taking on dragon claws through an impatient glare.

"Nunu. Do you really think you're that annoying?"

"Well you had to use the word 'that', so clearly I must to a degree. I definitely think so."

I crossed my arms.

She rolled her eyes and took a breath, some kind of smirk tugging at her lips.

"Oh my god, here you go with all that Nunu! I'm trying to ask you a simple favor."

"This is asking?"

Her laugh was quiet, almost fond, and her voice eased into something more endearing,

"Dammit, Kid, can you come with me or not?"

I glanced at the screen of my phone that had lit up suddenly. A text message from Katie.

OMGGGG!!!! I JUST WON GREENDAY TICKETS!!!!! Can't hang this weekend :(((yikes :((((BUT CALL ME WHEN YOU SEE THIS BITCH!!!

I glanced back at Irene and resigned, eyes even heavier. "Okay, I will."

"Thank you." She said through a sigh, and just as suddenly as she appeared, she left, twirled off elsewhere.

I sat in silence for a little while, sweaty, last night's clothes stuck to my skin, wondering as the seconds passed why Jonah hadn't said good morning yet and why I couldn't feel him nearby.

The walls snapped suddenly, like a gang of thugs leaning against an alley wall. I flinched and glanced all around. I watched the shadows seize all the spaces they could inhabit. Even the thinnest slivers of darkness cast by mundane objects pulsed and took a deep breath. I pressed my teeth together and shriveled in—like despite the board daylight the darkness was inches from biting me.

Eyes to the shadow behind a large vase in the corner, to the large framed photo of my late Nanna Victoria and Uncle Richard, into the dining room that hid from the sun, at the table, to the gap between the fridge and the counter, to the black silhouette behind the drape.

The slats of the laundry room closet rattled. CREAK. I looked, and past them I could make out another shadow cowering into the static, watchful and timid.

"Jonah?"

No reply.

I let out a breath that fractured into a pathetic moan and caught my face in my hands.

I followed Irene out the door with my head low, lingering a few moments longer than I should have. I stared at the empty chair by the banister and imagined my mother in the empty space. I could feel the back of my neck sting hot like I'd run poison ivy over it, and began to itch as I thought of the awful nightmare I had a few nights ago.

"Release his spirit. It doesn't belong to you."

A heavy, swirling, churning dread still lingered. Board daylight and the porch was dark like the night. I clenched my fists to stop my hands from trembling... *Wh—*

"Nunu!" She shouted, already opening the driver's seat door. *Saved by the bell.* "Chop chop! Vamoose! *Whatever, come on get your butt in the car."*

I imagined my mother there again and felt my nerves jolt like I'd clutched a fist around livewire. *Vision or intrusion? Nightmare or hallucination?* I still don't know.

I stared wistfully out the passenger seat window in a white collar and blue plaid tie, chewing on a fingernail. Irene didn't bother with small talk, perhaps because she was too preoccupied by her task at hand. The passengers didn't often acknowledge my presence, either. Only one spoke to me, a grubby man with white paint all over his jeans who complained about his truck having broke down. He asked me if I was some kind of instructor, and Irene laughed at his comment in a way that made me feel like a joke.

"Ahah! HAHAHAHAHA."

She explained otherwise and things got awkward he reasonably asked,

"Is that even allowed? I thought ya'll get in trouble for that?"

"I don't think that's any of your buisness."

Her low-volume worship music created just a lovely atmosphere. They exchanged tense eye contact through the rear-view mirror while the man on the radio sang:

♪♪ Jesus! I feel you deep inside me–! ♪♪

In downtown we picked up a chatty fellow about her age. I liked his hat. I did not speak to him, but I listened intently when he and Irene spoke. They overshared like old people do all the way to Inglewood. He seemed kind and decent in spirit, though. His sultry voice and gentle perspectives loosened that nihilistic knot in my chest just a little. Reminded me that there are decent people out there in this treacherous world. I was eased enough to close my eyes and doze against the windowsill.

"Okay~!" Irene sang. Mid-sentence, without breaking away from the man, she jabbed my thigh with her long acrylic nail to wake me up. " —I think we're here."

A shabby Motel 6. I grumbled and sat up, from the side mirror I saw that my hair took on a massive cowlick. The car rolled to a stop. He tore off his seat belt and hurried out while Irene nodded and waved him off with a smile. He met her at the open window beside her, still smiling, and leaned one arm on the roof.

"God bless you, Miss Irene. Have a lovely day." He said, and ducked to meet my gaze, "And you too, young man!"

I nodded indifferently.

"Thank you, God bless you too," Irene nudged me discreetly.

I threw a hand high into the air and waved theatrically, withholding inflection.

"Yeah, Shalom, Sir!"

He walked away a little strung by my attitude. His face made me realize I had taken my anger out on him unjustifiably. Ugh.

She drove off. I watched him from across the intersection wrestling with a key card and a stubborn door on the bottom level. I hid my hand from Irene and twirled my fingers, imagining a green check mark, eyes fixed on the door. It unlocked. He sighed and went inside to be never seen by me ever again. Even gone, my eyes still lingered. I just stared as the red light held us there. Traffic hummed, a diesel engine somewhere behind us gurgled loudly, I let out a quiet sigh and looked away once the light turned green and the building was gone.

Whatever.

Irene's phone started going off again. Another ride request, this time to LAX.

"Oh, hell no!" She exclaimed, *"Tell it no!"*

Although I'm desperate for this little ride-along to end, I know that she needs the money.

"It's only a ten-minute commute from here, and besides, it's worth it, I think. Look. Thirty-eight-dollars."

She squinted her eyes and leaned in closer to look at the screen.

"Tuh! Trust me, you've never had to drive to LAX. You couldn't pay me. Or anyone from Los Angeles, matter a' fact. "

"Is it really that bad?"

"Oh, yes. A nightmare. You're better off jumping in a cannon and getting blown up."

Geeze. She made a hard right turn into the entrance of a McDonalds out of nowhere. Everything in the car slid to the left—even me.

"This is why people don't want seniors to drive—" I said as the seatbelt squeezed my gut like a hang-noose.

She ignored me. "Can you deny the request and turn it off?"

"We're done for the day?" I asked, a little relieved, tugging at the belt. I had chosen to be supportive in good faith but I wasn't gonna argue to keep at it. I denied the request and closed the application.

"No, I need me a coffee break. Do you want anything?"

"No, I'm okay."

"Are you *sure*?"

I went mute. I already answered her question.

"When *do* you eat? You're never at dinner..."

I thought about a response and something clicked then, the strange ritual habit that'd formed in lieu of this great depression which devours me.

"Um, actually, I kind of eat the same thing every day. It's just... easier that way.

"Eating is more *necessity* rather than a pleasure. Appetite often eludes me.

"So, I consider the food pyramid and I make a huge sandwich with everything in it, buy a bag of chips, and a can of Coke.

"I know it doesn't *sound* healthy but everything is there. Bread, meat, cheese, veggies, carbs, sugar, all that jazz. And you buy everything from the good stores, so, it doesn't make me feel gross like how you'd think."

I let out a long-drawn-out breath and smiled a little manically, "Yeah..."

She hit the brakes just before the mic and looked at me, a bit puzzled, a bit concerned, with her lips bent in an odd shape.

"Every day, like, *every day*?"

"Yes."

She shook her head and kept forward, "You boys and your strange ways. No sandwich today, Nunu, I'm getting you some real food. And you better order something."

"I don't think McDonald's constitutes real food."

She glared at me, still insisting, "Okay, fine, then, I'll get you something else. I'm still ordering my coffee though."

"Thank you for choosing McDonalds. What can I get started for you today?" A little girl voice burst though the metal box.

Irene poked her head out of the window, "Hi, yes, can I get a senior coffee, please? Decaf! And I want two creamers!"

I wondered, *what's the point of drinking coffee when you're tired if you're gonna order decaf?* She must know something about coffee that I don't. I also wondered why she was being so nice.n Still *charming as ever*, but nice. Her statement hit me a little late.

"Okay, fine, then, I'll get you something else. I'm still ..."

"Why?" I blurted.

"Why what?"

"Why go through the trouble of driving somewhere else to get me something to eat?"

"My god, Nunu, what's wrong with you? You talk like everybody hates you."

I shrunk inward.

"I brought you on this little field trip with me, it's the least I can do." She seemed a bit annoyed I thought so little of her. My ears were burning red like hot steel.

A teenaged girl with thick braces and a collar hanging loose at her neck passed Irene the coffee with a quick, practiced motion.

"Thank you, dear!" Irene called and then rolled up her window. "So, where do you wanna go, buddy?"

Truthfully, nowhere. For some reason I felt ashamed and hesitant, retreating into jokes to avoid any sort of true desire for anything. Another mad smirk took to my lips,

"What if I say something crazy like Olive Garden?"

She chuckled insincerely. "Hah! Nice try."

"I'm kidding... I don't even like Olive Garden."

"Yeah, I know. So quit kidding around, where am I taking you?" She glanced at the digital clock in her console. "You got thirty minutes."

"Okay..." I muttered. Pretending to think and not coming up with anything of course. My nail was back between my teeth. I'd chewed off a whole inch of black nail polish.

She was impatient again, but trying to be helpful.

"How about this, pick somewhere by the house and we'll just eat there—I'll get something with you so you'll stop being all coy."

Is that how I come off? I turned to the side and glanced up. *What's even by the house?*

I had an idea then.

"I am sick and tired of this place." Irene fussed.

Troy's BURGERS #10 on Valley Boulevard.

She sat back in her side of the booth with her arms folded. The two of us were wildly out of place amongst all the locals in jersey shorts and t-shirts. I sat with my tie tucked into my shirt and Irene wore buisness casual. The handsome man who took our order at the counter asked if she and I had just got back from Church.

I cracked a little smile and shook my head at her. "You said that already." Amused by the face she was making and the fact that she refused to take off her cat-eye cheetah sunglasses indoors.

"We eat here too much." She continued, loudly enough that the family in the booth adjacent to us eavesdropped. "Every time I say screw it, let's go out to eat, it's always Troy's. Troy's, Wingstop, and Canes! I don't know how you guys don't get tired of it."

"Forgive the misunderstanding. I mean, initially it seemed to me that you liked it here. I chose it because you said you were also gonna eat, I-I didn't want to pick something that wasn't agreeable."

She settled down and grumbled, "Well that's considerate of you," looking down at a plate of asada fries I thought to be a bad choice for someone her age. I ordered a spicy chicken sandwich with fries and a horchata.

Before she took her first bite she reached into her purse and dry-swallowed three antacids.

"I don't feel it yet, I'm just preparing." She deadpanned before I could comment. I laughed a little—and she seemed to smile at it. Suddenly the day was a lot less monotonous and kind of decent.

We ate quickly because she didn't want to stay long, and so we didn't do very much chatting in the booth. Just enjoyed each other's company which, I suppose, was something I had forgotten we used to do, and something that I was even capable of. I remembered how she was my favorite when I was young. Every moment she could she'd drop everything just to hang out with me. And I always wanted to. Even if it was a monotonous ride-along or a trip to Burlington... she wanted me there.

One day all of that just... stopped. The thought made me so sad I didn't swallow my last bite. I kind of slowed the chew to a stop with a glassy look in my eye and sneakily spit it out into a napkin.

Back on the road she noticed how silent I'd become after lunch. The melancholy I cast into the car made it three tons heavier. Her shoulders were never fully relaxed, she had a hard time focusing on the road over the presence pressing on her. I caught her glancing at me every now and then as if still considering whether or not it was actually me and not just in her head. Every time it appeared she was about to ask, another ride request came in. After the fourth passenger following our detour she shut off the app and asked finally,

"What's wrong, buddy?"

I didn't know what to say, or what I was even upset about this time. Certainly not the state of our rapport. I'd be ridiculous to be upset over my grandma when I have much worse things going on. . .

The realization definitely triggered something in me, however. I guess I'd gone too far and let myself remember that there was a point in time where I could say the same for everyone in my family. That we used to get along well.

Bonnie and I used to watch horror films together and go to city walk. Valene would brag to her friends about her 'smart nephew' and show them my art and tell them about my writing.

And my mom.... well she loved me.

Certainly she did.

Fifteen years old wasn't that long ago. I remember when she used to make pizza from scratch for dinner and film silly videos with me and Tommy on iMovie. Once she let us all drag her across the living room floor in old Halloween masks she'd horded for a scene in our scary movie.

I frowned harder.

I remember when I submitted that god awful self-portrait to SoHDa's art showcase and I had to present it on stage. She brought Irene and whoever else she could grab just to see me speak for like two minutes. Afterward she and Irene ambushed me in the gallery and made me take photos with it. When we got home she bragged to all her friends on the phone that I "won" despite it not at all being a competition.

We were once a rising sun.

"Nunu. Do you really think you're that annoying?"

Had I done something wrong? And, even if—if I had done something wrong... Am I not worth the patience for redemption? What could I have done to warrant estrangement at such a young age?

Or did I just grow up and lose my novelty?

What a pain it is to live in a house with ten people and always feel so alone. And feel it harder because that wasn't how it used to be. I sleep in the living room for crying out loud... they all see me splayed out on the couch with last night's tears still clung to my face. But no one cares to lift me up in their arms and make me feel like I have stake in the world. And for why?

"You talk like everybody hates you."

God. We were once a rising sun.

"Who are you to me?"

No... I think, really, we were a setting sun.

And it is Midnight.

"Nothing, I'm just tired." I muttered. Her frown implied that she didn't believe me, but certainly she was so used to my mood swings that she didn't prod any further. Although I really, really wanted her to. Even if I don't plan to budge. Is that petty? Am I petty now? Petty and dull like the rest of them?

Her phone started to ring. It was my mother. I brought my shoes to the seat and curled in. I would've plugged my ears with my fingers were it not so theatrical. I bit down harder and turned, pretending to stare out the window.

"My lover! What's up my lover!" She shouted overexcitedly into the mic. My mother didn't match Irene's enthusiasm but she was polite.

"How's it going, mom? There's no one in the car with you is there?"

"No, just your son, he's right here." She said airily, taking another peek at me. "Guess how much I made today!"

"How much?"

"Two-hundred-fourty dollars and ninety cents!"

"Damn, how much are those rides?"

"Ah it depends. Most of 'em had me driving all over the damn place. I got one all the way out in La Puente, can you believe it?"

"Did you pick up any weirdos?"

"No, praise the Lord, but one of them thought Nunu was an instructor or something! Hahah. It was so funny,"

My mother chuckled a little, her voice suddenly distorted by a burst of static that startled Irene. I didn't react.

"Hey, am I on speaker? What is that?" My mother asked. A little rattled.

"Yeah, lover, I'm still driving!"

"I'll just see you when you get home."

"Aye!" Irene shouted right as she was about to hang up, "Are you still making me that rice for bible study tonight, yes or no, because you always say you will and then some BS happens, Priscilla!"

"Yes, mom!" She nagged, "It's on the stove right now."

I knew she was lying. You can hear it in the way vowels are a pitch higher than the rest of the letters in the sentence. I let my forehead press into the glass.

"Okay, Good. Thank you."

My mother's little chuckle made my chest hurt. "Kay, I love you, see you later." She said.

"I love you too."

Call ended.

I wish that I could slam my head into the dashboard. Melt into the car seat. Hearing my mother say *I love you* felt like a pickaxe to the heart. Everything that had been boiling up inside was beginning to make my lid shake and bubble over.

Irene rolled down the windows to relieve the pressure building up in the car. It didn't help, but the ambiance of the busy street spared her from having to acknowledge me and my awful face.

I peeked at the backseat through the sideview mirror and hoped to find Jonah there, making that overly anxious expression he has whenever I'm in a bad mood. But nothing still. No one there. I clenched my fist so hard my skin squeaked like a leather glove.

Both hands on the steering wheel, Irene tapped her fingers to the beat of Little Drummer Boy. *Bah Rum-pum-pum-pum* to distract herself for a while.

"My lover... My lover..." She cooed to herself with distant reminisce. *The name was a needle-prick to my ear drum.*

"Why do you call her that?" I asked, blurting, my voice gruff and bitter.

Irene hesitated for a moment, then answered sincerely, warmed in some creeping memory.

"It was this thing she would do when she was a little girl. She'd come out of nowhere and wrap herself around my legs, babbling, *I love you! I love you!*"

She gave a quick, incredulous laugh.

"Always worse before bedtime. I'd have to lift her by the arm and drag her to bed, and the whole way she'd still be whining, *'No, Mom, no! I love you! I love you!'* She never left me alone. Not even to go to the bathroom. It became her argument for everything."

She mimicked my mother in a shrill, childlike voice, *"'No, I love you! I love you!'"* then exhaled. That distant look in her took on a pensive gleam.

"One day I yanked her up and said, *'Okay, lover! I get it!'* And it just stuck. Everyone started calling her that."

The tires hummed against the asphalt. Irene seemed less focused on the road now. And that massive ache in my chest began to churn slowly, like magma under the surface.

"Well, anyway, Val asked her once, *'Priscilla, why do you always say that?'* And she said *'So my mommy will never leave me.'...*"

"My lover..." She muttered one last time, pressing her lips back into a smile.

Irene continued. "She, uh—" She sniffed, "—By the time she grew out of it I realized that she'd only started doing it after her dad died. I guess she was just scared to be alone."

For a beat, the only sound in the car was the steady whoosh of passing traffic.

I felt myself slipping away again. Into the fog. But her words waded through it, lantern in hand, to find me. And crush me.

"I was so worried about her..." She went on. "I know how girls who lose their dad young can end up. I would know—I was one. Bad with men, bad with themselves, low self-esteem... just trouble.

"It rattled her for a long time. Bad dreams. Seeing and hearing things. And she got so clingy. But she grew out of it.

"You know, by the time she was your age she was getting ready to join the Air Force. She had good grades, she was very bright. Kind of a rocker, but so responsible."

Irene's laugh cracked a little deeper. "One time she came home with liberty spikes. Her hair was all stiff and two feet high! I asked how in the hell she did that and she said she used the eggs from the fridge! My eggs!"

The right blinker clicked as she eased the car to a stop at the light on Huntington and Morant Boulevard. *TIK-TIK TIK-TIK TIK-TIK.* We were almost there.

"You know she told me something I'll never forget. After nine-eleven, she came up to me—all serious and pregnant—and said, *"'Mom, if I go to war, I'll keep a picture of you in my helmet.'"*

"She really thought she was gonna go join the military."

I felt my hard face shatter. The light turned green, and she was silent until we made it to the house. She parked on the street but didn't shut off the engine right away.

"I know your mom hurts you sometimes, my Nunu, but I promise you she loves you.

"She's just very lost right now. I feel bad for her... After your uncle was killed and my mom died, she just hasn't been the same, baby.

"There's just this big part of her missing. And, I think, with Jacob still being so little and now this new baby she's having... it's just a lot, you know?"

I was silent.

Irene sighed again, face troubled and droopy.

"Sometimes I think you're too hard on her." She said as politely as she could. "She's been through a lot. But she's trying, I know it. She's doing better than I was at her age.

"I didn't get my act right until Adriana was born, can you believe it? It took me that long to wake up and say, 'Hey, I need to make a change,'

"All my daughters ever wanted from me was to try. I mean, I think I'm doing phenomenal now compared to how I used to be. But they always tell me it's too late. Especially Bonnie. You know she's the one I have the hardest time with.

"I just don't want you and your mother to end up like me and Bonnie. Because your mom is different. Out of all my babies, she's the only one who's never told me it was too late. Even at my worst she still loved me. And, although I didn't appreciate it back then, it made a difference. Sometimes all a mother needs is someone to just believe in her.

"Underneath all that drinking and pain I know my sweet girl is still in there. People just break. Do you understand?"

My throat had grown so tight I could hardly breathe. It was like my mouth had been vacuum sealed shut. More than anything in the world I did not want to talk about this right now. Irene seems to have forgotten how much I have tried to reason with my mother. How much I'd bled to hold her hand. And all for not. Either that or she just never saw it.

Like mother, like daughter.

I couldn't look at her anymore. I didn't want to be mean, but I just couldn't shield her from the vicious temper of my words.

"I could be anywhere and this... turmoil between us clings to me like a second skin. Every time I trust her, or get too close, my feelings get abused. She's too hard on *me*. After everything, she's too hard on *me*.

"It wasn't easy, Nanna, growing up how I did. House to house, hands to hands, always being so brave beyond my means.

"I took care of my brothers when we were in foster care. I was robotic and high-strung, yes, but I did my best to keep them safe. I put all of me on hold to keep us safe for my mother. Waiting. Until I'd see her again.

"I shouldn't have expected her to be this, plucky, LA mom but at the very least I thought she'd have space for me. I always had it for her..."

I swallowed hard.

"It's hard for me, never seeing eye to eye with her on anything. This isn't what I want. But to say I'm too hard on her, or that she needs me to "just believe in her" is just... ignorant.

"I've always been on her team. I've always clung to her legs. But she doesn't want that. She doesn't want *me*. She'd rather me just... disappear.

"I was the one that tried in this relationship. She's never tried enough. Nowhere near what I've done to keep her close."

I swallowed hard again, feeling like I was soon to be out of breath.

"I understand. But not in the way you would like, and not in a way that brings me any peace."

I unbuckled my seatbelt and stormed out of the car, slamming the door shut behind me. Irene shouted after me,

"Nunu! Nunu!" But I had completely lost it. I sobbed into the palms of my hands and stumbled haphazardly past the gate and up the stairs onto the porch. I couldn't see a thing, but I opened the door and trudged inside, barged into Valene's empty room, threw myself into the bed and cried myself to sleep.

In dreams, there was darkness, and one side of a conversation I don't think I was supposed to hear. Jonah, broken down, speaking in a voice swollen with lament I could only half-understand as a living man. Lifetimes of fear and despair hidden between every note.

When he speaks, the sound isn't really there in the way my voice or your voice is. Not soundwaves, but an intrusion of the heart. In any tone, whether loving, angry, or sad, it seeps like in and stains like blood on anything.

I laid in bed with my eyes pressed shut, twitching, drifting in and out of that place between sleeping and awake. I did not know where he was, but I could see his face in my mind's eye. Swelling with tears as if he had the eyes to shed them, and not an afterimage.

"O-h m–y G–od," He squeaked, chattering. ***"W-hat are y—"*** a sharp gasp snipped the last part of his sentence into something unintelligible. Just syllables scrambled by a whimper.

A reply I could not hear. Shuddering and shaking.

His voice cracked, shouting, ***"Don't touch him!"***

Another beat of silence.

And as if summoned by that silence, a body manifested on the ground a few feet ahead of me, bright white that came slowly into view like someone slowly shed a spotlight upon him.

Further away, Jonah rattled. *"... Me. . ?"*

A sorcerer of some kind, or wizard maybe. Short and raven haired just like me. He glinted and shimmered like a brilliant diamond. He laid there face shoved in the ground, the back of his hands to the floor, fingers curled in like a dead spider's legs. Skin blue and ashen as if he'd been dead forever, fingertips blackened with soot.

"... Are you. . ?"

Beside him, shattered into bits and chips, was a star-tipped magic wand. The hilt was adorned with twisting filigree and garnet, silver bands spiraling upward the base from a crystal orb. One finger of his left hand seemed to be reaching for it in his last moments.

On the right, a chrome pistol, dead and cold, having been there so long I could see pills of dust collecting in the fine grooves of its body. Then I noticed it, a massive exit hole on the side of his back where his heart was. His thick ritual garment, blood soaked white and tattered all over.

"I'm already dead." Jonah said in a grim voice. Hardly there anymore.

I got closer to the magician and reached down to grab him with a slow, creeping, hand. My fingers curled around his shoulder one by one, pinky to thumb. When I flipped him over I gasped.

He wore my face, dirtied by years of time yet to pass and the shadow of a patchy beard.

"I'm already dead."

A violent tremor woke me up. I clutched the edges of the mattress, the old metal frame creaking and twisting. All of Valene's knicknacks on the high shelf fell over, as did the loose cosmetics on her vanity and a few picture frames off the wall.

Jonah appeared at the edge of the bed in a sudden green haze, frightened, hair on end like a wary animal.

"What's going on!?" He cried.

After a few seconds it ceased.

I sat up, trembling, and rubbed my eyes. "An earthquake?" I'd never experienced an earthquake before. I ran past Jonah and out the door and into the living room. At the same time my mother barged downstairs.

My heart stopped like it had been dropped into a pit of tar. Thick, sinking, suffocating. She seemed surprised to see me too.

"Are you okay?" I asked, a little breathless.

She exhaled, hand over her bosom, "Yeah,"

"Where is everyone?" I glanced around expecting the whole house. It was just the two of us.

"I don't know, everybody left."

"And the boys?"

"The boys are at the park. Tommy texted me and said they're okay."

I let out a breath of relief, still trembling a little. "Good." I muttered.

We stood at opposite ends of the rug. The awkward silence between was a terrible chasm. She scratched at her ear and glanced around.

"Well, I'm gonna go upstairs."

"Wait!" I whined. Despite myself I asked, "Ca-an I join you? I'm scared."

Her face hardly changed. Her brow was still tight and muddled. She nodded and I followed behind with my head down. Halfway up the stairs she said,

"You know you don't have to ask." With a bit of a tone but I said nothing.

Her living room was in complete disarray. Clothes everywhere, in assorted piles. Some folded, some not. I glanced around and noticed how different the layout was. I haven't been up stairs in months.

"Laundry day?" I asked. She turned the dial on her stereo, simultaneously swiping a small shirt that was haphazardly tossed on the same shelf. Metallica's *Garage, Inc.* CD resumed playing from where she'd left off.

♪♪ *There's a devil waiting outside your door...* ♪♪

I took a seat on the couch next to a bunch of folded jeans, hands folded in my lap and my back straight. Even though she wasn't looking at me she somehow sensed how stiff I was.

"Relax!" she squawked, tossing the folded shirt into a small basket.

I shifted and curled up into a little ball with my knees to my chest and my head against the armrest, staring up at the ceiling.

"That can't be comfortable." She said.

I never really am, I droned internally.

She walked over to me and grabbed the stack of jeans, plopped them onto the carpet, and put out a pillow for me to rest my legs on.

I stirred, a bit surprised by the gesture. I stretched out my legs and put my arms behind my head, back still aching.

"Will there be an aftershock?" I asked, still uneasy.

"It was a baby one, I doubt it."

"It shook the walls."

"Yeah that's how earthquakes work, Son." She said a bit sarcastically. I rolled my eyes.

// 185 //

"I thought you were going to Katie's this weekend?" She asked, back to folding clothes.

I spoke of it a bit distantly. "She won some Green Day tickets so she's blowing me off for that. I think she might end up taking her friend Gabby with her."

"That's pretty cool, I like some of the Green Day songs. Why isn't she taking you with her?"

"I don't like Green Day. Although I don't think she cares about that, so maybe that isn't why. I don't know. Girls are a mystery to me."

She hummed a bit dismissively and changed the subject. "If you're hungry I made taquitos."

"No thank you."

She grumbled a little. "I made them from scratch."

"Still, I am alright."

I closed my eyes. In flashes the conversation between Irene and I lashed at me like a mauling cougar. I cringed and stuffed all the words as deep down as I could. Though, I peeked over at my mother every now and then.

For a time my mind was quiet. Sadness returned when the earthquake was no longer a concern. I just watched her fold clothes and took mental notes on the way she moved. I noticed her favoring her left side and wondered how she'd hurt herself this time. She's deathly clumsy. When she'd turn my way I'd look to the ceiling again and pretend my thoughts were elsewhere. She didn't seem terribly bothered by my silence, but she did peek at me often. Maybe to check if I was still there.

I thought about that little girl Irene described. This time I rolled over, less subtle, and watched her with heavy eyes. It all kind of sank in then...

The passage of time. Once Irene's sweet girl, now a mother barely holding on. Folding little shirts and making dinner.

Ugh. The magma is turning again. I thought about what Irene said... About her past interests and aspirations. And how Irene's words made it seem like being knocked up with me is what severed the vine. I didn't know for sure, but I had a feeling.

I saw her wince and press a fist into her thigh to soothe it... And that feeling became a knowing.

I wondered what kind of life she would have had if I'd never been born. Or if Irene wasn't so cruel and made her keep me. Maybe she'd be happy. Maybe she'd been spared my father and that haunted house in Oklahoma, and, now, in Woodrow. *Ugh.* Maybe she'd still be that sweet girl Irene remembers so fondly.

Oh isn't the universe so cruel? I had a vision of my mother's child-face and pressed my eyes shut in agony.

Justice, like revenge, only exists in dreams. She is who she is now. And I am who I am now. What could be done to save the versions of us who now live in dreams?

I turned away and went back to the ceiling.

"Mom?"

"Hm?"

"Nanna told me something about you I hadn't known before... Can I ask you about it?"

She stopped what she was doing and turned around, leaning against the dresser with her hands behind her back and blew a strand of hair out of her sweaty face. Through her white tee I could see the early stages of a pregnant belly. It almost killed the thought.

"What did she say?"

"She said something about you in the air force or something."

She smirked a little fondly and glanced at her bare feet. "Oh," she blurted, trying not to chuckle, "Yeah, I was pretty into it. You know I was the Alpha Flight commander of my JROTC class senior year?"

"Really?"

"Yeah, let me show you something," She called over her shoulder as she walked into her room. I sat up, unsure whether or not to follow her. Then she returned with a tattered vinyl photo-album in her hand that looked like it hadn't been opened in years. She grabbed me by the legs and moved them over to sit beside me on the couch. I scurried up tense.

We sat shoulder to shoulder.

Before she opened it, she ran a hand over the cover, holographic purple and there were imprints of stickers long gone. I tilted my head as she browsed, catching quick glimpses of photos I'd never seen before. She stopped about in the middle, and I think the pictures there would have made the old Alexander smile. It was her, about my age, in front of an American flag wearing a flight cap and ABU's. Her hair was pulled back slick and tight and she smiled with squinty eyes a few shades brighter than they are now.

So pretty.

"H-how old were you here?"

She turned the page, more pictures. She and an ex-best friend named DeeDee she didn't like to talk about.

"Like, sixteen or seventeen." She muttered, turning the page again. Another photo of her in her uniform, this time a portrait. She wore blues and her face was serious and her hair was a different color. Dyed jet black.

"Wanna hear something so messed up?"

Not really.

"How come I found out I was pregnant with you at MEPS?"

I felt hot pricks in my neck like I did this morning. "What's MEPS?"

"Basically where you start the process to join the military. I was getting a physical and the doctor said,

"'Ms. Priscilla, are you aware that you are pregnant?'"

She did a funny man voice to imitate him.

"I was so embarrassed. Because I was still a minor they had to call my mother, and oh my god, she brought your Nanna Vicky too. It was so embarrassing. Everybody knew."

So it is true. I crumpled in so we were no longer touching.

"So that's why you didn't join? Because of me?" The implication was so wounding. She flipped back to the middle page with the picture of her smiling.

"Well, no," She began, glancing up in thought as if trying to recall, fingertip on her bottom lip,

"This was in the summer so I wasn't sure what I was gonna do after graduating. I still wanted to do it but, you know, I had a new responsibility coming. Then September came around and nine-eleven happened. Looking back maybe it was a blessing in disguise."

She shrugged. "Some kid from a different flight went to MEPs with me ended up being sent to Afghanistan and I never heard from him after that."

"Oh my. ."

She tossed a hand. "He wanted to go. Was' a long time ago, I barely remember him. But yeah."

My eyes were fixed on the picture of her.

"Can I see it?" I asked, pointing a crooked finger.

She swiped it from the cellophane and handed it over to me. On closer inspection I noticed even there she wore that crazy orange eyeshadow she always wears. *I guess some things stay the same.* I flipped it over. On the back there was a handwritten note from her.

"To my Mommy. I love you so much!

-   Lover."

Another punch in the throat. I gave it back to her. She stood, dusted off her lap, and put it back in her room. She returned with a different CD and popped it in the stereo. She hit play and bent over to pick up a bundle of socks and underwear, marching it over to an open drawer and chucking it all in there.

Some metal band I didn't know played in low volume—music I like— but the volcano was about to finally erupt. The sound was so incessant.

"Mom?" I blurted once more.

She hummed again, with some strain as she fought to fit all of Franky's clothes in a bottom dresser drawer. I kept my head low and timidly pressed my fingers together.

"Do you... Do you ever wish that it worked out for you?"

The CD came to an abrupt stop. My mother shot up and seemed startled by the timing.

"What are you talking about?" She asked as she paced over to the stereo. She took out the CD and checked for scratches. There were none.

I continued, the pricks in my neck had gone into a full burning sensation. I clasped a hand over it.

"Uh. You know—the Air Force."

Something beneath her face shifted. And for a moment, half a second, she seemed... frozen.

"No." She said tonelessly, "I don't like to think like that."

She wasn't looking at me still. She let out a full breath on the shiny part of the CD and polished it with her shirt and the fog.

"Mom."

She looked at me.

"Can I say something?"

Her eyes squinted just a little, hardly enough for any normal person to notice. But I'm not normal. I'm me. I noticed.

"Shoot."

"Learning this h-has been very heavy on my heart. And I want to say, mother, that I see your folly. A-And that I understand you, better now, I believe."

Her face sank deeper into an expression I wasn't liking—one that was making me reluctant to continue. But I did.

"I wish the adults in your life were more responsible when you were my age. I wish that you had been allowed to have the life you were supposed to have. You know."

I shrugged a bit nervously and took a deep breath. She stared at me speechlessly.

"You're like me. You wanted to be bigger than this place, a-all these people... this broken town. I see that was taken from you. And I'm sorry."

I felt a spark in my chest that betrayed my instincts. Maybe finally, just finally, I had found something that would bring us closer. Maybe my understanding could reach her—and she would know that I see her—and she would see... Me.

But she looked completely beguiled, still staring at me in shock as if I'd said something crass.

"Alex, don't say stuff like that, I'm serious. I don't wanna hear it."

The hurt manifested physically. There was a sudden sharp pain in my heart.

"But I mean it, mom. I'm trying to say that—I see you. I understand, and maybe we can—"

"We?" She spat. "Always "We!" what is this "We?" Alexander, *enough, enough! Enough, okay!?"* "I hate when you do that!"

I recoiled. "Do... What?"

"Psychoanalyze me or whatever it is you're trying to do. It's inappropriate." She shouted, then exhaled with stress.

"I don't appreciate it. Sometimes..." She trailed off, seeming reluctant to say. But she did anyway.

"Sometimes I feel like you love me more than a son should."

I was disgusted. All breath stripped from my lungs in one exhale.

"Wh— like Norman Bates or something!? Is that how you see me!?" My fingers were pressed into my chest like I was trying to rip my chest open.

"No!" She shouted, equally disgusted by the idea. "No! You just..." She sighed again, seeming frustrated.

"I never ask you to do all that. You shouldn't be digging through my past and trying to put yourself in it or hash it out with me like it's got anything to do with you, it doesn't.

"If something was meant to be, then things would fall where they oughta be. End of story."

She turned away from me and put her CD back in. But she didn't hit play. She sighed and shook her head, reaching over to grab another shirt to fold. She thwipped the shirt so hard it cracked like a whip in my face. I stammered and went back downstairs with tears in my eyes. End of discussion.

I dragged my sorry self back to Valene's room with tear swollen eyes and thought about Irene's pep-talk in the car, wishing she could see me now and know just how wrong she was and how right I am to feel the way I do.

I fucking told you so.

But to everyone it doesn't matter anyway. Clearly. I wiped my eyes three times over and still I could not see ahead of me. It was too much. My tears are a sea.

As I walked down the hall, I heard a muffled voice from behind the door of Bonnie's bathroom. Words I couldn't make out, but a cadence that brought me to a dead stop.

"GE-KEN-OUT"

A terribly strange phrase. Perhaps misheard entirely. It wasn't Jonah. The voice was deeper... Scarier... Familiar. I sniffed and reached for the handle.

Then, *"Alex!"* Jonah called behind me in a hush.

I flinched and spun around to face him. In the light he was hard to see, but he was there, a faint impression of an adolescent boy against the wall. A shadow with a shadow. I took a second to blink and wipe my tears away. He seemed saddened by the sight but for once didn't ask.

"Alex I s..." He trailed off with a hiss, twiddling his fingers. "Alex I... I know it's a bad time but I need to tell you something."

I sniffed and averted my eyes from him. "Where have you been? I haven't seen you in days."

"You've seen me."

"Yes, I've *seen* you, but you've barely been around."

His form compressed a little, he inched into the shadow cast by the curtains.

"Wh—Well, I... I've just been sleeping a lot. Very tired. Unwell."

Is that even possible?

"Apperently." He spat with a frantic edge. "Nevermind that right now—Alex, I-I've seen something troubling. Something that's frightened me. I don't want to tell you, but I must. It is the only way I can protect you."

I got goosebumps. I felt them hard under my sleeves. I brought myself close and listened.

"What did you see, Jonah?" I whispered, thoughts still buzzing to the closed door behind me.

He shifted around a little, glancing those anxious shiny eyes around the hall and in dimensions I couldn't perceive. When he deemed it safe, he exited the shadow and got in my face. Nose to nose almost. I fell cold. So cold my teeth began to chatter.

"J-J-Jonah?"

He touched me. His fingers lingered on my loose hand.

"I saw Death in the room where you sleep."

My heart sank.

His head fell a little helplessly.

"What do you mean by that, Jonah? Death like the grim reaper? Is that even real?"

He let out a stressed sigh. "I've always understood Death as a force of nature... a feature of the natural order of things. Not personified, but a state. What I saw was malicious and—"

He gasped, his head shot to the foot of the stairs.

I looked—there was nothing.

When I turned back to Jonah he was gone.

He didn't return. I asked him about it when I saw him the next day. He brushed it off as a bad dream and went back to being distant. Haunting the corridors like a real ghost. And my mother went a whole week without talking to me and really committed to it.

That night I got on my knees to pray. I told God that all else was failing, and that my softness was almost gone. I asked if I could trade every dream I've ever had for another way. For something brighter. I offered him the last of my heart.

But of course he didn't reply. He just watched me cry my eyes out in the dark. And how I wished someone would come and wash this heaviness away.

"Lord I know there is so much suffering in the world, and I am but one in a sea of voices, but please God, please. Hear me... Hear me... Why has death come for me and not taken? What is your intent?"

I tried one last time. But I feel the language of love leaving me. I simply begged. I begged him and my mother, saying,

"Just tell me what to change."

Nothing.

February. . .

March. . .

April. . .

May. . .

June.

Chapter Seven

Time seems to slow down when things are unpleasant. More time, more life, when I'd give anything to just die. It's now a funny thought, that I tried to kill myself a year ago. To think any of this could end on my terms.

Life does not end. It only happens to you until it stops. When I'm gone the sun will rise and the birds will live to sing again. Time will still exist. Life will go on.

I live on. I have, despite a hollow frame. I live on, not because I want to, but because living is a cross I must bear until I'm done bleeding out. I guess, in a way, it is a cross we all must bear. A crucifixion that begins in the womb.

As for me, afflicted and in pain, I was born crucified like the Saint Peter. Pinned down to mine reversed, to be made a mockery for all to see. But nobody cares. And the ones who do have their hands bound to governor who presides over the land. There is one watches from the crowd. And he is me. And I shout, and curse, and cast stones at myself.

I awoke this morning to the sound of my mother's voice in the hallway, pacing back and forth as she wagered on the phone. I stirred, curious by nature, and listened, eyes blank, fixed on the light that broke in from the sill of the door.

I braced myself and waited for her to barge in.

But she didn't.

I got up and got ready for another day.

"Hey!" My mother called after me. I took a deep breath and turned.

"Are you gonna pick up Tommy after school?" She nagged, as if this were some chore she'd assigned. As if she *asked* me to do it. Which she hadn't.

"I volunteered." I glowered at her, "Why are you asking me like I'm unreliable?"

She blinked, middle finger tapping the ash of her cigarette. I watched it crumble onto the floor and into nothing.

"Did I say that?" She shot back.

I exhaled sharply. "Nevermind. Yes, I'm walking him home."

A curd nod. No words.

"You know today's my last day of school and you haven't asked me a thing about it."

She sighed before taking in a slow drag, metal fence between us. Through the bars I met her eyes, usually hard and wounding to mine, seemed distracted. Far away. I wondered,

What do you think about when you stare off into the clouds?

"Son." She said this stern, it hit my ears like the snap of a finger. "What are you talking about?" Her words curled in the air with the smoke. The breeze sent it my way, arcid and sharp.

I inhaled it, not wanting to admit to myself that I liked the smell of her cigarettes. I tell myself it's the only piece of me she shares anymore. I covet every discarded fume.

"I guess it's too late now." I muttered over my shoulder as I walked away.

"Nunu!"

I turned one last time. "I don't know how many times people gotta tell you that you shouldn't smoke while pregnant. It's bad for the kid."

I was gone before she could react and didn't look back.

The bus lurched to an abrupt stop. The force sent me hard against my seatbelt. The lady next to me seemed frightened by my stone-cold face. I didn't react. Then, a sudden shift in the air. My hairs stood on end. I glanced up and saw Leonel with his boys.

They entered the bus smiling, giggly. Surely having a better day than me. Down the aisle he froze mid step once he saw me. Eyes locked onto mine, a second of stillness. Then his face contorted, like he'd seen something he wasn't supposed to. One of his friends noticed the tension with mischievous curiosity. Leonel shoved his hands into his pocket and dismissed me like I wasn't somebody he once knew. He did it to be cruel, but that was actually the correct response.

There was a boy amongst them that held my attention more than him. A threatening aura clung to him. But, not in the sense that I found him a personal danger. He was just a little unsettling. It radiated from him like heat off summer pavement. And his resemblance to me was a bit uncanny. All but the tan and the green eyes, we could be brothers.

He sat at the far end of the back row. He and everyone else roared with careless laughter, the sound made the cabin feel packed-full. Leonel didn't look at me again. *But his friend...* From the window's reflection I caught him staring at me. Each time our eyes met he grinned. Something wicked and knowing.

I had never seen him before in my life. *What's his deal?* The fourth time it happened I snapped, my stomach fell to knots as I spun around to confront him—But he was gone!

I froze in place.

Leonel noticed instantly, as if he'd been expecting me to try and make a scene. He shook his head and muttered something to the guy next to him. I turned away, white faced as what I had just seen fully sank in.

The bus hissed to a stop. I gripped the rail and swung out the door, I practically launched myself off the seat and into a full sprint toward the high school.

I entered the room with a grim face. Mrs.Blanco stood tip-toed on top of her desk with a banner between her teeth as she fought against a stubborn thumbtack lodged into the wall.

She gasped and quickly tore it out of her mouth, red-faced.

"Alexander, welcome!" She called happily, stepping down carefully. My eyes shot to her bare feet on the linoleum that hadn't been buffed in God knows how long—a choice.

"Hello." I said in a flat voice, though the back of my neck stung. I was in awe for a moment—it was sad. How quickly the room had been reduced to cardboard boxes and blank walls. I couldn't name one poster that was there if she'd asked, but I could feel their absence everywhere.

"You're too late, Alexander." She laughed. Friendly. "I'm basically done, Coach Santi's boys came in here and helped me pack. There's still Rice Krispies on the table if you want."

I had noticed it empty on the way in. "No, I'm okay." I said gruffly. She smiled and gestured for me to sit down. I glanced at the chair and got a headrush. How many times had I been in that seat? I couldn't remember. The thought made me so uneasy—some faceless terror.

I shrugged, "Nah, I'm okay—If I'm all good to go I don't wanna impose. It's your summer too."

"I wish." She muttered. "I might have to work this summer with everything going on at home, I'm not sure."

I frowned at the implications. I can barely handle life now. I imagined a nine-to-five on top of that and felt immense dread.

"Are you gonna be okay?" I asked.

She looked at me, muddled for a moment, and then smiled.

"Of course I will be, Alexander." She sat down, gesturing again. "How are you? C'mon, what if I don't see you next year. You never know."

I sat, albeit reluctantly. "What do you mean? Are you not gonna work here anymore?"

"No, that's not what I'm saying." She said in a high pitch, "Life happens. What if you get a change of heart and try out public school?"

I tittered. Empty. Devoid of any real humor in it. "Hard pass." The wry smile on my face was nice. Muscles I hadn't moved in so long.

"You look tired." She noted, her presence trailing off into her thoughts. Then her face lit up in a bit suspiciously.

"What time did you wake up?" She asked, peeking, covering her face with her mug as she took a two-handed sip of her latte.

The odd question threw me. "Like... an hour ago." I answered without giving it much thought.

Her eyes flashed to her desk for a moment and then back at me as she set down her glass.

"What are your plans this summer?" She asked.

"I don't have any plans." I learned the hard way that what can go wrong will absolutely go wrong.

She dropped her head theatrically and sighed, "You're a bright kid, Alexander you gotta get it together,"

"Does intelligence constitute brightness? Nikola Tesla was extremely inventive but I don't think I would call him bright."

"Why not? He's probably the reason we're sitting in a room with light and air conditioner. I'd call that bright."

She smiled. I guess she missed our little chats.

I shook my head—unable to fight back a smile. But still, past my teeth I could feel the horror of what I had seen on the bus.

"He also worked on a death ray and a phone that can call the dead." The chill in my bones was evident. She wagged a finger at me, trying to be charming, but it fell on a dead man.

"Bright kid." She insisted.

I glanced away a moment. "Patent pending."

I would have rolled my eyes were it not for the fact I pledged kindness to her after my outburst in the beginning of the year. She'd all but forgotten about it by now.

"Are you someone that I can be honest with? I'm asking sincerely."

She was serious in an instant—shifted in her seat, hands collapsed together on her desk like a lawyer ready to make a plea deal.

"Of course. Is everything okay, Alexander?"

I huffed. Shattering my pledge when I rolled my eyes at her overly nice tone. "Everyone is always asking me that. I don't even know what the question means anymore."

She frowned and got a little closer. When she spoke her voice was softer than I'd ever heard it before. She said to me, "I talk to your mom often and I know there's some tension at home."

My eyes went dark. "You don't know how bad it is." I muttered. "But that's not what I want to say."

Her eyes were eager. Concerned. I continued.

"I-I just wanted to say, um, your remark got me thinking. Life happens."

Until it doesn't. "If I don't see you in the fall, I want to say that you've done me an immense kindness over the last few months. I don't really have a lot of friends right now, so, these little conversations, um, I know I act like I hate being here all the time but now that's its done I, uh—"

I inhaled.

"—Sorry. What I mean to say is, I enjoy your presence and I always have. I guess now that it's up in the air I regret taking your kindness for granted. Even now. I'm kind of an asshole."

Her lips pressed into a genuine smile, but her eyes were the same. My hands were too close—she reached over and placed hers upon mine and gave a maternal squeeze that made something inside of me shatter. I felt every shard sink into the outline of my heart. But I did not move an inch, or pull away. I accepted it.

"Aw. Alexander. That's very sweet of you. Listen to me—"

I looked away and sniffed—feeling my tear ducts start to turn over like an old car struggling to life. I couldn't bear to look at her any longer, but I was listening.

She waited for my eyes. Despite myself I looked back.

"—It's hard, it's really hard. But the most brilliant, beautiful people come from the darkest places. Don't give up on yourself, Alexander. You're gonna do great things one day."

"And how do you know that?" I croaked.

"Those capable of great pain are capable of even greater love." She let go of my hands and gave me a final smile before I was out the door.

I walked to Tommy's school from Woodrow. It's not very far, just past the park and the baseball field. I thought about him on my way there. Crazy to think that when I was a kid I used to break down in nervous fits if I didn't know where he was every second of the day. I was very protective of him and Franky. It kind of robbed me of a childhood but I'd do it again in a heartbeat and probably do it better. I was always hard on myself but in the end I think it was worth it. They trust me more than anyone else. We didn't have it easy as wayward boys. I thank God my mother isn't cruel to them. Pragmatic and aloof, yes, but she isn't cruel. These days I'm a ghost like the others. There's not much I can be for my brothers other than a benign presence. I send love all the way from sheol.

"I saw something weird on the bus." I blurted into the silence. Tommy dragged his feet behind him as we walked. I tried to change the subject as he requested, but his lack of a response informed me that he didn't wish to speak at all.

I sighed, "Buddy—" and placed my hand on his shoulder to stop him. He wouldn't meet my eyes. I leaned down and met his. There were tears in his eyes.

"Tommy—?" "Buddy, hey—what's wrong?" I prodded, wishing I could sound as worried as I was. I hate to see him cry.

He was frustrated, I knew that much. He got in trouble for something stupid at school and it wasn't his fault. He's a skater boy with stick and poke tattoos so no one ever believes a word he has to say. It's been that way since we were young. It makes him so mad he goes numb. So it's dire when he cries—especially in front of me. I reserve the most of his trust and tears are the line he seldom crosses. I'd give anything to know his heart but I've accepted my role in his life a long time ago.

I believe him. Always. I wrapped him in my arms. He stood straight as a board but I felt his shoulders ease at least. We both knew he was in for a mouthful once we got home.

"Can you tell me what's wrong?" I asked again, making a real effort to speak as delicately as I could. The sound of my indifference angered me. The anger was a rush. It was like inhaling flames. He finally met my eyes and stepped away, face a stern mask. Though the traces of dry tears betrayed him.

I used to find comfort in the idea that he and I would be alike as we got older. We're cut from the same cloth, afterall. I've always been the black sheep of the family, even when I was relatively tolerated by them. There were still things about me that put off my aunts. Namely my opinionated nature. Can't help that I'm not a liar like the rest of them. It makes me an outsider. At least I had the possibility of like minded brothers.

Yet, as I behold his budding identity outside of us, we cursed people, it's clear that our commonality ends at the face. And I think I'm okay with that. I hate being me. Why would I wish such a curse upon him?

That being said... I don't know if being *him* is any better for his spirit. He *is* a Hunsucker. I wonder how that's going to distort him. I pray he's stronger than ten of me and it never does. Tommy is sensitive. I see the way his face shatters when he feels betrayed. I'm there as much as I can be but at this age he'd rather be alone.

I never wanted to be and it's all I have. Even Jonah can't save me from *that*. If anything my friendly ghost has finally got with the program.

"No. It's fine." He sniffed, absolute. I broke our gaze in shame. I wanted to know. His eyes, another pair that break me. Not because of malice, but something else... maybe that great love the teacher talked about.

"Did you tell Mom I got out of school early?" He chided, like he already had an answer in his mind and it angered him. His curt tone upset me, but that's just how he talks sometimes. I used to think he got it from our mother but he never means to cause harm with his words.

"No." I said robotically. "I speak to her as minimally as possible." I rubbed the back of my neck—that stinging feeling again. The bus sped past us down the road suddenly—the same bus I rode this morning. I shivered and imagined the grinning boy from earlier still aboard, staring at me from the large window.

"Okay, well, Ima go to the skate park. Can you come with me so Mom thinks we walked home right after school? Or are you gonna snitch on me?"

I took a step back. "W-Why would I do that? I just said I speak to her as minimally as possible."

He glared at me. "You snitched on me last time, bro."

I sighed and spoke with emphasis on every word to ensure that he understood me.

"Tommy, look—you're a kid, okay?"

He cringed at the word. *Kid.* More than anything he hates being infantilized, but he's too young to care about that. It's the least of his worries. It would be different if he was my age being called *kid.* And even then it would still be true.

"This is a shady town. And although mom and I don't get along, your safety trumps my personal feelings. I only 'snitched' on you last time because it was after dark and no one knew where you were, not even me. What if the worst happened?"

"I was at my girlfriend's house!" He groaned.

I crossed my arms. "Enough. You're lucky I talked her out of shipping you off to boot camp over the whole ordeal, she's a maniac."

He wasn't looking at me anymore. I sighed. "You're not a bad kid, Tommy. I'm on your side. Even when I tell on you. I just want to keep you safe."

Silent treatment.

"I'll spare you and never mind. Yes I'll go to the skate park with you and, no, I won't tell mom. I promise."

I smiled at him in an attempt to alleviate the attention.

He blinked. "Why couldn't you just say that last part, dude?" and stormed off ahead.

I stammered and resigned, simply following behind. I chose not to take it personally. He's just a boy.

I sat in the dirt by the trees and watched him from afar. It was nice to see that he has a plethora of friends. He didn't want me to meet them, of course. If I'm known at all I'm his weird goth brother. To spare him the embarrassment I told him that I would linger nearby and keep to myself. He appreciated that. Most of them are stoners and scrappers but they seem genuine. The way their faces lit up as he approached told me everything I needed to know, that he's in good hands.

To my displeasure I noticed Leonel and his pals on the other side of the park doing God knows what under the bleachers. Their absent giggles crept all the way up the hill to annoy me. He must've noticed me at some point because when I looked back he was already halfway toward me, having snuck away from his clique. I made sure to mad dog him the entire time so he knew that I wasn't in a friendly mood.

"What do you want, Leonel?" I spat once he was close enough to hear me. He seemed surprised by the acid in my voice. Although I'm not sure why, it's not like we ever *really* had a good rapport.

"Creeper, you're the one stalking me from the bushes. What's up with you?"

"I'm not stalking you, retard. You don't even exist to me. I'm here for my brother. I just so happened to notice you and your friends down there." I peeked over at them. The troublesome lot dispersed from the bleachers to find him.

He smirked and shrugged, though his gaze seemed a bit stung. "I thought you missed me or something, jotito."

Something rolled in my chest—some snarl or growl. Nasty and inhuman. Unintentional but so appropriate that I didn't even stop to question it.

"Can I help you?" I asked curtly. He got closer, inching toward the hidden patch by the trees. I didn't budge, my feet firm in place.

"How have you been?" He asked, pulling a half-burnt joint out of his pocket and sticking it between his teeth as he fished around for the lighter. My eyes fixed on a face down by the field—immediately recognizable. I turned white. He turned to see who I was looking at—It was the guy I saw on the bus. The one that vanished. Same face, same everything. Only now he wore athletic gear and had his headphones on.

"Who is that?" I blurted. Stressed.

Leonel seemed amused by my dramatic expression, but I was mortified.

"Who? Jacob? That's my homeboy. Why are you looking at him like that?"

"Was he on the bus with you earlier?" A chill ran up my spine. So vivid it made me wince. I couldn't look away.

His little smirk fell and he answered me seriously. "No. He met us here. Why? Do you know him?"

"No." I said quickly, to swallow the thought. "Nevermind."

His smirk slowly crept back in. It infuriated me. My hands curled into fists. *It's all shits and giggles with these boys.* What a torture it is to be so far removed from the reality of my peers! If only he knew the restraint it takes not to—

"Oh you know him, don't you?" He teased. Whatever he meant to imply, I hadn't a clue.

"No, I don't." I hissed. Honest. He was still smiling at me through hooded eyes. I tilted my head and came to the conclusion he must be under the influence. He brought his hands together and lit his cigarette against the breeze, facing away a moment to get it right. Just for a second my fury settled so I could get a better look at him. At his face.

His profile was sharp. Handsome. Perfect angles in the right places, jaw, cheek, beautiful roma nose for character. His wavy, vanta-black, hair. He's always been very blessed in appearance. I noticed a small tattoo hidden behind his ear, three little stars. I wondered what it meant and when he had gotten it.

He then blew a puff of smoke to the side of him. It smelled terrible.

"You know Jacob's a little jotito like you." He said. The fury returned. It washed away all lingering guilt and sexual frustration. Hateful ants took to my skin—my white face began to go red. That fearful tremor I'd gotten from the boy in the field rolled over into a rage. I exhaled sharply—like there was steam trapped in my chest.

And I knew he was misreading all of these queues. He got even closer. I took a few steps back, and he and I were hidden—still separated by an arm's length—but hidden. Under the trees. He stared at me, really trying to read my face, eyes struggling against mine. *Nobody's home, Leonel.* I thought.

"Fuck you. I know your secret." I reminded him.

His face shifted—no longer friendly, if you could call it that, and he paced toward me.

"You're not gonna tell anyone, you know it'll be your ass." He hissed.

I grimaced and shot to an inch of his face. He seemed surprised by my gull. Leonel lurched back just enough.

"Did you tell anyone?" I asked in a tone just as threatening. And I can't speak for him, but mine wasn't an act. I felt the air shift around us until it was vacant.

"No? What are you on?"

"I got some weird emails a few months ago from a guy named Adrian. He called me gay and accused me of making moves on you when we both know that's not what the fuck happened."

He burrowed into me with both arms and pinned me to the tree. The ash of his cigarette crumpled onto my arm.

He spoke through his teeth, *"And what did you say?"*

I found his breath intolerable. I turned a little, but I kept his eyes locked to mine.

"I said nothing. I'm not an idiot. Getting cyberbullied is pathetic. You ever heard the phrase 'pick your battles?'"

He let go and stepped back in thought. I adjusted my collar and tucked it back into my jumper.

He took another hit. And let out one lone chuckle.

"You said his name was Adrian?" Smoke followed every letter. I swatted my hand to clear the air.

"Yes. Adrian Lazo. The last email I got was in March. It was some fucked up chain email called *'Mandingo Party'* and it was just a bunch of—really *lude* porn!"

He shook his head and blew the smoke in my face this time, trying his hardest not to laugh. When it cleared I saw that he was still smiling.

"Nah, I don't know an Adrian. And I don't know anybody who uses email like that. It was probably one of your weird friends."

I crossed my arms and scoffed. "Where do you get that, anyway? You're a fuckin' minor."

He raised an eyebrow, incredulous. "You've always been a little fed, you know that, creeper? Why do you wanna know? You want some?"

He passed it to me. I put out a finger and removed it from my face.

"No. I heard somebody in town is selling it to you guys and my little brother recently became another one of his victims. I don't give a single flying fuck what happens to any of you—but Tommy? I'm not gonna let anyone corrupt my little brother. He has a good heart. When I find out who it is I'm gonna kill him."

He was utterly shocked by my words. Smile gone again. Eyes wide.

He huffed. "You're fucked up, Alexander."

He then muttered something to himself that I missed. I stood silent and stared off elsewhere. He continued when it got awkward for him. Rudely, of course.

"Who'd you hear that from? Nobody knows you."

His cigarette burnt out spontaneously to his surprise. Like invisible fingers had pinched it out. It happened with a loud hiss. He was muddled as he tried to relight it and it wouldn't take.

"You're such a prude." He said through pressed lips. Finally when it relit he tried to pass it to me again. I declined.

"I'm surprised that's even a word in your vocabulary."

"Fuck you, I'm not illiterate. What's your problem, fool? Forreal. You got a fuckin attitude."

I rolled my eyes and ignored him. I looked at the boy in the soccer field again. Jacob. The one from the bus. His face was softer than the others, less threatening. Friendly, even. I imagined the boy from the bus— same exact face as the young man down there. But that can't be. It doesn't make sense.

I reminded myself that I'm crazy. *I was just seeing things again.* But even still... it was the same boy. It was.

"So he's really gay?" I asked. Not interested but curious. An attempt to rewire the terror the ambiguity his face inspired. I've never seen him before and Woodrow is small. He's definitely someone I would remember. Maybe even know.

Leonel chuckled. I glared at him. I would ask myself why I bother but he was the one who approached *me*. This conversation was doomed from the quotation mark.

"You think he's cute?" He asked, rocking and smiling in humor of himself like an imbecile.

"Do you? You're always friends with the prettiest boys. Makes me wonder if it's intentional."

He laughed. "No mames. Yeah, he's gay. And I didn't try shit, I'm not a fag, so don't start, jotito."

I shook my head, eyes still lingering on this Jacob boy.

"He probably likes you." I said. A hunch. He still scanned around the field for Leonel whereas everyone else went back to the bleachers. Leonel stood beside me and looked down at him, curious. I uncrossed my arms when he crossed his to mirror me. He was silent for so long I thought he hadn't heard me. Then he said,

"Nah. What makes you think that?"

I shot him a glance up and down. "Well, clearly you haven't changed at all. You're extremely difficult to be around." *"And even worse to be alone with."* I added with disdain. His face shifted from offense to something else as I continued.

"You're always flashing your body, standing too close, too touchy."

He was closer now. Shoulder practically against mine. He turned suddenly.

"Yeah?" He asked before pulling me in for an unwanted kiss by the collar of my shirt. I shoved him away from me and punched him in the jaw.

"Don't fucking touch me!"

He tumbled over and scurried to his feet. Before I could even process the act he leapt toward me and tackled me onto the ground. Suddenly he and I were exchanging fists.

I blacked out.

When I came to Leonel and I were both on opposite ends fighting against arms holding us back. And he looked pretty dinged up. His friends eased their grip when he calmed down but I struggled in an unknown boy's arms. I slammed the back of my head into his face and kicked back into his knee. I would have jumped straight into Leonel had they all not shouted their friend's name—Jacob—with the horror and distress of small children. They all fled past me and shuffled to lift his head off the ground. There was blood dripping from his nose. I winced and felt a weight dissipate. A shroud I had not even noticed was there. A blind rage that consumed me like fire—gone in an instant. I stepped back modified by what I had done.

He cried out in spanish, a language I did not understand, but every word was laced with pain. Amid the chaos we met eyes and he stared at me with betrayal. I wondered if Leonel had mentioned me before. My intuition informed me that he had. The look in his eyes was so telling.

I yanked my backpack off the ground and ran toward the Ascott Hill. A few boys gave chase until I heard Leonel shout for them to stop. My heart was pounding so hard I could feel it in my ears.

They all left after that.

Tommy was none the wiser of this incident. Although he did ask why I was covered in dirt and bruises. I lied and said that I had fallen down the hill while exploring.

When we walked through the door my Great Aunt Val slapped her knee and laughed when she saw me. The whole family was sitting in the living room watching some straight-to-DVD-release indie horror and eating Adriana's home-made lasagna.

"What the fuck happend to you, Buddy!?"

"You're already laughing. Your imagination is way funnier than the truth, I assure you."

She frowned and went back to her conversation with Irene about all the excessive sex scenes.

"Just tell us what happened, Nunu, you're so dramatic." Valene droned. I ignored her. My mother stepped past Tommy, to my surprise, and marched straight toward me.

"Are you okay?" She asked. It rolled off the tongue so crisp I could swear she meant it.

"Yes." I muttered quickly, eyes downtrodden. "I fell down the Ascott Hill and rolled all the way to the bottom."

Val overhead and burst out in laughter. Saying *"Only you, Nuners!"*

My mother sucked in a breath through her teeth and leaned in close, picking at the dirty nick on my cheekbone with her sleeve stretched over her thumb.

"We don't need to take you to the hospital, do we?"

"No." I said, flat. "I'm fine. I just have to shower." I trudged past her and down the hall. Irene watched the whole way with a long face but said nothing. Everyone went back to what they were doing.

I stared into the mirror for a while after I was done washing the dirt and gravel off my body, frigid and shaking, cleaning the little nips on my face and hands with saline and cotton pads.

Dark red blood spatters bloomed across the white of the sink from the scabs I peeled away. Some had matted itself into my right eyebrow from a cut I couldn't remember receiving. I swiped a pair of tweezers and plucked at it until it gave. Dried gash, open again. I saved that one for last. By the time I was finished a stripe of my eyebrow was gone, leaving the little wound raw and pink right in the center. I dropped my head in sorrow.

The sky is utter darkness. A year ago I boarded a plane and went some other place. When I got off it was past midnight, and there were no stars in the sky. As if the moon had taken them with her. I remember, the people in town were afraid. There in Gig Harbor you can see the space clouds. But not that night. The light was never meant.

I returned to that beach suddenly. Like I was living it for the first time. A memories after image, my life and death in supersymmetry. I was in pain. It was late. Beneath a starless night sky I stood at the edge of a cliff, hovering just above my oblivion. And that darkness went on forever, I could not tell apart the sky from the sea. That treacherous black static was everywhere. I thought of my mother and felt her frailty all around me. I wept. I couldn't tell you how many mornings I'd awaken with tears in my eyes over a dream she were dead. Waking life is a continuation of that nightmare. She lives, but her absence shrouds me like smoke. The promise of her love... the static of her embrace. A love I clawed at the fabric of time and space to receive... only to find myself in a dead universe all alone. Not one star to shine upon me. Not even the sun.

I truly felt like nothing mattered anymore. *It's over.* I felt over. *I feel over*. It's over.

And yet... I hesitated.

The macabre embrace of death was terrifying. That my life would end. Life—all we will ever know. I may believe in God and ghosts, but in truth my beliefs about it are nothing compared to the cold hard fact; no one alive *really* knows what's on the other side. My greatest pain is that, perhaps, there *is* nothing. My greatest fear is that I may have already traveled there, to that great and terrible nothing. But is that nothingness any worse than this loveless existence?

I think I realized that I didn't actually want to die when I stepped over the edge and fell down. I just wanted my suffering to end. But it was done. It was all over. I tossed myself below with eyes wide open to snuff out the seemingly timeless agony of being unloved by you, Mother.

I didn't die when my body smashed through the surface of the sea. I'd simply gotten the wind, and maybe, my soul, knocked out of me. I went under and sloshed about every which way. The sea is so powerful... for a moment I thought I had died and went straight to hell. The water felt like hands gripping me from all sides... I started to panic. I screamed until my voice tore like cheap cotton. I gasped and swallowed pints of dark water.

The only thing I could see when I glanced above were the blinking red lights that shone from an airplane high above me.

My body truly was the only thing that survived the fall. I see that now. As for the soul I once possessed? Gone with my last breaths and sunken away entirely. Into the dark. Suspended in moment that forever.

The wind picked up and a large wave slammed into me—I went flying into the rocks, the entire left side of my body and head rammed against it. The shock, fear and pain only led to more water in my lungs. I was drowning.

I used to hear people say that your life flashes before your eyes when you're dying. Mines did not. As I drowned wearing leather shoes, a necktie, and a trenchcoat, I was really frustrated that this is how I would be found—if at all. Ready for the casket. Soggy, sad, and unwanted. And I was also really upset about the fact that I was actually going out like this. A part of me still had hope things would get better. He was betrayed by me as I passed away under the waves.

Sometime later I woke up on shore thorwing up all of the saltwater I'd swallowed. It gushed out of me like glass shards out of my throat. I felt all the little bits of seaweed, salt, and sand tearing me up from the inside. My eyes bulged out and my mouth was so wide I felt like my jaw would unhinge. I hurled until I passed out again, face planted in the sand. I woke up a few moments later to throw up some more.

When it stopped I stared blankly ahead like a boy already gone. And there in the distance I saw someone watching me. A silhouette. An impossibly large man.

Who are you?

I rolled over on my side and the ground began to shake beneath me. Before my eyes I saw individual grains of sand dance and warp in the force of it, taking mathematical shapes on the floor. A plane flew close above me, so close I could count the rivets on the undercarriage. It was so loud the sound hardly registered. Its lights shone red on my skin. I thought it to be work of the devil.

I couldn't breathe. I just laid there and wheezed for a while. Every breath in tandem with the folding waves along the shore.

New moon. Motionless beneath its static. A perfect view of the black sea. Dead on arrival. The light was never meant.

Two knocks at the door frame snapped me out of the fog. I was startled to see that I was laid back in Irene's room. An hour passed.

"You left your phone in my car." Irene announced, said phone clasped in her hand. She tossed it to me—way off the mark. It shattered like Legos on the floor. Shell under the sofa, battery under the vanity and screen face down against the tile. She gasped and covered her mouth in shock. I hardly even shifted. I only moved my eyes, a slow glance at her blurry knees.

"Nunu!" She shouted, suppressing laughter. And it was funny. How can this horrible day get any worse?

"Oh my god!" She groaned as she bent over to pick up the pieces. Her spine popped and she winced. "Sorry, buddy, you're gonna have to pick that up yourself." Her voice was light. Happy. I didn't move.

"Are you okay?" She asked, that happiness now laced with doubt. She got down on her knees with hardly any grace, one hand still lodged firmly in her aching back.

I didn't speak. At my side she asked again, voice firm as always, "Hey. What's up with you? You said you fell down the hill?"

"I did." I lied. "I'm fine, I was just spacing out a little."

"I don't like that." She said, face and voice an impossible pair. Pouty eyes, curt tone. "I don't like that one bit. Your friend called asking for you."

I tensed up to attention immediately and turned. "And you answered? Which one?"

"The red head. And yes, I told him you left your phone in my car. He wanted to come pick you up, he said to call him back."

I sat up, already frustrated and groaned. I didn't even bother asking whom she referred to. I'd find out when I put my phone back together.

"Ugh, I don't hangout anymore, I've been avoiding—well. I don't know who you're talking about, but regardless, I'm avoiding them."

"Why? Do you have anything better to do than mope around all day?"

"Are you trying to comfort me or scold me?"

Her face hardened. "Hey, buddy, watch the attitude." She stood. "He's, like, one of your best friends, Nunu. Katie too. You don't wanna lose them."

Another pop in her hip. She cursed under her breath and whined, "I wish I had friends to come pick me up and take me camping."

Now I really have no idea who she's talking about. Nevertheless it isn't an urgent situation.

Before I went to sleep I sat alone in the kitchen and put my phone back together. I'll be sleeping in the living room tonight. Some nights, like tonight, I dream of putting a gun in my mouth and pulling the trigger. No bullets. I imagine the hard metal against the roof of my mouth and feel an echo of satisfaction.

Instinctively I glanced at the wall to check the time. No clock. The kitchen clock has been missing since I had that nervous breakdown with the pen ink. I had yet to get used to it no longer being there.

Adriana baselessly accused me of getting rid of it. She and Bonnie screamed in my face and claimed that I was "doing it to make a fool out of everyone." Irene was unconvinced, but only because her anger extended to everyone. We were all at fault given that it never turned up. My mother considered the possibility a spirit had taken it and accused Jonah. Of course it wasn't Jonah. Out of spite he knocked over three of her vases and her hummingbird feeder for good measure. That, she also accused him of.

Irene tore up the entire house looking for it, even lifting the cushions off the couch like that made any sense at all. Leave no stone unturned, I suppose. She adores her vintage decor. I often mistake her aesthetic for anachronism instead of the tragedy it actually is. I imagined her again, decades earlier doing the same exact thing and sighed at the thought.

I stuck to my guns. "I didn't do it." But for once I was actually the trouble maker they've always seen me as. Little did they know they were right about me getting rid of the clock. My reasoning, however, was not as malicious as Bonnie made it out to be. I threw it away because I was scared. All the gaps in time tore at an already frayed mind. The kitchen is my last safe haven now that Valene spends most her nights home. That clock was a constant reminder of all the bad dreams.

The screen lit an electric blue and stayed that way for a moment too long. A white line split it in two. I thought it was broken until it abruptly returned to life.

MISSED CALL   DANTE

MISSED CALL   TWINKLE

MISSED CALL   TWINKLE

MISSED CALL   KATIE

DANTE

Hey me and Jessie are going camping wanna come with?
Haven't heard from you in a while ;)

So it was Dante. *Irene has my social life all wrong.* He texted me a few nights ago wanting to come over. I've never actually hung out with just him before, so this was unexpected and impossible for a myriad of reasons. From what I could put together through the brain fog he'd taken a recent interest in reigniting our friendship. Even if I was in any condition for friends, hanging out *here* is a complete no go. Literally before he sent me that text Adriana pummeled me into the couch over a stupid argument she started. You can imagine why I said no.

Dante likes me. He thinks I'm interesting. And I find him charming. But he lives a life so far removed from the nature of mine he couldn't possibly understand me. I know that's shallow but it's the truth. I suggested another time and swore on it. I guess I have to be a man of my word or weave together a new lie to get out of it.

"Whatever! I don't have the mind for it!" I shouted as I slammed the phone on the table. The screen fractured. I frowned and gazed into it, my reflection was split in two.

Jonah shifted in the closet beside me. My eyes shot to meet his, little green lights shining through the slats. I stormed off and went to sleep on the sofa.

No dreams. I closed my eyes and tried to sleep. But I could not. I fell plaid and trembling. I shot up in the quilts and covered my eyes with my right arm as I broke down into a fit of tears. Loud and unbidden.

CHAPTER EIGHT

The cicadas sang a nasty shrieking song. It was almost as loud as the shouting from the other side of the wall. But not louder than the high frequency from the television. I sat in an otherwise dark room and wept into the quilt I clutched close. At some point I fell asleep, basked in neon blue light and static.

Something unexpected shocked me awake. Some electric feeling. My pajamas soaked in sweat, I sat up, disconcerted by the pitch darkness of the room. Tommy laid beside me, even sweatier, curled into a little ball at my side. I began to shove him in a desperate attempt to wake him up. I felt the panic burning in my lungs as Tommy lay there, limp and cold. I couldn't see him, but my other senses remained, sharp and unmerciful. The hum of the ceiling vent had taken on a low, animal growl. I could still hear the high-pitched whine of the television bleeding into my skull, and the dying fire alarm gave a final shriek that echoed through the walls, impossibly distant and unbearably close. BEEP.

I began to whimper his name over and over again. Out cold on cough medicine my father had fed him to sleep. But he wasn't sick. Even as a child I understood this was cruel. My father hates to be bothered by any of us in the night. I ate coffee grounds when I was his age to fight against it. I saw a girl in a scary movie do it to keep her from sleeping.

"Tommy!" I stressed through my teeth. Still nothing. My little heart sank. I held a lone finger under his nostril to make sure he was still breathing. And to my relief he was. Carefully, I climbed out of bed, holding myself close against the darkness, and went for the door. I was barely tall enough to reach the knob. I twisted slowly, as to not make a sound and risk waking my father.

The hallway was just as dark. I was afraid. I called out into it, "Hello?" and recoiled from how booming my little voice was against this dark night. Nothing. Just that lone chirp again. BEEP.

A shape emerged from the darkness suddenly. A hazy outline of a boy, glowing green all over. I froze and watched him turn the corner of the kitchen and straight for me. His visage cut in and out like the darkness was trying to eat him too. I could feel my heartbeat in my ears. His eyes were white and his skin was see-through. Feet an inch off the floor, unwound shoelaces dragged behind him as he hovered down the hall with neck limp. The aglets tore against the floorboards like scratching fingernails.

I remained right where I stood. Barely past the foot of my door, shaking violently like a wet dog. Never once looking away from the specter. An older boy dressed like an old man. He wore a dingy white shirt with pinstripes under a black vest with nicks and frays. And there was a large gaping tear that split the shoulder to his chest. His skin was sallow and bruised like a rotting apple, and his eyes had sunken so deep into his face the sockets were a black crust! Like he were Dead! Then it hit me—

I let out the loudest, blood curdling scream. The boy sped past me—heels to the ground full sprint into the end of the hall where I was. He stopped to take one last look at me before he vanished into the wall of my parents' room. His face was cold and emotionless, and his eyes were shinier than a cat's. A devilish shade of green. I wet my pants at the sight.

I pressed my knees together, disgusted, horrified, unable to make sense of what I had just seen. My father kicked down his door and flew toward me. My mother right behind him, frantic, shaking me, begging me to tell her what's the matter. Tommy woke up shrieking. We both stood there soiled and in tears like babies in the dark. My father was still at his wits end from the argument he and my mother had. He carried not one ounce of patience for "another bad dream." But it wasn't a dream. What I saw was real.

By the time I had calmed down I was already in the tub, my eyes red and wounded from how much I'd cried. As my mother sat there on her knees, weary, rinsing the suds off me with a bucket of hot water, she asked me again,

"Baby, what did you see?"

My father appeared in the doorway curt and mean. "Priscilla what the fuck did I tell you? Just leave it alone!"

I winced. She spun around and screamed at him, "Alex get the fuck out of here! This is all your fault! I tell you not to mess around with that ghost shit!" She threw the wet rag clutched in her hand at his face. It hit him so hard it made a sound. *Splat!*

He balled his fists and made a sudden jerk. My mother and I both flinched, but he stopped himself from taking it any further and stormed down the hall while cursing her name.

She sighed and turned back to me, cupping her hands around my face, trying to keep my eyes on hers so I wouldn't start crying again. That was the first time I had noticed the color of her eyes. Then, green and sparkling, even late at night. Like emeralds. She was a young mother, only twenty-three or twenty-four years old. Homesick and lonely outside of my father and our haunted house.

"You're gonna be okay, my baby." She said. "He's not gonna come back, I promise."

She was talking about the ghost but in my little heart I had wished she was referring to my father. She poured more hot water over my head to soothe me. I was still trembling.

"Mommy, I'm scared."

"I promise you he's not coming back. I'm your mom. I just know these things."

I believed her. But I was still afraid. I kept quiet as she finished rinsing me off, eyes lingering on the empty hallway. She brought my face back to hers.

"No, stop looking, my love. If you keep imagining him there he'll come back. He's not there, I promise you baby."

The idea frightened me even more. Every time I blinked I saw his face behind my eyes. *Dead. Dead. Dead!* I believed her. But her knuckles turned white how hard she gripped the bucket. I wonder if she believed herself.

She tucked me in bed and remained there a while after that, watching the clock on the wall. Tommy was asleep in their room to my father's annoyance.

As young as I was, I was clever. I made a smart remark once. I said it was stupid to put a clock in my bedroom since I couldn't read it. The teachers at school tried hard to teach me, but like cursive, I didn't get it. My father thought it was funny. They didn't even know the word stupid had made it into my vocabulary. My mother wasn't impressed. She said, "It's important you understand the time. That's how you know whether you're sleeping or awake."

"But I can't tell the time." I insisted. "Even when I am awake." And she teased me and told me, *"Then I guess you're dreaming right now."* I knew I wasn't. But the thought was horrifying enough that I quickly learned how to tell the time. I had nightmares almost every day that I had woken up and it was all a dream. It got so bad I had to start wearing a wristwatch to school. But it only lasted a few weeks on my arm. A pair of boys on the school bus beat me up and took it from me. Said it was "faggy,"

It was Buzz Lightyear.

The clock struck Midnight. She smiled and kissed my forehead.

"It's Midnight, Son." She sang, *"Happy Birthday."* She wiggled a finger at me, "You're my, what? Baby?"

I giggled, still tense, but happy, and brought a pointed finger to meet hers. Like the hands in The Creation of Adam by Michaelangelo. It was our thing. We've done it for as long as I can remember.

I whispered, *"I'm your number one, mommy."* And tapped the tip of her finger with mine. She made a buzzing sound through her teeth. *"Zzzzzzzz,"*

And kissed my forehead one last time. Her eyes glanced below a moment and I caught her sigh a heavy sigh. A sound I couldn't yet comprehend as sadness. She glanced back at me and her face softened, a little smile before shutting off the lights.

I was so drowsy in the morning I could hardly speak. My father dropped me off at school. Not even his loud diesel truck and the coffee my mother told him not to give me was enough to snap me awake from the fog and the looming terror.

On the playground I stared off into nothing, tossing a volleyball into the fence repeatedly. Eyes dark and some other place. That game of one-player catch that lasted the whole recess. On top of the melancholy of being friendless in second grade it was a particularly frigid October morning. My mother fell sick overnight and couldn't get out of bed, so my father had to get me up and ready. He's an inattentive man. I learned that word from my mother. That's what she tells Nanna Irene on the phone when she smokes her cigarettes. And because of that I was underdressed for the weather. I wore a white and blue striped collar and school shorts.

I waited for what seemed like ages for the bell to ring. I thought about the ghost in the hallway the entire time.

A few kids stopped by to call me names and I didn't even acknowledge them. They left when my eight-year-old catatonia was too uncomfortable. Still, the boy's cold dead face was hidden in everything. I wasn't sure if I was imagining it or not. But my mother said if I imagined it he would come... the stress was too much to bear. I couldn't stop thinking about it.

"Your teacher said you were distracted all day today." My mom said when I met her arms after stepping off the bus. She seemed to be feeling better. She told me that my father would be working overnight in Nichols Hills and she said it with a smile on her face. I already knew she and Trina planned on burying their heads in a bottle of wine.

"Did you stay up all night?" She asked, a little annoyed.

"I was scared." I admitted. Reluctant to lie, because she smacked me in the mouth the last time I did. I didn't even think it was that big of a deal. The teacher went around the class and asked us if we'd ever been to the dentist. I never had before, but I didn't want to be made fun of, so I made up a story where the dentist took all my teeth because my mom let me have too many sweets. My mom didn't like that one bit. She said, *"It's one thing to lie! It's another thing to make me look bad!"*

She sighed and brushed my hair out of my face with her pale fingers. I held onto her leg up the stairs.

"I know baby. I'm sorry. Let's go."

We didn't have a birthday party because my father spent all the money on candy and costumes for trick r' treating. I didn't mind this, however. I love halloween. It's my favorite holiday. Because I wasn't having a party she let me stay up and miss school the next day so I could make cookies and tea with her and Aunt Terry.

I sat alone in front of the TV watching transformers in my SpongeBob costume. It was almost Midnight. The only light in the house came from the TV and the fireplace. Tommy was asleep on the couch and my father was at the bars with his friend Mike. My mom was next door with her friend Trina and said to ring the doorbell if I needed her. Now that I'm eight years old she said I was old enough to hold down the fort. She called me a big boy. But I didn't feel any different or any older. I was still terrified of the dark. Just as I have always been.

The TV shut off suddenly. And it hissed for a few seconds after that, the black screen dancing with static electricity. The sound was like fingers tapping all over the glass how intense it was. I walked up to it and got zapped in the finger. I could even see the spark. Electric blue and impossibly quick. It felt like a hot bee sting. I yelped and got startled by the volume of my own voice as it bounced off the walls. I had forgotten that I was all alone. The echos made it very clear.

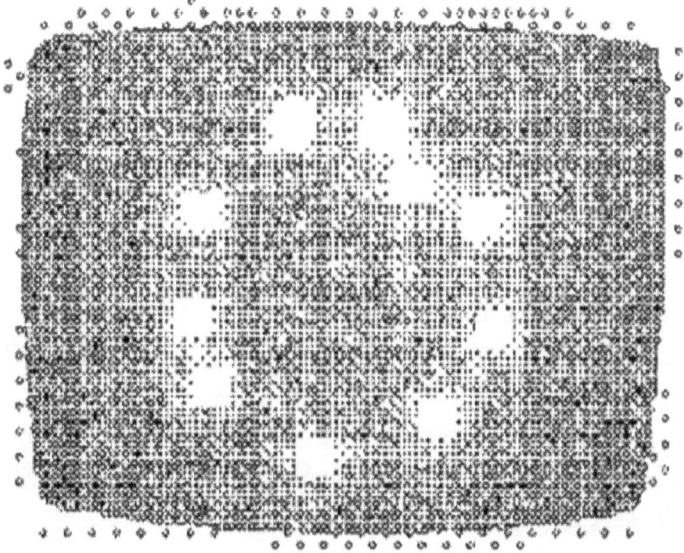

I hit the knob on the TV twice and the screen burst to life with black and white pixels that juddered and whined all over. The pitch was so high I could hardly think. I felt its radio waves get all tangled up in mine. There on the screen, in the shifting static, were several spaces missing. Perfect square panels of white light. Uniform, arranged in an odd shape, the other pixels seemed to come them rather than apart from.

I got down on my knees and pressed my nose against the screen just to get a better look. Then some commotion from the kitchen sent me a foot into the air.

Nothing.

I turned back to the screen, the panels had taken on color. Red, yellow, orange, blue, blue again, green, yellow, red, red, and purple in that order. The squares bobbed up and down, then took a clockwise spin around the screen in broken frames, every square clicked abruptly into place.

From the kitchen again, an awful banging sound. Like someone had taken a jagged stone into the hardwood floors. I lept up to my feet, hands clutched to my sleeves and scrambled to find the source of that sound.

The flames behind me gobbled up all the light. Everything past the couch was black, but still recognizable. Then a particularly dark corner of the kitchen caught my eye. It was an impossible void. Like instead of shadow it was a portal to some other dimension.

I brought anxious hands to my face.

A horrific metal clanging came from that dark corner. Heavy and mechanical. *CLICK CLICK CLICK CLICK CLICK*—GRRHN!

I screamed so loud it tore my throat this time, the sound small and shrill against the air that had gone vacant in an instant. *WOM WOM WOM WOM WOM WOM*—**GRRHN**—!

Quiet.

Then it manifested in the corner just as I imagined it, with all the details I had missed and filled in myself. The ghost from the hallway.

"Whut tis' this? Whut tis' this please?" Every word struggled to break through his wheezing. And his voice was foreign, like he was from another time and another place. I became so frantic I started curling my fingers to stimulate myself. I just stood there, knees buckled and this close to having a nervous breakdown. When I took a step back the floor moaned and he gasped. The fire behind me made his eyes shine just like my mothers. Like glinting gemstones.

He crawled toward me with movements that didn't make any sense. One second he's slithering out of the shadow like he's made of liquid, and the next he's stuttering across the floor on all fours. I fell over and begged him to stop. The silence that followed my command meant that he had.

I peeled open my eyes after a moment and there he was hidden just behind the couch where Tommy snored. I could see the spikes of his wild blonde hair and the tips of his dress shoes peeking at me over the edge.

I held my breath and mustered up all the courage to creep over and look at him. Once I had he was no longer as scary as he once was. Just a sad teenaged boy with his knees to his chest and emerald green eyes.

My father once said ghosts used to be people, too. I remembered that when he glanced at me and then away with a frown and tears in his eyes.

"H-Hello." I squeaked, holding out my hand to shake his. My face turned away and my eyes pinched shut. "What's your name?"

There was a long pause before he answered. Between the silence I imagined his name was Jonah.

"My name *is* Jonah." He muttered in reply. I gasped. For a ghost his voice was so pensive and warm. I looked at him.

"Are you a friendly ghost?" I asked with a chill.

His brows knit together. *"Something like that."*

"Where did you come from?" I asked, tense. His lips pressed into a hard line and he hummed in thought as if he too didn't know the answer.

He didn't speak after that. I just stared at him until my mother came home. He vanished the moment she stepped foot past the door. Him and the dancing lights on the TV.

When she came home the clock read 3:12 A.M.

A sharp pain in my chest woke me up. I clutched my hand over my heart and stammered off the couch, lost in the dark, desperate for a wall to lean against for respite. I found no such wall no matter where I threw myself. And that was, of course, impossible.

Drip... .

I froze. In an instant I knew what was happening. I spun around on my heels and tried to make sense of this senselessness. Before I could freak the light switch clicked and I was back in the living room.

Jonah leaned against the wall, fingers still on it. "What are you doing?" he asked. My eyes shot to the wall—no clock.

"What time is it?" I asked.

He yawned and read it off the microwave. "3:12 A.M."

Figured as much. I sighed, the pain in my chest fizzled into nothing and I threw myself onto the sofa with crossed arms. He hovered over to me and put a hand on my shoulder.

"What are *you* doing?" I asked, clipped.

He was indifferent to my tone. "I heard a weird noise." He answered in a quick mutter. My eyes wandered off to where I was standing when Jonah turned on the light.

My stomach twisted. I was standing right next to the window, curtains drawn, moonlight pouring in. He sensed the distress and asked me,

"Is something the matter?"

I glanced at him and then back at the window. A draft sent the chiffon into a twirl. He sat next to me, knees to his chest, feet on the couch.

His bare feet took me by surprise.

"Where are your shoes?" I asked.

He chuckled. "Shoes on the couch? Irene'll love that."

"I'm serious."

He shifted. "Geeze." Seeming unable to brush off my voice that time.

"I guess it's jost one of those things. I dunno." He shrugged, "Maybe I imagined myself without shoes the split second before I joined you here on the couch. Figured it would make you feel more comfortable."

"I'm sorry, Jonah." I sighed. "You just—" struggling to find the right word. "—*surprise* me sometimes."

He broke our gaze.

"You said you heard a weird noise? What did you hear?" I asked.

He seemed lighter again. He glanced around in thought.

"I dunno. Can't describe it. Normally something like that wouldn't even stir my attention but it was just the strangest thing."

"Well what was it?"

"Alex I just said I can't describe it, what do you want me to do? Imitate it?"

I nodded yes absently, still reeling from what had just happened. Eyes locked onto the window. He shook his head and hesitated. Then. . .

"—*grrhn*—"

My head spun fast toward him like I'd just heard a gun cock.

"What?" He whined. "You know it?"

I wasn't sure. "I don't remember. But I swear I've heard something like that before. Should I be afraid?"

His face was unreadable. Stone cold. "I don't know." "Should you?" he said, voice deep, nasty, and vicious.

I gasped. He grabbed his face and pulled the Jonah mask melted off in clumps that splattered all over the couch. I screamed and threw myself over the edge as The Wayback crawled out of his mouth and exploded the remains all over the house.

"Oh my God this is so Good. This is really really Good." He said over and over again, sick and twisted. His limbs snapped back into place and he joined me on the floor in a cannon ball that shattered reality.

No sense. No existence. Only nothingness everywhere.

A place beyond strength. *Enveloping me.* I've been here once before— and as I watched this horrible monster flick Jonah's goop off his sharp fingers I knew it to be true. And I also knew I'd been here the entire time. I let out a cry that vanished to thin air. Like he pressed mute on my voice. I clutched my hand over my heart and fell to my knees.

Is this death? Am I dreaming?

"No." The Wayback answered, blunt and simple. **"This is not a dream."** A monstrous snarl rolled between every word. He towered over me as I beheld his full form for the first time. White face and horns bloomed from the darkness. He was gargantuan. At least three times my size. His body bulged with massive, veiny, muscles covered by coarse black skin—rough and prickly like a cat's tongue. His hands were massive and taloned, nails black and razor sharp. And he stood completely in the nude.

The rings in his eyes cycled through every color of the light before settling a ghastly shade of blue. I tried to speak but I couldn't. I wanted to scream. I couldn't. In horror my eyes began to waver in the sockets and roll back. My breath stopped dead in the lung, my eyes rolled over, I suffocated and fell to the ground.

A waft of hot breath against my skin. His breath smelled like nickels and pennies in a sweaty fist. Rusty, humid and sharp. Tears broke and gushed down my face.

What is this? What is this please? What do you want from me?

He paced around me in circles. Every step shook the ground.

"I don't want anything from you." He corrected.

He wiped a tear from my cheek with a talon—a sharp pain snapped my eyes open. A thick red drop burst and rolled down my cheek. Quickly I clasped my palm over the wound.

He was barely a foot from my face, looking right into my eyes. In a stuttering flicker, the array of color resolved itself in his gaze. Like some kind of bootlegged divine code. A code that gave him life, unpermitted. I tried to look away—with a massive hand he pinched my face and held me still.

"A—AA—AA—GRRHN!"

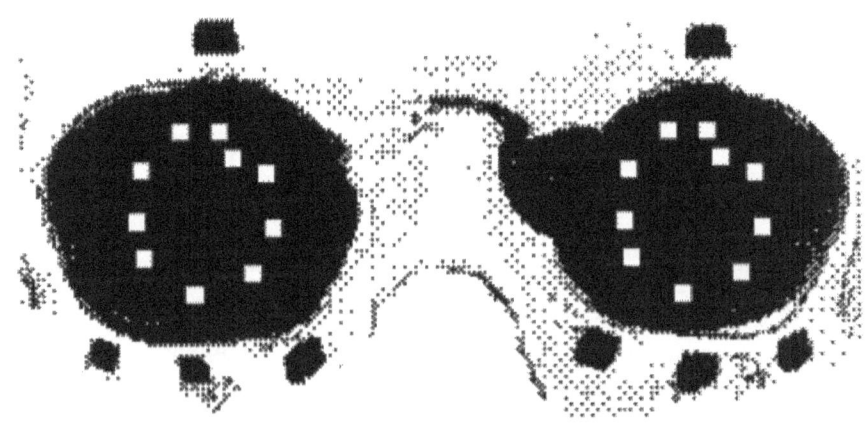

"Do you see it now?" He snarled, chest clanging like a diesel engine, drool oozing off his teeth and spilling all over my face. ***"Is it sinking in?"***

"I'm one of YOURS!"

He let go. I scrambled to my feet and slipped on some impossibly smooth surface. Like the ground had been clipped out from right under me just to make me trip. My hands and knees hit down hard, searching, but the surface gave no grip.

Man down. *Broken man down.*

And this beast, this horrible fucking beast, stood there twiddling his fingers like a tweaker and watched. That crude smile twisted on his face.

My eyes staggered on a reflection—an infinite black mirror beneath me—and in it I locked eyes with my own gaze. My burning, ringed eyes.

In that moment I saw everything. And I hated what I saw. I was too stunned to consider anything else other than the fact that I hated myself and my mother doesn't love me. I felt the jerk in my chest when my heart stopped before I *really* felt it. And then I *did* feel it.

Dying.

My eyes were closing. My consciousness was fading. I heard the muffled, gurgled, steps of The Wayback shuffling around behind me as if I was underwater.

Even dying I found that ironic.

I remembered. I remembered that it was he who saved my life a year ago today. The Wayback was the one who dragged me out of the ocean. Death and me, hand in hand.

My eyes closed and I drifted. My final breath escaped, thin and cold. And with it I was gone. His muffled voice was the last thing I heard.

There were flashes and screams. Souls everywhere, moaned and wailed as they grabbed at me with desperation. Then, slowly, my writhing lulled into a peace unlike any other. A weight lifted. The feeling came like a rush of cold through shattered glass. Swaths of my spirit, bright red, radiant, poured out of me in gleaming ribbons into the ether. The release was so, so, sweet. Soft upon me like the fizz of spilled wine on carpet. All my fibers, all my strings, the most fabulous shade of crimson.

In life I had always been made to feel like nothing. Not no one. *No thing.* But not tonight.

On this night... in this red light... I know who I am. . .

I am... The—

My eyes opened and I caught my breath in shock. My body and heart were still like I had been dreaming peacefully the whole time. The shadow of the ceiling fan's slow turning blades were the first thing I saw.

I jerked up, sheets clung to my body in a cold sweat. It was all so fleeting. Like a bad dream. I sighed and stared at the floor while my mind snapped back in place. I quickly noticed the massive leathery handprint burned into my arm. I fled out the door in a panic.

JONAH.

Outside there was an oppressive fog that shrouded everything. I stopped not even a foot past the door like I'd just slammed into a lead wall. The streetlights cast blurry shapes all around that looked like monsters. I unlatched the gate and ran into the road wailing his name into the night, my jaded shell shattered.

"PLEASE GOD DON'T LET IT BE TRUE!?"
I stepped on a small shard of glass that dug viciously into my bare heel. I didn't react—all I could do was scream for Jonah like a mad man as my face began to numb from the strain. I didn't care if anyone heard me—and that was another futility. No one came, but I know everyone who lived on my street heard me.

I can so much as sneeze and Jonah appears at my side to pester me. By the second time I had called his name into the vacant road I already knew he was dead.

Really dead.

I was just in denial. Until I wasn't.

The image of The Wayback, giddy, flicking Jonah's flesh off his fingers—

I can't.

I fell to my knees and sobbed into the asphalt.

This is how I know with certainty there is no binary. If Absolute Good exists then so does Destructive Evil. But this. This timeless, senseless pain!? No light to shine through dust! No love. No love!

I roared in anger and raised my fist at God.

"There is no love! And so this evil is not truly evil! It's worse! It's just a state! With no collapse because you don't fucking care to observe it!

I flew out of your mouth like a cough and into nothing! Just a speck, ejected! That is how I know with certainty there is no binary!

DO YOU HEAR ME!?"

There was nothing. Just the night. I don't know what hurt me more. The echo of my own voice, or his silence. I winced and smashed my head into the ground.

"You're absolutely correct." The Wayback said. I turned, eyes swollen with tears and burning with hatred. He stood some feet away, body obscured by the light and the rolling fog. And those shapes like monsters I thought where shadows had all congregated behind him—eyes piercing and watchful.

I stood. A feeling far past frustration. Something gnawing at me, gnashing at my spirit. I didn't know what else to say.

"How can I keep losing when I'm so sincere?"

"The sincere are doomed because the world is rigged for people who manipulate, perform and lie. The sincere are crucified.

"You betrayed and destroyed yourself for nothing, Alexander. It was so unnecessary. So fucking cruel. In that you, like all the other bugs on his back, were born to be destroyed. That is God's ultimate betrayal. Not that he even allowed a little freak like you to exist in the first place, but that he gave you love and cursed you for having it."

He teleported in front of me and smacked me onto the ground in one sweep like I was a measly fly. My back slammed into Irene's car and made a dent in the fender. All of my breath, anger, and despair was ejected from my body with the air in my lungs.

I wheezed. *"What did you do to my Jonah!?"*

My sight zoomed in on his corrupted face. Still smiling he said,

"I ate him."

Some legion erupted in a chorus of shrill, taunting laughter — the kind that echoes on schoolyards when a child slips and splatters into mud. The voices jeered and pointed in glee, as if my soul's collapse was the funniest thing they'd ever seen. Their eyes, hundreds of them, glimmered with delight — expectant, hungry, and wanting. And The Wayback stood there, with my seal still reflected in his eyes, and savored the moment.

I swallowed a whimper, gathering what little strength clung to my bones, every muscle burning, my heart raw.

"All magical phenomena manifests from the conscious or unconscious will of the self. Not something outside the self. Not angels, not demons, not spirits or God.

"Thy own power.

"If you invest belief in "energies", "ghosts", or "currents", then even so it must originate within the mind and body's psychic temple."

And just like that — they vanished in a sudden jerk, swept away with the fog as if none of it was ever there at all.

I clutched myself and stood on wobbly legs, slipping into the alley and curling against the rubble and all the other broken things hidden there. The cold came in swift and unnatural for a June night in urban California. It crept over me like a second skin and seeped into my blood.

I remembered something on the floor. Something tender that flickered in the abyss like a dying candlelight. A time small and faint that slipped between the cracks before I could save it. The way Jonah and I played together when I was a kid.

I imagined him there with me. And there he stood, my friendly ghost. The boy I once knew beaten into nothing more than an echo. His voice but a recollection of it in my head. His presence but a final crushing blow I would never recover from. Gone with the last of me.

I let out a shaking breath that turned to smoke.

"Come to me." I begged him. The words hushed and pitiful.

His visage did not speak. His visage did not move. I writhed, guts wrung tight like a blood-soaked rag dripping with the weight of everything I had done in vain. The blood of my own flesh. The blood of my own eviscerated heart.

No love. No love. "Jonah. Please."

Still he remained. Just two solemn lights in the dark, staring as if he too was in mourning of the end. A flicker. A blink. A breath too shallow to be called a goodbye. Then—nothing.

Silence snuffed out the flame of his eyes and it was cavernous.

I was alone.

My mind reeled backward, dragged against time's splintered edges, back to my birthday. The last night anything was as it was. I saw the red candles flicker. I saw the breath pass my lips.

I saw the kitchen, hollowed out in the wake of extinguished light and knew that was the first time I visited The Empty.

And I felt it all over again. That terrible aching feeling. The same as before. I laid there too frayed to even mutter a final, pathetic, *"I'm sorry,"* to the only friend who had ever truly known me. My regrets lingered, circling like vultures over carrion. The last of my love frittered away with the memory.

TWINKLE

I miss you buddy. Are you awake?

MISSED CALL   TWINKLE

Chapter Nine

"Oh my God, what's with that slit in your eyebrow? Are you trying to be edgy?" Valene needled.

I glared at her over my shoulder with the strap of my bag gripped tight in my fist. Irene and Adriana whipped their heads around to look, Adriana going as far as to shout, *"Let me see!"* as if I'd committed a crime. I kept forward to the door to shine her on.

"Hey, I'm talking to you! Rude!" She called after me. Adriana began muttering to her and Irene about me being always being "so disrespectful." My eyes darkened. I spun around and answered her.

"Why do you care!? Do you wanna tease me or is it just killing you to know?"

She laughed and glanced around the table where she and everyone else sat at breakfast, seeming amused and unthreatened by my tone.

"Yes, Nunu, I am absolutely *dying* to know."

Sarcasm. Fun. "Okay. Well if you must know—I got a cut, it turned into a scab, and picking at it cost me part of my eyebrow."

I walked away.

"Suuuuure." She teased. In the foyer I could still hear her voice. "I'm gonna talk to Priscilla, that boy is unbelievable."

I snapped. Suddenly I was in the middle of the kitchen entrance staring her down. They all jumped.

"Weren't you pregnant at my age? You should reevaluate your standards given that the bar is already so low for teenagers in this accursed family!" I spat.

She gasped.

"What the ef did you just say!?" Adriana nearly knocked her chair over as she jumped up and charged toward me with balled fists.

"You know what! I'm getting real freakin' tired of you, Nunu, you better watch it!"

"Adrian!" Irene barked. *"Stop!"*

Adriana towered over me, staring straight into my eyes but not really seeing *me*. An angry girl like her couldn't fathom the idea that other people have souls. And although it is true, that I am fucked up and not worth shit, I still have a soul.

She stood an inch from my face. My eyes shot to my baby brother's Jack In The Box laying on the ground and then back to hers. I wanted to push her into the floor so she could snap her spine on the hard edge of the metal. I probably would have done it had it not been for the fact that out of all the unhinged women I live with Adriana is the only one that scares me.

Not because I find her intimidating, no, sincerely I think she's a fucking loser. Adriana scares me because she's a big demented oath who doesn't know how to keep her fucking hands to herself. You wouldn't believe how many of my things she'd destroyed just because she felt like it. When my mother first brought our family to California Adriana took my Ben-10 Omnitrix and dismantled it piece by piece using a little screwdriver. She threw the bits into a Ziplock bag and smashed it on the floor. Ten years later she's exactly the same. I find her disturbed and completely sadistic.

I remember the first time I brought Katie over, she grabbed me by the neck and dragged me out of my seat and body slammed me—just to give Katie a scare. It must've traumatized the poor girl because she still brings it up to this very day.

I seeth. I hate her. I hate her! But I know that I can't take her... at least... not with my fists.

My gaze gobbled up all the light. She seemed unable to look away for a moment—And I liked that. I kept her there. Then I released her when I felt like my hatred had been communicated clearly. She blinked and stormed off to her room without saying a word. The slam of the door made me jump and it snapped me out of it. Valene went back to her room with her head down.

Irene's sigh caught my attention. When I met her eyes she had a frown and looked at me like I was a disappointment to her. Seeing myself from her perspective made me clench my jaw. It made me hate her for not seeing my pain. My fist tightened around the strap of my bag and I left without another word and slammed the door behind me.

I barged into the convenience store, startling the man behind the counter. The little bell above the door jingled loud and hard like a cymbal right into the tight space. A woman gasped too. I froze when I saw that it was my mother hidden behind a rack of crisps. She seemed just as unsettled as him.

"Speak of the devil and he will come." The man blurted, trying to be funny. My mother let out an uncomfortable titter in response to his words. Though she tried to keep her composure, her porcelain skin betrayed her when it went red. Something I picked up on immediately because it's so out of character for her.

"I beg your pardon?" I hissed.

She tucked a loose strand of hair behind her ear. "Nothing, Son." She said quickly. "I was just talking about you, and—" She laughed again, nervous, "Here you are. Kinda creepy."

Creepy? I locked eyes with the man and his face was outrageous. He looked at me like I was some thug or something. Frown full of disapproval and judgement. Eyes observant. I clenched my fists.

"Well I can assure you this wasn't premeditated. And *creepy* is a bit much." I stormed past her.

The clerk broke our gaze and muttered something in spanish to my mother. His speech was fast but I caught it. And despite not knowing the language I kind of knew what he said.

"Tu hijo tiene un espiritu malo con el, Pan Blanco."

I took in a dense breath. She's rather chummy with the locals. I hadn't considered the idea before but now I wonder—Just how chummy is she? And why on earth would she be talking to a cashier about *me?*

"What are you doing here?" She asked. Tone deliberately neutral. Like she was actually trying *not* to set me off. Smart, for once. She'd picked the right day to tiptoe around me.

I snatched a bag of Planters trail mix off the shelf beside me, "What do you think?" I hissed, so tired, and slammed it on the counter.

Her face twisted. I pulled out my wallet and placed my last bill on the counter. The man looked at her—as if seeking approval—and rang me up when she didn't acknowledge him. I couldn't help but notice him staring at me the entire time. Not even bothering to check that my change was correct. I found it wildly inappropriate.

"Where'd you get money from?" She asked.

I shrugged. "I wouldn't call a measly twenty dollars money. I sold one of my paintings to some older gay man in West Hollywood. He was a creep, so I didn't wager a better price. I just wanted to get out of there."

The atmosphere around her settled a bit. She let out an easy breath like she had been holding one the entire time I stood there. She approached me.

"Only twenty dollars, though?"

"No, he paid me sixty. I bought Tommy and I lunch the other day and a few things for myself here and there."

"Wow. When was this, Son?"

I glared at her. "Nevermind that." I said dismissively. She gave the man a look and followed me outside.

"Do you think you can help me out with some money to buy meat down the hill? I'll make something you like if you do." She asked sheepishly.

I stopped walking. Her eyes lingered on me carefully—and I wasn't sure why. Their gleam lacked the usual disdain... there was something else behind her words. I had a feeling she was stalling. But why? I couldn't say. Her mind eludes me.

"Um—Sure." I said to get her away from me.

I packed a bag when the sun came up. Where to, I don't know. But I know one thing. I can't bear to stay here another night. I shoved my hand into my pocket.

"What is it, like, five or six bucks a pound?" I licked my thumb and started counting out dollar bills.

She seemed too eager. "Come down to the carniceria with me. Please."

Any form of collaboration between us was uncharted waters. Even if it is as small as walking alone together. Before I could spit out a bitter *No!* her phone began to ring.

She answered.

"What? No—He's with me, Mom, calm down." She said. There was a moment of silence and I watched her face shift through every variation of irritation and annoyance. I couldn't hear the other end of the call but I knew it was Irene complaining to her about my rude exit. I rolled my eyes.

"Okay, yes, fine, I'll talk to him—Okay mom, fuck—OKAY! Yes, Yes, Okay now bye, Mom. Bye—Okay, yes, I will. Bye Mother!"

She hung up, jaw hung loose for a moment. "Alex—" She said through a breath. "What the fuck happend before you left?"

I groaned a little too theatrically. Luckily it was too early in the morning for there to be any traffic in the parking lot. Or else she would have lost her head. Instead she started to lecture me like a reasonable mother would.

For once her words lacked any added cruelty or carelessness. She seemed genuinely upset about my hostile demeanor. Said I seemed "off."

I tuned her out and started counting sheep in my head. *One sheep, two sheep, red sheep, blue sheep. . .*

"Alexander!" She clapped. I blinked. She said the next thing with genuine concern. It rattled me.

"Wh... Where do you go, Son?" It was clear to me that she was afraid.

I let out a dark chuckle and shoved my hands into my pockets, peeking at her.

"Do you really wanna know?"

"I'm sorry?"

I shook my head and wiped the smirk away. "Nevermind." "It doesn't matter. We gonna go or what? Why are we just standing here?"

We stood under the canopy a moment more. She just stared at me. And that echo of who I once was wanted her to ask just one more time: *Where do you go, Son?* But I know her well enough. And he's dead. Of course we left it at that and continued walking.

When we left the butcher's my mother looked to the sky in unease as black clouds rolled in, ginormous and unrelenting. Together we watched the last section of blue shrink like an iris and pop with a roll of thunder. Despite the bad weather that came from out of nowhere it was still very hot outside. I chucked it up to global warming.

She got a chill and folded her arms. "It was just sunny out." She blurted. "Kinda creepy out here."

I gave her an acknowledging look and left it at that. Eyes back to my shoes. I'm past small talk and I'm not good at it anyway. I didn't notice that she'd stopped walking after a while. I turned to see her some feet behind, wrestling with the drawstring of her jacket that had gotten snagged by the zipper of her handbag. I was by her side in an instant.

She jumped like I'd teleported or something. I could feel her heartbeat in her clenched teeth. Doe eyes a sickly shade of green. I reached over and yanked it free in one swipe. She gave me a pressed lip smile that didn't meet her eyes and uttered, "Thank you." through a breath.

She seemed to be leaning away from me. Her shoulders to her hips were all off kilter. I didn't like that. I then noticed the way she held herself—arms wrapped close around her torso like she was cold—a gesture that made no sense in this weather.

"What were you and that man talking about before I walked in?" I asked bluntly. She gulped and nodded down the opposite direction of the house.

"Walk with me." She muttered. I followed, saying nothing else.

We trudged along Morant Boulevard and deeper into the neighborhood. And she didn't say it right away. She waited. She waited until we were away from the house, on another block, under the trees.

"Mrs.Blanco called me yesterday... Early in the morning..." She began, almost hesitant to say.

I was already irate. *Of course* she did.

"She was very angry, yelling at me—*'Priscilla! Your son's trespassing on campus again! If it keeps it up, I'm reporting him!'* And I was mad too, cuz like, how many times do I have to tell you—"

She lifted a finger. Instinct. To shut me up before I could launch into a rebuttal.

I wasn't there in the morning. I was asleep. Yesterday was the worst day of my life. I remember every excruciating detail of it. I bit my tongue just this once.

"—So I go downstairs to get my mom so we can pick you up—But she said you were still asleep in my sister's room. I checked and it was true. I saw you there. So I tell Mrs.Blanco,

"'I'm looking at my son right now. He's here. He's asleep.' But she didn't believe me. She kept *insisting* that it was you." She glanced at me like she wanted me to explain something she couldn't say out loud. But I was simply lost.

"I tried waking you up so you could get on the phone but you just... you just wouldn't wake up no matter what. Then all of a sudden your eyes pop open and you sit up like a mummy—screaming at me."

Something twisted inside of me. Wretched and sharp, curling like a hook in my gut. I got goosebumps. I remembered hearing her on the phone when I woke up—but I don't remember *that*. She caught the shift in my face and struggled to look me in the eye.

"I hung up. I didn't want her hearing all that. But at least she heard you. She called in the afternoon and apologized for the whole thing. I didn't think much of it until it happened again this morning."

I stopped walking. The heel of my shoe skid against the sidewalk.

"What are you talking about, mother?"

She drew in a shaky breath, reached out to touch my shoulders—then pulled away as if she was too frightened to even touch me.

"Zero said he saw you before sunrise just standing there, out in the parking lot. Staring straight into the camera. He went out to check on you because he knows you're my Son—he thought you were in trouble. He said something seemed off—

"But when he went outside you vanished. *Vanished.* Like—he saw you, literally saw you just—disappear right in front of him."

She paused. And then said the last thing in a whisper that broke her. "That's what we were talking about before you walked in..." Her eyes waxy and tense.

I was silent.

"Son... Do you know anything about this?" She asked, almost pleading. "Are you... doing this?"

If I was holding a pencil in my hand I'd have snapped it.

"What!? No, Mother!" I stepped away from her. "What are y—" I sighed. "Are you crazy?"

I felt like I was trying to convince myself, however. That what she was saying couldn't be further from the truth. But the entire time she spoke I fought back the image of that boy on the bus who looked strikingly similar to me. *Similar.* Not exact. And how he, too, vanished right in front of me. Maybe these are isolated incidents. I'm not sure. Maybe none of it's true.

She sighed. Desperate. "I'm not! I swear I'm telling you the truth— Why would I lie!?"

I glared at the sidewalk. "I never *said* you were lying."

"And then you just appear earlier in the store—right when I was about to tell him about what Mrs.Blanco said—it was scary!" She blurted.

"I got scared, Son. I got scared."

Her eyes locked onto mine. The idea that I frightened her made something in me shrivel. Yet—isn't that what she always does? Treat me like I'm some ticking time bomb? The pang morphed into resentment. I just shook my head at her.

"Do you have anything to say?"

I scoffed. "What do you expect me to say? Seriously? Do you want me to scream!?"

She resigned to a quiet shame and the look in her eyes was serious. She shuddered.

"Remember when you were little... when you would—"

I stopped her right there, a hand in between us.

"No. Trust me you're onto nothing. And another thing, I'm glad I barged into that store when I did—maybe it was fate. People talk. It's bad enough I got the fucking cashier at 7-Eleven thinking I got 'bad spirits,' Jesus mom!"

Her eyes got sharp. She crossed her arms. "So fuck me, right?" her voice cracked slightly.

I shrugged. "No—! No—But can't you hear yourself? You're on about doppelgangers like—like that's—" I cut myself off with a sharp breath.

"I just thought, for once, we were about to talk about something real. It's one thing to notice a weird coincidence but to talk about me like that to some stranger—and n-not even bring it up with me first? What am I supposed to feel? What do you want!? Fear? Intrigue? I'm offended!"

"No, *I'm* offended. You wanna know why *I'm* offended!?" She screamed, pointing a shaky finger at me.

"First of all—you aren't even listening to me—I saw—"

"Oh I have been listening and I've heard enough, Priscilla!"

"I'm telling you the truth! I would recognize my own goddamn Son! I'm a mother. You're the only kid walking around dressed like he's selling fucking bibles! I saw you on the cameras, Alex! He showed me!"

I lurched away with a narrow, stinging, gaze.

"It was you... except—it wasn't you. Or maybe it was... I don't know. He said he felt something evil staring at him through the screen... but I just felt you... I know my Son... What aren't you telling me?"

I was stunned.

"You think I'm evil. . ?"

She was quiet long enough that it gave me the answer I needed.

I pressed my lips into a hard frown. "You're fucking ridiculous. When was the last time I ever felt like I could fucking tell you anything? I can't even look you in the eyes any other day without feeling like I'm made of smoke. Fuck! *Fuck! Fuck! Fuck!*"

I threw my leg to the side and sent a rock flying into the street!

She shook her head, shoulders sagging and muttered something indecipherable. Her eyes shot below—suddenly gone wide. I looked—to see my hand bent into a claw. I wasn't even aware that I was doing it. I let go and sighed.

"Mom—"

She turned on her heel and walked away, leaving me alone on the sidewalk.

I lingered there, watching her retreat, my breaths loud and heavy like my face was covered by a rubber mask. Chest tightening with another wretched feeling I couldn't yet name. The humidity pressed in, thick and unfeeling, swallowing the space where she once stood. Somewhere in the wind I caught the sound of a faint sob and wondered if it was her or my conscience. Tormenting me as it likes to.

I couldn't tell.

I nearly ran after her in response to that sound. I traced a finger around that void in the shape of my ghost. Of the boy who once ached for her love. But the weight of what she had become—of what *I've* become—held me fast and held me right where I stood. It's silent cruelty like a ball and chain to my ankle.

I just watched her walk away. As I always do.

Extant.

By the time I conjured up enough will to move she had all but dissolved away. I jogged uphill, catching only the dim glow of her cigarette flicking near the house—then the slam of the door. The last trace of her smothered like a dying ember under my heel. I gave up and started heading for the train station.

I tried not to think about Jonah as I walked but it just kept happening. Waves crashing onto me. *Dead. Dead. Dead.* I traced the cracks in the pavement and kicked rocks but nothing helped. His face was hidden in everything. *God I can't stop thinking about it.* Waves crashing onto me.

The dark storm clouds seemed to follow me all the way down Huntington Drive into South Pasadena. The women in lovely tracksuits and athletic gear who jogged in gaggles all stopped to remove their sunglasses and look at the sky in shock. I passed through them dressed like a marching funeral, head down, shoulders down, eyes dark and some other place. When I reached the station I curled up to my knees and watched people board for a while.

Then it started to rain. I heard an old woman say something about 'June gloom.'

I found the expression extremely fitting. June gloom indeed. I snuck onto the train with a group of disgruntled young men in soccer gear. The most handsome of the group cursed the news forecaster for "having the weather all wrong."

I came to the conclusion that I was causing the bad weather. And that little voice in my head that sounds just like mine who hates me said I was a conceited freak for even considering the idea. Let alone believing it. But there couldn't be any other explanation.

I'm evil and I cause things.

Love never collapses into truth, but my stillness and woe sure do. It always seems to pour and rain when I'm going through something unpleasant. Or when I'm angry.

And I'm angry. Very, very, angry. At least on the metro I can tune myself out in the sea of voices. Everyone had someone to speak to.

But not me. I'm evil and I'm alone.

I guess that's fair.

The caboose groaned and clattered. Rain streaked against the windows in jagged lashes, like it was alive and trying to shatter the glass to find me. I saw a woman who looked a whole lot like my mother. That alone I didn't find suspicious or cause of metaphysical concern. My mother's a blonde with fair skin and colored eyes. Pretty girls like her come a dime a dozen in California. There was a young man sat next to her, however. A little boy no older than seven or eight years old dressed in his best clothes with a bundle of dandelions clutched in his hands.

The woman seemed young. Too young to be his mother but that kind of thing happens. I mean, it happened with mine. Sat beside each other they bore a striking resemblance to my mother and I some lifetime ago. They didn't speak. The little boy stared out the window humming to himself and the woman seemed lost in her thoughts. It hurt to see. And I couldn't help my face. She caught me mad dogging them and moved down the aisle to get away from me. In the empty seats they left behind I saw something in the window that felt like acid thrown straight into my face.

On the pane in tiny inconspicuous letters the phrase ABRACADABRA had been scratched into the surface. I turned away and pressed into the rail beside me. My eyes settled on the little boys then, all the way at the end of the cabin. He was looking at me, curious and innocent. When the train stopped he waved at me before he and the woman disappeared into the exiting crowd. By the time I waved back it was too late. He was gone.

I was a little surprised how nervous I was at the foot of Katie's door given everything. Here in my suit I felt like I was a morose sibling trying to get invited to the wedding before its too late. I suppose all this time apart has left me feeling a bit estranged.

It took me a lot longer than it should have but I rang the doorbell twice and knocked three times. Her grandpa peeked at me from blinds. I pretended not to notice him while I waited.

Katie opened the door, face torn between a myriad of emotions I couldn't even begin to guess. She didn't even step forward or back to join me outside or allow me in. Her hand still clutched around the doorknob was a strong indicator that I was uninvited.

And I was, yes that's true. I haven't spoken to her in weeks. Missed calls turned to unopened texts. Unopened texts turned to... nothing. A year ago I could have shown up unannounced and taken a seat at the dinner table. Not today, I guess.

"I don't even know what to say." She blurted. "Where have you been?"

I didn't want to stir in a way that communicated obvious shame. And I didn't want to just blurt out that the worst has happened. My toes curled against the confines of my dress shoes the entire time we spoke.

She took my silence as a queue to prod even further. "What happened to your face? Why are you all—cut up everywhere?"

The little scars were more obvious to me all of a sudden. She seemed a bit distressed. But not enough to ignite any of the warmth in her voice that I desperately needed.

"Can I come inside?" I asked. Stiff. Inching closer.

She let out a breath and glanced around before turning me down in a mutter.

"It's my dad's weekend, Alexander. I can't. He and Shirley got us tickets to see Ocean's Eight."

I frowned. The anger she wore cracked a little and she blurted,

"Alexander, you've been ignoring me since, like, April. I-I don't know what you expect me to say right now.

I'm... angry... I miss you. I can tell that something's wrong—I mean—You're all wet, frowning. But I can't just drop everything for you, Dude. Not right now. I have a lot going on."

The way she crossed her arms and hunched her shoulders revealed that I had missed quite a bit. Ditto.

I shook my head. Stung. "When have you ever dropped anything for me, Katie?" I spat.

Her brows knit together. *"What!"*

I exhaled sharply. Shaking. And recoiled. "Katie—Please. Forget I said that. Just throw me a bone. Please."

"No! What the fuck do you mean by that? You can't just say something like that to my face and expect me to just take it. *I'm not your mom!"*

I cringed. *Ugh.* "Katie—Please. I'm begging you. Can't you just see him some other weekend? It's not like you don't have the freedom—" I took another step forward. "Please."

She laughed. But nothing was funny. She was irate.

"Alexander, no!" She shouted, hands back to the door like she had already decided our conversation would end with it being slammed in my face.

I was frantic. "Katie—Katie, please!"

"I said *no!* Go home, Alexander! I'll call you when I'm back home— And you **better** answer!"

"WILL—YOU—JUST—LISTEN TO ME!?" I screamed, voice way more ferocious than I intended. Her red face spiraled quickly into terror as she slammed the door and turned the lock.

"GO AWAY ALEXANDER, WHAT THE FUCK IS WRONG WITH YOU!?" She cried through the door—voice torn and shrill like a child. I shoved stressed fingers through my hair and fled down the street in a fit.

When I got to the end of the block I buckled onto the ground with my back against a metal gate.

"Oh you've really done it this time, Alexander Hunsucker." I said to myself in a gravelly voice, rocking back and forth. I buried my face in my hands and mashed it all around like that would help the feeling. It didn't. I let go and stared at my palms. A strange thought occurred to me then.

Whenever I mean to behold myself I look at my hands. Not my reflection. Not my eyes in the mirror. My hands. As if they hold more truth than my face ever could. As if they are the true window into my soul. These manipulating hands.

"My God, what have I done?" I sobbed. It got even hotter all of a sudden. I unfastened a button and ripped off my tie—discarding it into a puddle to the right of me and slammed my fists into the ground.

"AUGHHHH—"

BING!

My heart jumped. *Katie!?*

Dude are you dead? Talk to me □Leaving tmr I really want you to come with don't miss out x :p

Dante. I sighed. But as I was about to shove my phone back in my pocket my eyes skimmed the last text he'd sent me.

Hey me and Jessie are going camping wanna come with? Haven't heard from you in a while ;)

I sniffed.

Chapter Ten

Conveniently for me Dante was only a short bus ride a walk from Katie's. His house was a lot bigger and nicer than I would have assumed. On my way up I wondered if he'd given me the right address. I knew he was well-taken-care-of but he didn't come off as wealthy.

I approached a nice modern home that sat atop the winding hills of Eagle Rock. So high up, in fact, it seemed spared from the rolling black clouds that followed me all over Los Angeles County. I rang the doorbell and waited.

I was greeted by his mother Gretchen, who introduced herself as such. Right away her beauty was the first thing I noticed. A name like that inspires the image of an old grandma already dead, but on her it was glamorous. Anachronistic. She welcomed me in with a hug and a smile like I was someone she'd seen a thousand times before. I accepted sheepishly, I'm not a hugger, but anyone who welcomes a stranger with kindness deserves a little bit of effort, so I tried my best not to be awkward despite the air buzzing around me.

I entered, following behind her and into the foyer where I met an ecstatic Dante at the stairs.

"You made it!" He shouted, grinning, thumb up in accomplishment. "Woah. You're all wet. Did you walk here or something?"

"No!" I lied. Chipper. "Uh, my Nanna left me at the bottom of the hill. Bad tires."

"Ah. Makes sense." He stretched out his arms and spun. "Welcome to my crib!" He announced in a funny voice, before pulling me into a second hug that I received as gracefully as a housecat. I glanced around, curious. Indeed a lovely crib. So much... light. There were windows and glass doors all over. All cranked ajar, breeze wafting through.

"Great house." I said—shock slipping out as something like praise. He was giddy, grabbed me by the hand. The boy practically yanked me along.

Right away he dove into an impromptu tour. Balcony, kitchen, living room. He stumbled around a bit rehearsed like he'd done it a million times before. But he was extremely polite. I guess I'd never actually been shown true hospitality until now.

In the living room he started making small talk about the weather and hoped that there would be snow in Big Bear given the sudden cold front that had come in. He likes sledding, he said.

I raised an eyebrow. "Snow in June?" and leaned in to get a better look at a photo of his family. He, his mother, a goth man and a lavishly dressed girl with red hair just like his.

"That's my sister." He announced, pointing to the girl. He then flicked at the goth man. *"Oh, and that's my mom's..."* he trailed off.

The photos hung on the walls were all framed genuinely and well taken. I saw another of just the sister, a whole lot younger in the photo, an even younger Dante who clung to her leg, smiling.

"Will she be coming with us?" I asked.

"No, she's in London right now, actually."

I nodded. "Wow. What for? Is she on holiday?"

He smiled at me and answered but I wasn't listening. I went back to the pictures.

"Your family seems very close." I said, tone a bit clinical. Back hunched, nail in between my teeth. There aren't any pictures of me on the walls at Irene's house. You couldn't even tell I live there. But here Dante and his sister were stars mounted and, surely, loved. I swallowed a sigh at the observation.

He shrugged a little dismissively and said, "Eh."

We turned the corner and walked down another small flight of stairs that led to another floor. At the first door he announced, "This is where I hang out," and led me into an office-sized room that had been reproposed into a lounge.

I followed and muttered, *"Cool."*

He turned around and really looked at me. How I kept my body close. Noticed my damp crumpled clothes, sleepless eyes and stiff frame. Made an attempt to diffuse the air.

"Are you nervous? Or just a chill guy? I don't bite unless you ask. Hahah."

I tittered. "I'm just super chill." I said, though my hands still clung to the drawstrings of my backpack. "I see you have a keyboard. Do you play?"

He was shy suddenly and walked over to it. *"I try,"* He said with a little smile, "I'm really thinking about picking up guitar, actually. Do you play any instruments?"

"Oh—No, I don't. I think I've tried a few times here and there but..." I shrugged, "No dice. I usually have a lot going on."

He hummed. "Homeschool stuff?"

"Yeah." Though that wasn't what I was referring to at all. I sat down timidly as he began setting up his gaming console. I found it cool that he had an additional room all his own. A lounge with a flat-screen and a collapsing sofa that didn't quite match the elegant glass table in front of it.

He began babbling about his last sexual encounter that he had with his former girlfriend on said sofa. The sofa where I was sitting. My internal reaction was mixed. A part of me, the existentialist, did not think much of it other than acknowledge that fact sex is intrinsic to the human experience. Okay, yeah. No big deal. Dante is sexually active. But the other part of me... that teenager I sometimes forget that I am was... uncomfortable.

I may not be human, I know that now, but I am a man. A young man. Sex and intimacy is definitely something that crosses my mind once in a blue moon, but it is a tough subject to reconcile with. Sure, I've kissed a few boys here and there and let Leonel tug me off the one time, but it's never been something I feel like I can just speak about freely—let alone participate in. It just feels so wildly inappropriate given the nature of my life. I can't even masturbate without the painful awareness that my mother doesn't love me.

I like to think about it in third person. Although, knowing how this is gonna sound, I proabably shouldn't. But it is the truth.

Little hyper-evolved money tugging on his penis in the shower while his mother who hates him is three doors down. Little hyper evolved monkey kissing a boy while the spirit of a dead trans-Atlantic settler child watches from a dark corner. Little hyper-evolved monkey lusting over a physician after being kidnapped into a dimension of his own making. Just sounds so fucking ridiculous. Isn't all utterly so fucking ridiculous!?

I moaned in agony, far too deep in my thoughts

"Huh?" Dante blurted, hands still buried in wires.

I blinked. "Oh nothing. Continue."

He smirked and went on.

There are nights when I think about the first time Leonel kissed me. But it isn't because I yearn for the softness of his lips. Nay, I think about it because the only thing on my mind when that all went down was how heartbroken over my mother I was. Instead of catharsis and ecstasy I got my mother staring back at me, ashamed.

"—And then I pulled out and shot on her back!"

"Oh dear!" I said through a slightly distressed grin. My fingertips pressed into my knees as I caught sight of a suspicious stain beside me.

He saw my face and snorted, "Grease stain, I swear!"

I laughed and let my shoulders loose a little so he'd have less reason to be concerned about me. He didn't say anything but I could tell he was watchful how high strung I seemed.

It's like instead of a glass ceiling, there's a dimensional boundary that separates me from everyone else. I can't even imagine what else I'm *supposed* to say. I figured I'd play along.

"Suuuure." I teased. But I don't think I was very convincing. He chuckled and began browsing through YouTube.

"So what kind of stuff do you watch?" I asked with put-on nonchalance. He stood and leaned on the balls of his feet, still glued to the screen and spoke over his shoulder.

"Oh, man, all kinds of stuff." He beamed. He began flicking buttons frantically. "Have you ever seen Rubber Johnny?"

Rubber Johnny? I raised an eyebrow. "Sounds—" I stammered. *Be friendly.* "—sounds interesting! Let's see it."

The next thirty minutes ensued in a blur as I tried my best to pay attention. Obscure videos and music. After Rubber Johnny he ran me through an Aphex Twin crash course that sent me spiraling even deeper into my thoughts. I couldn't even remember when exactly I stopped listening to the music. Depression is one of those things that doesn't really register until... well, I guess until some tragic point where it's less an ailment and more of a mute acknowledgement.

He went on to show me some more of his favorite music. I liked the one Gus Dapperton music video titled *Prune, You Talk Funny.* But of course, I can't allow myself to enjoy anything. I imagined Jonah's goop splattered all over the walls and felt the cognitive dissonance hard.

There was one song in particular that actually snapped me out of the fog for a second. A song by an artist called *Boy Pablo.* Quite a sad song, in fact. My mind couldn't help but conjure up a montage of my life's worst hits over the haze in my eyes.

♪♪ *These days gone to waste is what we're left with,* ♪♪

I would have cried were it not for the fact that he sat beside me so eager, analyzing my facial expressions for approval. I maintained an air of intrigue throughout. He was pleased.

When he hit play on the last video he wanted to show me the TV burst into static and shut off suddenly. It was so aggressive we both flinched. Dante stood and apologized, fiddling with the wires in the back and cursing under his breath.

"It's a new TV! What the shit!" He muttered in frustration. *ZAP—POP!* The outlet burst with a little white flash and a puff of black smoke. He laughed in disbelief. When he wasn't looking I pulled out my phone and took the name of the song so I could give it another listen later.

Thunder rolled outside. So close it rattled the windows in their frame. A moment later it began pouring rain. I looked out the window anxious as I watched the last of the sun vanish over the horizon.

"H-Hey, so is Jessie still coming?" I asked, mainly in an attempt to distract myself. Dante stood scratching his head as the TV came back to life with a sudden jolt and a white buffering screen.

"He's coming over in the morning, I guess he had something with his dad, I dunno." Then he turned and looked at me with a crooked smile, rearing back into the theatrics of himself.

"You're all mine tonight, big boy," He winked, and plopped himself right back beside me criss-cross.

"So what's in the bag?" He prodded, eyeing me.

"Huh?"

He smiled and nudged me. "Your backpack, man, you've been wearing it since you came in."

The weight suddenly clicked. "Oh. Um—" I slid out of the straps and opened it,

"I mean, I just have a change of clothes, some peanuts—which, was actually a good call—"

I met his gaze. I felt a bit crazy then, coming all this way. Sitting in his house like there wasn't a horned monster somewhere lurking.

"Actually, I think I'm a bit ill equipped for this camping trip." I said. I dug into the bag sifted through my slacks, collars, and tube socks. Curled my toes in my dress shoes.

The air was getting thin again. I tried to make a joke. "If anybody sees me out in the woods dressed like this they'd probably mistake me for slender-man or something."

He nudged me again. "Too short. Maybe boss baby."

Funny. I made an effort to laugh a little—but the sound was just slightly off. His ear twitched like a dog. "HahHah. Heard that one before."

A loud eight-bit kind of song played suddenly. We looked at the screen.

"Oh shit, it's starting! You're gonna love this one." He said. Another treatsforbeasts video.

A crude drawing of the earth emerged from black before cutting to a green man wielding a cleaver who sang,

I am the beast that cuts the meat

Now that they're dead, you can sink in your teeth

I am the beast that grows the wheat, I make bread to go with the meat,

I am the beast that makes the fleece, keeps you warm, keeps out fleas!

I am the beast that handles deeds

I am the beast that keeps things clean, Give it a shine, Give it a sheen!

I am the beast that likes to preach, Don't face your problems, resort to belief!

I am the beast that chops down trees, They're put here for us, so we can do as we please!

I am the beast that sails the seas, I find new worlds to claim for the beasts!

I am the beast that must compete,

It's so much fun to put a thing in a thing!

I am the best that makes decrees,

As long as I smile, I can treat them like sheep!

I am the beast that loves to teach,

Work on your mind, or you'll work on the streets!

I am the beast that's on TV, I make you think you need to be like me!

I am the beast with your deceased, I make 'em look nice before they go underneath!

I am the beast that sports the teat, I nurse the young so we can have more

Beasts. . .

And then the music took haunting turn as the world came back into view. Melancholic synths as, slowly, the world turned brown and died. The beasts stood in mighty legions upon it with crooked faces, they, responsible for its decay. And then I understood it—what it all meant. Like the universe uses itself to speak to me.

We are the beasts.

He turned to me and asked, *"What kind of beast are you?"*

I shuddered. *"I don't think I wanna be a beast."*

His mock-serious face shattered into laughter. "You didn't like the video?"

"I didn't say that. It's definitely layered." I recoiled. "Why did you show me this?"

He stirred, perhaps a bit surprised by how heavy handed my reaction was to a cartoon that was meant to be sardonic. He was sensitive all of a sudden.

"I dunno, it's the kind of stuff I'm into. I guess I have dark humor. I'm sorry."

"No—It's good conversation. I mean—How do you feel about all this?"

"Uh—Hahah. I mean, consumerism, war, it's just one of those things. A condition of the world. It is what it is. We still gotta live, regardless, so." He gave me a friendly tap on my leg. "Sometimes it's just nice to laugh at the absurdity of it. And make time to have a little fun, too. It's crude but you gotta realize there was a cool as fuck guy who made this.

Everyone has something to say. Some people are just a bit more honest than the rest."

I hummed in thought. The room, the entire house, the silence between us yet again. There was a great pause before I spoke.

"There are those religious types that think God is going to destroy the world with fire.

"I think it ends with us. With our conquest, war, and famine.

"Everything we do—from survival to empire-building is a form of violence. And violence for violence is the rule of beasts.

"How could anyone—how could you, or I, contribute to a society that was built for beasts. Kinda makes me wonder about Adam and Eve... the knowledge of Good and Evil was their original sin. Passed down to us like other chains. Like the curls in your hair... or my desire to create.

"Just stuff that... makes us.

"Whether or not it's true, what a metaphor it is. Moses was really onto something, I think. Maybe the binary itself is what makes us... beasts."

He blinked, but his little smile never wavered.

"Wow. That was deep. I like that. Yeah, the world is pretty fucked. But you can take care of your people. And if you look in the right places you'll find some good stuff, too. It's not all darkness."

Thunder rolled again.

Despite the creeping midnight hour, I was able to settle down a little. Our talk about beasts softened my edges just enough. And his constant joyous chattering filled the space with a light ten times stronger than my darkness. I found myself able to pay attention the rest of the evening. After the beasts he insisted on lightening the mood and went back to playing music off his PlayStation, and I got to listen to a few of my favorite bands I hadn't heard in a while. At some point his mother had left and came back, knocking on the door around nine o' clock to make sure we were asleep. Long drive in the morning. It was then the last twenty-four hours slammed into me like a violent wave. Pangs of dizziness, body aches, and turmoil ravaged me. My back and shoulder throbbed like I had just been beaten with a mace.

I snuck off to the bathroom to wash my face and took a lot longer than was appropriate. I didn't want to pass out in front of him. A little voice in my head, an imitation of Jonah, told me to drink water from the faucet and I listened.

Dante had already fallen asleep. Which I found really surprising. I could not name one person in my life who was asleep by nine. He laid there on his belly over a blanket, snoring. Insisted I take the bed despite my protest. I was genuinely so scared, I didn't want to sleep alone.

I woke him and asked if he could sleep next to me, but he made a joke about "not swinging that way." I knew it was an innocent joke, and I guess, in a way I was bit grateful he was so comfortable with me. I took the bed disappointedly and closed my eyes, but I couldn't sleep a wink.

I tossed and turned, utterly terrified that The Wayback would return, but too tired to keep myself fully alert. It was unbearable. I literally slept with eyes half closed. At some point I did fall asleep. My body was so heavy I had no choice but to succumb to it.

MEANWHILE...

Valene's room was swollen with the presence of pure evil. Churning, writhing darkness that awaited her insidiously. Violence for the sake of it. Terror for the pleasure of inflicting it upon one. It could have been anyone, but on this night, it was her.

She stumbled into her room with the straps of her red heels twirled in her fist. The hall light cast her shadow on the floor in solid black. She looked to the ground, noting that even her silhouette looked completely, totally, trashed. She sighed and ran the fingers of her free hand through a large tangle in her hair.

"Ugh." She shook her head and fiddled with the wall until her fingers found the light switch. *FLICK. FLICK. "What the f—" FLICK.*

She kissed her cheek. *"Mom–ugh!"* wafting over to Irene's door and letting her head thud against it. Her toes lit up when Irene pulled the chain on her lamp. She looked down at the little gap of light that broke in from under her door and watched the shadow of Irene's legs approach her.

CREEEEEAAAAAKK. Irene took one look at her, door half-open and sighed.

"Really? Valene, what in the hells' the matter with you?"

She scoffed. "Oh my God, mom, I had, like, two seltzers, chill out."

"Your daughter is asleep in my room again." Irene whispered with emphasis on 'again.'

Valene peeked over Irene's shoulder and saw her daughter Stevie in a deep, sweaty slumber at the foot of her mother's bed. She wore off-season fleece pajamas and her dark curls were slicked to her forehead. The tail end of the blanket clutched in her hands. A single guilt-ridden tear formed in her eye.

Irene said nothing. And she was unmoved. Having grown used it all the nights years ago. She opened the door all the way and stepped aside so Valene could enter and fetch her little girl.

Gently, she bent down and tapped Stevie's shoulder. *"Baby."* She whispered, and then sniffed. Another pair of taps. "Wake up, my baby, let's go."

Stevie stirred, curled in tighter, and tiredly muttered, *"No."*

Valene sighed and stood, throwing a hand on her hip and feeling a pang of nausea. "Just—I'll get her in the morning, Mom." Valene said through a breath.

Irene kept her arms crossed the whole time and wore the same look of stone on her face. She hummed disapprovingly, reaching out and tucking herself back into bed in one move.

Valene was stung, eyes back to her daughter who faced away from her now. She took in a deep breath that made the room spin a little faster, and went back to her room, closing Irene's door behind her. A soft click and then back to the cavernous room that awaited her.

FLICK. FLICK. FLICK. She gave up and shut the door. Nothingness everywhere, the shifting of her dress and her stockings was the only sound. A pair of blue ringed lights stood in the corner unbeknownst to her, watching her undress, standing in the dark.

She carelessly fumbled onto the mattress, the ancient metal frame and the springboard groaned and squealed under her as if it had been punched in the gut with her sudden force. Head still spinning. Head still thumping. Ringing in the ears. But yes, *oh yes,* the lull of drunken-sleep came upon her. She could see the morning approaching now, the smell of avocado toast and egg whites. She sank deeper into that feeling and smiled a little. *Sleep. Yes. Sleep.*

Then she sensed something. A presence. Dangerous, wicked, and staring right at her. Her eyes burst open and locked straight onto those God awful rings that watched her from above.

The air in her throat slammed to a violent stop. So hard she squeaked through tight lips.

The rings pulsed like a dancing flame. Slow and dreamlike, responsive to the currents surrounding it. They exchanged a macabre embrace of the eyes, when she shuttered, the light fluttered with excitement. The bed creaked again, the high pitch bellowing out so loudly it scared her even more. She winced and aimed the screen of her phone at it—brightness all the way up—the darkness scurried away in a perfect rectangle, illuminating the plush cat that sat innocently on top of her high dresser.

She let out a loud sigh of relief, recalling its glow in the dark eyes. *"Oh my God, what the fuck!"* hand clasped over her forehead, eyes pressed shut and jaw tight. She sniffed, and opened her eyes right when the screen timed out. *The cat's eyes aren't blue. They're green.*

A large, kettle-hot-hand gripped her by the throat and gripped tight, with a force more powerful than that of any man. He jumped on top of her, body crashing down and snapping a few wires in the bedframe, as heavy and brutal as a meteorite. With the other hand, he made a fist and pressed his bare knuckles in her face and scuffed them around, moaning and humming with ecstasy as if he were eating the most delicious food and savoring every tasty mouthful.

"Mmmmmmmmmmmm. MMMMmmmmmmmmmmm!!!!!!"

Her body gave out not even a second after her attempt to thrash around. All the bands of muscle she employed were snapped in the effort. Not even adrenaline could hold a finger to The Wayback's crushing body on top of her. She cried out in wretched beeps and chirps, face slicked with tears and the black grease of his fingers.

He laughed, like a choir of children being tickled to hysterics. The atrocity sent her eyes rolling back into her head and her spit to foam in her popped lips.

"IF SOMEONE KNOCKS ON THE DOOR—! DON'T—! FUCKING—! OPEN IT—!" He roared maniacally.
Then he snarled in his throat, the sound rolling nasty and slow like a gunky engine. Thick with the blackest tar. His breath was putrid, kissed her in all the wrong places. He bent down and brought his teeth inches from her smeared up face.

Another roll of breath that cracked like a Lion.

"—GRRHN—"

The poor girl lost it—she began to seize and scream in her throat, with what she thought was the last of her breath. The whole-time heart broken, picturing her daughter's sweet face and damning herself for all the time missed and the time running out.

My baby! MY BABY—!

The monster let go and vanished so suddenly the bed snapped back together and jumped a foot into the air—Valene still in it, purple all over her neck and body. It crashed back down with a nasty metallic skid against the tile.

The shock held her in place for a moment. The light was on. The ceiling fan turned slowly. The pull chain swung in the draft it cast over her. Which meant the darkness hadn't been darkness at all. It was The monster.

From deep in her gut, the silence shattered into a scream so raw, so endless, it didn't even sound human anymore—just one long, blood-curdling wail that clawed at the walls and refused to stop.

I dreamt for the first time in months. Despite myself, I dreamt. I dreamt that I had turned to smoke and flew all the way to my mother. My spirit cast a huge shadow over the city, something like a massive, reaching hand that blocked out the moonlight and cast everything beneath me in darkness. I entered the house through the windows and began knocking pots and pans around in the kitchen because I was so angry with her. I flew into her room and hovered over her body to watch her sleep.

And she was sleeping, but not peacefully. Hair damp with sweat and limbs spread out in a star, blankets tossed off her and onto the floor. She wore boy shorts with a white tank top, pregnant belly exposed to the cold air in her room.

I heard a clicking sound. Something like old gears fighting against rust as they turned. *CHCHCHCHC—GRHN—* I stared at her belly and I could hear the low hum of her baby's heartbeat. Loud and maddening in my ears. A red arm extended out and reached down toward her navel, about to press its long black talons into her flesh.

"—*Psst!*"

I flinched—realizing then that it was my hand reaching for her. I spun around to see who, or what, was hollering at me.

There was nothing. I flew through the wall and into the living room to look around. Still nothing. I then noticed my laptop tossed lazily on the couch—And not in my dresser where I had left it. As if someone had been using it unpermitted.

"Are you an angel?" The voice whispered. Curious. Uncertain. My sight flew toward it in an instant.

He stood in the darkest shadow of the house, where the moonlight barely reached. He wore his sweatpants tucked into ratty socks and a red christmas sweater. So much pomade his hair looked like plastic.

"No." I answered.

// 287 //

"Are you dead?"

"No."

"Then why do you look like that?"

I turned back to my mother and she was gone.

—KNOCK! KNOCK!—

My eyes shot all the way open—and it hurt so damn bad. The scant light that came in from the window was blinding. I felt my eyeballs sizzle and shrink.

Then I heard footsteps walking away from the door. Soft, hardly there. My heart thumped in my chest. My ears were sharp as a fox. I could hear them in my skull.

I sat up and watched the shadow that danced on the floor from the crack in the door. I couldn't tell if it was a person or not. Then my eyes adjusted to the light and it disappeared. I rubbed my eyes and sat in woe for a little moment. Then I heard it again, further away.

—KNOCK! KNOCK!—

It was down the hall. I looked at Dante who was still asleep, neat in the blankets, and felt extremely anxious. I snuck out of the room and went to go look.

The floors were cold. Ridiculously cold. Like they had the AC on high. But the transoms were all open and I could hear the bugs outside. Cicadas, crickets, and other crawling things. The storm had passed. It was eighty degrees and humid.

I went into the lounge and pretended to look around for my backpack in case anyone caught me snooping. I sifted through all the shadows to make sure nothing was there hiding.

Then I felt a presence behind me. I spun around and saw the boy from my dream standing in the doorway with his arms crossed and his back against the crown molding.

I opened my eyes and saw Dante standing over me. Morning. I sat up in shock, looking to my palms for reassurance.

"You alright?"

"Yeah." I said through a sharp breath, like he'd asked a stupid question. He swallowed my tone and asked what I wanted for breakfast. I just said "Yeah." to get it moving along because I only eat because I must or else I'll die. By the time we were in the car on the way to Big Bear I had already forgotten what we ate.

Jessie's father dropped him off right as we were all leaving. His dad showed up in a big van all loud and full of character. It was only my second time meeting him ever. The first time was when Dante invited Jesse and I to watch Weezer perform live. That was in march and I only believe that happened because I still have the pictures he'd taken with us there. March was a brutal month for me. I don't want to get into specifics but my dissociative episodes would last days. I can only imagine what I *don't* remember.

The pair talked and joshed the whole way. His mother brought a friend along whose name went in one ear and out the other. But she was very kind. In fact, I was with a lovely group of people. The fog lifted by the time all the pine trees appeared and I was actually a little curious. I had never seen a real pine tree before, but I just adored them in the pictures. I watched people pass us by in cars and walking in and out of little shops and couldn't believe that people could just come out here for leisure. What a life. Despite the circumstances, I was glad to be there. I'm not allowed many good memories. I cherish every good memory, believe it or not. They're so far and few that I wake up when I know I'm in the middle of one—like I want to soak up every detail so I never forget it. Even if it's insignificant. It's mine.

There were mountains in the distance, frost barely clung to the heights of it. I imagined Dante sledding that and kind of smirked to myself over it. When we made it to the "cabin" I was relieved to know that we were glamping and not camping.

Gretchen had rented a log house with heating, air, and television. No wonder everyone laughed when I stressed trail mix and jerky over oven ready pizzas when we were in the car.

The night settled in fast. To my fortune the streets were well lit despite all the trees. They wasted the day walking around town and window shopping. I had spent the last of my money on the bus to Dantes and felt awful when he and Jessie bought me an ice cream. I had to pretend that I didn't want one that bad but I really, really, did. It was abhorred.

In the middle of it all we actually drove to the next city to buy groceries because Gretchen wanted to cook. Dinner was a haze but I was sure I liked it because my stomach wasn't a gaping pit by the evening like it usually is.

Dante, Jessie and I played tag in the backyard under twilight. And it was kind of fun, but I was so terribly anxious. It seemed like with every gust of wind and every cloud that crept in the sky became even darker. The stars waned and waned. Even the moon. It wasn't long until we were playing tag in pitch darkness.

A set of arms yanked me from behind and jerked me back. *"Tag! Hahahah!"* Jessie whispered. I felt my guts fall to my feet.

"Hahah. You got me." I said through a chill. I began skipping the opposite way and hid behind a tree. I was so nervous that the sounds of my own breath were frustrating me.

Then I heard a few twigs snap in front of me. Trying to get a better look was no hope, it was so dark. But I had a feeling it was Dante. I crept over to him and shoved him a little.

Still whispering, *"Tag!"*

He laughed. "Aw, fuck!"

I was a bit amused. I laughed too, but my eyes were so heavy above my smile it hurt to make a face. And I was so irked out I just hoped he'd call it game over.

"Come with me–Come with me—" Dante urged. *"Mischievous alliance. We're gonna go find Jessie and tag him."*

I cracked a little smile, but the darkness was so perfect it made me feel sick. Like The Wayback could come and drag me into The Empty at any moment.

I glued my hand to his shoulder and we were off.

It took us a lot longer to find him than either of us thought made sense.

"Do you hear that?" I asked.

"Hear what?"

The sounds of the land had vanished, the chirping critters and the owls in the trees. It was dead silent.

"Exactly." I shuddered.

We both began shouting for Jessie. Loudly. Then we were shouting for too long. Dante was frantic on the last one.

"JESSIE—!?"

"Tag!" Jessie tackled him. Dante was immediately on the offensive. I was the only one of us who noticed the forest's abrupt return.

"Jessie what the fuck, man!" Dante chided.

Jessie was defensive, but chuckled. "The fuck did I do? It's just a game,"

Dante was annoyed. "You aren't even it, dude, you fucked up the whole thing. And we were calling you? Why were you all quiet?"

Jessie chuckled again. Uncomfortable. "What? No you weren't. And it's *tag*. Why am I gonna answer?"

Dante and I spoke over each other. "Yes I did!" "We did."

The knowledge that the backyard was just a twenty-by-twenty foot fence snapped like a sudden finger right in our ears. Because we all believed ourselves whole heartedly and only ourselves.

"Okay—well, I'm still it, guys." Jessie insisted.

"No, I'm it!" Dante corrected.

"Yeah because I just tagged you!"

"No, I tagged Dante after you tagged me." I interjected.

"Wait—who am I holding onto right now?" Jessie said.

"Me!" Dante shouted in frustration.

We waded closer together. Jessie started laughing out of sheer exhaustion over the confusion. But Dante and I were unsettled.

"Who the hell tagged Alexander, then, because I never tagged Alexander."

Dante shifted beside me. I could feel his gaze for answers.

"I mean—I'm certain it was you. I swear someone tagged me." I didn't bother lying or back tracking because I had a gut feeling someone else was out there playing tag with us.

Dante seemed to agree. "I'm getting a little freaked out, man. Let's just go inside."

Jessie protested but we went inside and didn't say another word about it.

I was deeply unsettled but tried my best not to think about it. We sat together in the theater room watching movies well into the night. Dante laid with his head in my lap and I sat uncomfortably beneath him for a while. Then, enough time passed and it was all I could pay attention to. I had never had a boy so close to me for so long before. I sat completely still, though I wanted to play with his hair a little. He didn't look at me once the entire time. We were watching The Void on netflix and he was blown away. I, on the other hand, was lost the entire time. It would have been terrifying if it had made any sense. Longest hour of my life. I did appreciate the practical effects, however.

Gretchen came downstairs to give us cokes and popcorn and flicked on the light in shock when she saw Dante laying in my lap.

I was utterly embarrassed when she questioned us because it wasn't my idea and I didn't have any explanation given that Dante just went ahead and done it.

We all went to bed then, taking separate beds all in the same room and babbled as we dozed off. At some point I ended up explaining the difference between seals and sigils because of a one-off comment Jessie had made. It got really windy outside the later it got and the patio door kept rattling and making me so nervous I couldn't fall asleep. I started thinking about what happened in the backyard again and got scared.

I woke up at the same time I wake up every night and woke extremely dizzy. There was more knocking and thumping coming from the stairs. The wood floors creaked, too, like someone was sneaking, trying not to wake us. I held my breath and listened.

Then I heard the bathroom door open shut. Toilet flushing a few moments later. I sighed and went back to sleep.

No dreams. I reminded myself.

I woke up just before sunrise, having slept and not dreamt. I was still tired, but I couldn't bring myself to fall back asleep. I felt like I was being watched.

And I was. Right by the patio door I saw him standing in the dark. The boy in the Christmas sweater.

"How can you see me?" He whispered. Curious. Eerie.

I froze, staring at him in shock and horror.

Who are you? I thought to him.

Nothing.

He spoke again. Suddenly more animated. "Can you hear me?"

Yes.

He sang this time, waging his fingers to get a reaction out of me. *"Helloooooo? The fuck."*

I gasped. He flinched. Both of us locked wide eyes.

"What do you want?" I whispered.

His face twisted. "What? I don't want anything—What the fuck are you? Are you a djinn?"

I looked around to make sure Dante and Jesse were still sleeping. Both snored steadily and Jessie still had his headphones on.

"What are *you?"* I asked.

He threw out his arms. "What do you think? I'm fucking *dead!"*

"You're a ghost..."

"Ghost? What are you, eight?"

I glanced around the room wondering if I was dreaming. Knowing I couldn't possibly be. This ghost is absolutely absurd. Catty, even.

"Would you prefer I call you 'spirit?'"

"My name is Ref." He huffed.

"Ref? Is that short for something?"

He lurched back into the shadow. *"That's none of your business."*

What the hell? "I never asked your name, you told me. Dialogue invites engagement."

He stirred. A little impressed, a little mean spirited. *"Well, aren't you a nerd!"* He spat in an obnoxious vocal fry. *"I demand you tell me at once! How can you see me?"*

"I don't know!" I stressed. Dante flipped over and startled me. He was still asleep.

Ref got down on his knees and gawked at me like a man looking at a gorilla in a glass enclosure, disposable camera in hand. His face was completely amused. Like I wasn't a danger at all and more a spectacle.

"The others here are scared of you." He said cryptically. "You don't scare me."

"Why are you telling me this, spirit?"

"Jesus, I'm not a fucking Ouija board, you can talk to me like a person."

"I—I don't know what to say. Yeah, I have, like, ESP or something, but you're just— you're just so mean for a ghost. I'm a bit confused."

He recoiled. "Excuse me? *Mean?* Zack Bagans over here, you look like the kind. How many ghosts do you know?"

The question stung a little. I saw Jonah in my mind and winced. And his *Ghost Adventures* reference was crazy to me. *"When did you die?"* I spat.

"Twenty-twelve."

"Oh. Okay..."

His animated demeanor disarmed me a tad. But it equally unsettled me. Still, I entertained him and sat up, scooting closer to the edge of the bed so I could get a better look at him.

He wasn't as transparent and dreary in form as... *Jonah*... But he was definitely not all there. I could make out the pattern of the carpet under his transparent shadows.

I extended my hand. "I'm Alexander Hunsucker."

He tilted his head skeptically. "Shut up. That's *my* last name."

I was immediately suspicious. "What? Are you serious? I'm starting to feel like..." I hesitated. "Like you're something I made up."

All the amusement in his face shattered like he figured me out in one second. "Oh God, you're crazy!? I should probably leave you alone, I'll only make it worse. Honestly I don't even think I exist. But that's only because I was a vehement atheist in life."

"... But you're a ghost?"

"And you're a guy that can see ghosts. We both sound pretty made up to me."

Dante's alarm went off, loud and piercing. He woke up with a loud groan.

Ref was gone.

Three nights passed and I did not see him again. I began to consider the idea that perhaps he was something I made up. Maybe even a figment of my dreams. Though I was sure I had not fallen asleep.

Even so... someone or something was, indeed, haunting me the whole trip. Perhaps my mother or maybe even Jonah... I don't know. Can ghosts have ghosts?

In the late of one evening Katie called me, saying Irene and my mother had stopped by looking for me. She was angry about that, assuming I had lied and used her as a "cover" but I did no such thing. And she seemed quite angry that I'd gone camping far away and didn't tell her, which confused me given the manner in which she and I last spoke.

"I left without saying a word to anyone, Katie. It kind of just... fell into my lap." I muttered, hoping Dante wasn't listening.

She tried to lecture me on the phone but I became cross with her rather quickly and we hung up on each other. Dante came up to me after, piqued.

"Fighting with your hot gamer girlfriend?" He asked.

My face soured. "What?"

He twiddled his fingers with boyish curiosity, lips pulled into a little smirk. "Her name's Katie, right? She's super hot. Do you think you can set me up with her, maybe?"

"Katie's a lesbian."

He didn't believe me. "Like actually? That's hot."

I shrugged. "Whatever."

He yawned and took a seat next to me, at the edge of my temporary bed which I'd grown somewhat attached to over the weekend. It's been quite some time since I've had my own bed. Which is crazy but those are the cards I'm dealt by God's clumsy hands.

"Can't sleep?" He asked.

I don't wanna talk about it. I conjured up a quick excuse. "You know when you have to wake up early for something and you can't sleep a wink?"

"Oh." He said through a breath, smiling. "Long drive."

"Yeah."

"Well, I had fun. I hope you did too."

I met his eyes, a bit pensively, and gave him a sincere smile of appreciation.

As we pulled out of the driveway the next morning I dug through my backpack under the impression I was missing something. And I was correct—my journal had suddenly vanished straight out of the bag. But I vividly recalled tucking it behind my clothes. I sifted through the bag frantically and shouted,

"Oh no, I think I forgot something!" before we drove too far down the street. Gretchen turned right around, as if it was not a problem for her.

"Oh no, what'd you lose?"

"My journal." I admitted sheepishly.

Everyone hummed like I was being completely reasonable. I was grateful. Most other people would have said rest in peace and buy a new one at the dollar store.

The car lurched to a stop in the gravel driveway with a loud crunch.

"The lockbox code is zero-three-one-two." Gretchen said. I repeated the sequence in my mind—*0312 0312*—again and again as I dashed for the door.

The moment I stepped inside everything was off. Ice cold air. Creaky floorboards. A looming dread. Black static bouncing in the shadows. I glanced at the thermostat on the wall that read seventy-two degrees.

Ugh. *"I've played this game enough times. I just want my journal."*

THUMP THUMP THUMP THUMP I ran down the stairs and barged straight into the bedroom.

The door was already open.

Jesus. Jesse closed it behind him as we left. I saw it.

I stood in the doorway, a bit horrified to see that my journal was laid out neatly on the center of the bed as if it had been placed that way intentionally by someone else. I glanced around, apprehensive, and went for it.

Ref appeared behind me once it was in hand. I did not turn and look, and tensed up when he spoke. Every single hair on my body rose in a violent shiver.

"Take me with you. Please." He whispered in a desperate, tear-ridden, voice. My eyes flitted a little and, without much thought, as if being compelled by something deep within me, I pulled a pen from my pocket and opened the journal to a blank page and scribbled on it a simple snowflake.

A snowflake just like the one embroidered on the chest of his turtleneck. I slammed the book shut and the chill in the air vanished. When I had enough bravery to look behind me I saw that he too had disappeared.

I called Irene when we made it to Los Angeles. To my surprise she wasn't at all angry with me. In fact, she seemed pleased that I had gotten out of the house and "had fun." However, she told me that I was playing a dangerous game with my mother. After her warning she asked me if I had a nice time, which was another surprise. Yet even in this rare interest, there was a distance in her tone I couldn't help but pick up on. I kept it simple and said, *"The woods were very pretty."* and left it at that. She sighed and spoke softly of her wish to see the sequoias one day.

Her little confession made me a bit sad. The idea that she in her big age and disposition can still dream. When I got too quiet Irene trailed off and said she'd send Bonnie to pick me up.

Dante and I had *In N' Out Burger* to conclude our time together. While we ate he questioned me further about my friendship with Katie and I found myself being a little too honest with him.

"So, what's the deal? Why are you guys fighting all of a sudden?"

I hesitated, no real answer blinking in my mind. Just uncertainty.

"I just think, maybe I've been looking at our relationship all wrong. I feel... silly to word it this way, but I fear that perhaps I've just been her 'gay best friend' this entire time and—I dunno—" I rubbed the back of my neck, "I definitely don't want to be *that."*

He tried to be comforting, rested a hand on my shoulder and said, "It'll get better." but he washed away all sense of security when he went back to prodding about her sexuality. To shut him up I gave him her number as a bit of thoughtless mischief. He changed the subject after that.

"Do you know you talk in your sleep?"

I felt a hot sensation in my chest. Like guilt. But for what? I held onto myself like that would bring me some comfort, but it didn't. When I asked if he remembered anything I'd said he could only recall one instance confidently. All the other times he was half asleep. But for this one he was awake. It was the morning after my first night at his house.

"You said, *"I am The..."* and only that." He laughed. "I poked you and asked what. You didn't say anything else. You just woke up on the wrong side of the bed."

"... how troubling."

On the way home, Bonnie freaked out about Dante's mother, who saw me off in the driveway and waved at my aunt who perked at her through the open car door. Apparently she's some kind of celebrity. Bonnie asked me about my friend's father whom she also knew by name, but I just shrugged; I didn't know a thing about him and Dante had never brought it up. I had no idea.

I stared out the window, a little anxious. A little ashamed. About a number of things. All faceless and gnashing only because I refused to really look. I just wanted to get back already, although there was nothing waiting for me at my Nanna's except more upheaval and pain. That, I knew for certain.

"I didn't know you had so many friends." Bonnie commented with half interest, still reeling from seeing Gretchen Bonaduce, trying to make small talk and hopefully learn more.

I don't know about that, I thought to myself.

"I think my mom said a group of boys came by looking for you when you were gone. Which, by the way, you're crazy for..." Her voice was snuffed out as I turned the volume up on the radio.

Right Now by *Akon* played. I closed my eyes and listened.

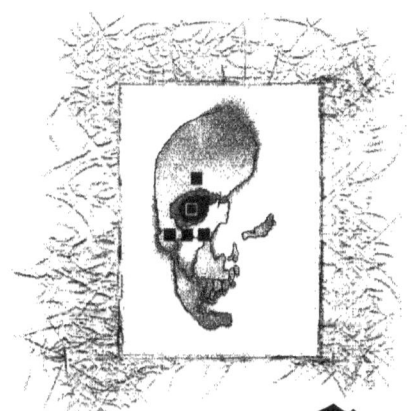

Chapter Eleven

When I got home my laptop was the very first thing I looked for. It was right where I left it. I felt foolish all of a sudden, for thinking that its appearance in my dream was some kind of omen—maybe someone was snooping. But no. It was right where I left it, buried under all my shirts and undisturbed. I sighed with relief—then I realized I had nothing to hide anyway.

Irene sat on her bed completely jaded, sipping on a mug of hot tea and reading a bizarre book titled 'MY JOURNEY TO HELL' By some Dr.Michael Yeager, who I was sure was in need of a doctor rather than being one himself.

I find her compulsive interest in the afterlife offensive. Always contemplating the fate of the soul without any passion for the living human condition. Especially since she considered my once interest in necromancy to be sinful—I couldn't see how her obsession with the dead was any more innocent than my bored musings.

As skewed by her faith and grief as I find her, I think at some point I figured her out. My beautiful grandmother, great matriarch of this family after her mother died of leukemia and left the title of 'Nanna' to her. She's no saint by any means, but I think she's actually made some effort to be a decent person after this family was dumped on her shoulders. She lost her only son to a tragic act of violence the summer after her mother passed. Heaven for Richard is her only way of finding any thread of peace over the turmoil his death inspired. And its human to look for meaning in an untenable situation, I know that. That fact makes me loathe her a bit less than the others.

However, I remember. I remember everything they wish to forget. She lost her only begotten son, and it makes her sad, but that doesn't mean she, alongside everyone else in this damned house, cannot be held accountable for my active murder at the hands of them.

All of them.

Not to mention, this family neglected my uncle for the larger part of his life. Much like they do me. Richard was always the odd one out, left to fend for himself all the while Irene gave her daughters everything undeserved. She not only mourns his end, I believe, she also mourns what she'd done and how her absence cast a dark shadow over his short life. As I stared at her I imagined my mother in a similar condition, in some other life—maybe one where I didn't survive the ocean. And it made me angry.

Welcome home, Alexander Hunsucker.

I tried to find kind words, but I realized I had nothing kind to say. So I decided to be frank about my business instead of making a wry comment about her book.

"Is Valene coming home tonight?" I asked tonelessly. She glanced at me once and went back to reading.

"Valene hasn't been home in days. Since you left, actually."

"What for?"

"She's crazy." Irene laughed to herself. A bit exasperated, maybe even a little wry.

"What?"

"Valene's telling everybody she got attacked by a monster in her room, can you believe it? She said, 'Mom, I don't feel comfortable being in that house.'

"I think she's a damn liar. Stevie's been acting up and she doesn't want to deal with it, so she's leaving it to me like always."

Despite the absolutely heinous nature of her claims, I was beaming. I hate sleeping in the living room.

"So... she's not gonna be here tonight?"

"Are you?" Irene snapped.

I sighed and rolled my eyes. All of our petty disagreements have conditioned me to answer 'yes' vacantly, but luckily I caught myself before I answered. I suddenly wasn't sure. *Valene said she got attacked by a monster in her room. . ?* I know with certainty that the monster she referred to was The Wayback.

I glanced at her closed door a bit fearfully.

"Nunu, what were you thinking!? It's like you want your mother to freak out on you!"

I grimmaced. *"That's what I'm used to!"*

She shook her head and broke out in another fit of dry chuckles, before silencing herself with a sip from her mug. "You're too much, Kid."

Tell me about it.

I walked out into the hall and flinched when I saw Adriana stumble out the bathroom in full back brace and crutches, glaring at me in mute agony as she hobbled into her room like brick on stilts.

I spun right back around. "What happened to Adriana!?" I exclaimed.

Irene clicked her tongue. "Adrian got hit by one of those big grocery trucks in the parking lot of Food-four-Less. Broke her leg and cracked her spine."

I chuckled darkly and tried to pass it off as clearing my throat. Irene noticed but didn't seem phased

"Oh my God. When?"

"Thursday." She sighed. *Also the day I left.* I scratched my ear, wondering if I was somehow responsible. That wonder very quickly spiraling into certainty. My fingers clenched around the doorframe.

"Oh my." I uttered. CREAK. "Did I miss anything else?"

I didn't expect an answer. But there was one more thing I missed. "Tommy almost burnt my face off."

"Jesus."

She closed her book over her lap. "Do not say The Lord's name in vain."

"Shit."

She snapped out of the daze and glared at me. She literally raised her arm and pointed to the door. *"Enough of you, get out!"*

I left, trouble starting to boil behind my gaze. Tommy and I walked into the living room at the same time. Me from the hall, him from the stairs. He threw his arms out in disbelief when he saw me,

"Dude, where the hell did you go?"

"I went camping."

He was disarmed. "Oh. That's... actually pretty cool. Did you have fun at least?"

"Kind of." I said a bit vacantly. "I saw a ghost."

"That's not surprising." He muttered darkly. Unsettled. "Did Nanna tell you about the fire?"

"I was just about to ask you about that."

He was annoyed and threw himself onto the couch.

"Dude, she swears I did something! She pisses me off, bro!" His hands were clenched around in the air.

"We were in the driveway setting up the grill and she told me to pass her the lighter fluid, right? Bro it isn't even in my fucking hand and this huge ass flame bursts in her face!

"It wasn't even me! It just—happened!

"You're lucky you weren't there bro, she freaked! She threw herself on the couch and started crying and said she would kill herself if she got burned. That she would never wanna live and be ugly. What the fuck is that?" He sighed and let his head drop dramatically.

I was sad. He looked just like me when I was his age. Stressed by these whack job women and paying the price with greys and stomach pain. His arms were clutched over his gut.

I sat next to him. *"What horrible antics."* I said, trying to be snarky to lighten the atmosphere around him. But he looked pale. *This is my fault.*

"Are you okay?" I asked.

"You're lucky you weren't there..." He said again under his breath. The story was a lot more serious all of a sudden. I frowned and saw flashes of it in my head. Irene frantic on the couch. Full blown melt down. I sat beside him, pensive, and stretched my arm over his shoulder.

"I'm sorry you had to go through that."

He shrugged. "It's whatever. It's just annoying."

I sighed. "Yeah."

As twilight fell I sat in the kitchen, actually taking the time to look through my phone. I had a missed text from Tyler that I felt a little guilty about. He texted me the night before—

... ... the night before... .

—I can't say it.

My eyes crept over to the closet where I last saw Jonah. I tossed my phone onto the table and shoved my hands in my hair.

The last few days started to buzz like a pesky fly in my brain. I pondered my sanity then. Something I try not to do often, but with everything being anxious about my sanity was actually a shred of hope that I wasn't entirely fragged out yet.

I tried very hard to make sense of things. Very hard. Of The Wayback, of Jonah, of the ghost Ref. Of the violent misfortune my family had in my absence. I couldn't help but feel responsible.

But why? I didn't wave my hands and intend any of this. Never once said or done anything to invoke such happenings. I'm very careful with my words. I already killed the family dog with a bad joke. Is it so impossible that I put Adriana in the hospital by giving her the evil eye? And what about Irene and Valene? They hadn't done anything to me. At least, nothing out of the ordinary complaisant abuse. The fire incident could very well be a case of bad luck, but the "monster" that attacked Valene. . ?

I wondered what exactly happened that morning. I wondered if it had anything to do with the fact that I *wanted* her out of the house for a few nights. Every time I wake up in the living room I'm bitter about my only privacy being taken from me. I know that's unfair. But I guess I learned that it's human nature to commandeer what you need. I used to think I was a monster. Inhuman, strange, and unmeant. Turns out I was correct. In the sense that being human makes you all of those things.

I felt like I was being watched then. *I have a habit of sleeping in her room. Maybe The Wayback was trying to pay me a visit.*

I wasn't sure. I moaned in frustration. *"Maybe this is all in my head."* I rolled up my sleeve and examined the flaky remnants of The Waybacks handprint that coiled my arm.

Or maybe I just want it to be. "Imagined or not, I still have to endure *it.*" I muttered to myself.

I let a moment of silence pass, for Jonah to say something uplifting. Of course he wasn't there. I just stared at the kitchen table and traced the lines in the wood while I waited in vain.

I opened my laptop after a while and dug through my inbox to see if I had missed anything there.

Tom Steyer - - Need To Impeach DONALD TRUMP   Republican

Obstr. . .

Quora Digest   So wtf

was that clown thing in 201. . .

Pinterest   **You have a good**

eye - - Doctor Strange i. . .

Quora Digest ─────────────── Does

anyone else think the mande. . .

Quora Digest   What

happens at a Mormon endow...

Thirteen more from *Quora Digest*. I unsubscribed, hoping that was a sign of progress. I've never met anyone mentally sound who's subscribed to Quora Digest.

Deep in the chain I caught a familiar name that made my heart skip a beat.

Adrian Lazo   l

wondered if you got my messages. N...

─────────────────────────

The air started buzzing like a fluorescent light in a liquor store. I opened it.

Reply: [deleted6n16S75....]

 Adrian Lazo ‹IncdrXML167D54E6AF7.kjev@instamail.com›
to me(444dreamcowboy@instamail.com)

Hey

I wondered if you got my messages. Now I know.
You're gonna wish you died when you jumped off that
cliff joto. Watch your back.

As quickly as being decimated by a lightning strike, so many kinds of anger surged through me in a single splintering second. For a young man with such an extensive vocabulary, I could conjure a single sentence to accurately describe the caliber of this feeling. The static in the air made my temples start to tingle.

The kitchen, once just dim and heavy with my thoughts, seemed to tilt under the weight of this feeling. The hum of the refrigerator deepened to a low growl. The shadows on the walls elongated, as if leaning in to see how I was about to react. The air tasted metallic, bloody on my tongue, like I had bit my lip until it popped!

Then—A voice broke through, low and venomous from the slats of the closet shutters.

"I know who's been pretending." he said in a snarl. From between the slats, I caught a glimpse of his rings: blue and cold as frost.

Oh I was so angry! **It's getting to be too much!** *It hurts! Angry about The Wayback! Angry about this! That someone would target me like this at a time like this!?*

I clucthed my head with both hands.

"WHAT DO YOU WANT FROM ME?" and shot up from my seat, tearing the doors open with a nasty, frustrated, snarl!

—There was Nothing. Literally Nothing. No dryer, no washing machine or room or floor or anything. Just The Empty. My nose burned with the sharp stench of bleach. I slammed it shut and locked it.

And stepped back in terror.

"I will reveal a great enemy to you. Not because he is a threat to your life, but because of what he represents: Another insult to your power.

"You are a force. Stop swallowing yourself and show the world what kind of force you are. One to not be reckoned with."

"Why are you saying this shit!? What the fuck do you want from me, really!?"

"A boy and his friends came looking for you after you left. They came to beat you up, but you were at Katie's by then.

"His name is Leonel Castillo."

My legs turned to jelly when I heard the name. And suddenly all the anonymous cyberbullying made sense.

"Honestly it's not even that big of a deal. But with everything going on I would imagine it to be such a nuisance.

"I've seen him. I've seen him send you hate like it cost him nothing. I see them all do it to you. And you wanna know something? It really does cost them nothing.

"I hate that for you, Alexander. Really I do.

"That's why I want you to shed all of this... mercy. They're cruel, they've turned you into Nothing. They killed you.

"Everyone's had a piece of the Alexander fucking pie. Even me. And this one is just another one to take.

"What are you gonna do about it?"

He vanished with a click and the light in the laundry room reappeared. The pull-chain swung violently and tapped against the glass of the bulb.

Stunned silence... ... .

Then a wrath beyond words, Lionel's face clear in my mind. My body ran cold.

For too long I have cursed my own life over the weak. The weak willed, the negligent, the narrow minded and the senseless. They all share one unforgivable trait. A cardinal sin in my eyes—

A profound weakness of the heart.

Even if Leonel and I are enemies, to say such a disgusting thing to anyone, let alone a boy who's been through what I've been through, is a fucking crime. *Especially if that boy is barely hanging on by the last atom of his last thread.*

It is a vile insult—*a mockery of the divine gift of GOD!* To wield free will, only to commit cruelty and malice for the sake of it!

I thought of the beasts.

I see it now.

No longer will I allow the weak to ruin me. No longer will I allow beasts to ravage me.

I will find him. I will make an example out of him for the next and the ones before him. I will ensure he lives with the regret of ever being born just like ME!

Because of his BLATANT ignorance, he will endure greater pain. He too will know the curse.

I know what I am. And he's going to be the first to know. And he will weep at the sight of it.

You're gonna wish you died when you jumped off that cliff joto

I did.

I jumped into fresh clothes and redid my nails, clipped and black, and used Irene's charcoal powder as kohl, smudging with the tip of my middle finger until my water lines were black. I took my time, either out of compulsion or stalling, but my heart never once stopped racing. I pondered whether or not I was having some kind of breakdown. Nevertheless, I did not intend on responding any other way.

Leonel will be a bloody pulp in my hands.

I looked in the mirror and watched the rings settle in, subtle, shiny like a coin in the dark. Through the reflection I glanced at Valene's door. I spun around and opened it.

Stale air flooded into the hall like it was a vacuum sealed tomb. Her room was terribly, utterly, dark. The only light that broke through was from the hallway, but even that was afraid to go any further than a measly foot past the door. I walked in and shut the door behind me, lights off.

The room was an oppressive void. I walked over to the window and tore the curtains all the way open so the night would flood into the room and cleanse the darkness. It was like all the sound was allowed entry all of a sudden. Her window was wide open, and there was a dead Jerusalem cricket laying on the sill —sun bleached and shriveled up.

I mourned him. A stranger to me, but I mourned him. I wondered how many others just like it were out there, living lives we often consider disposable and insignificant.

God put them here with us. It is a miracle that these little creatures live and fight on alongside us. I got down on my knees and spoke to him, because they are all pure and beautiful. Our angels are not babies in loincloths, they are the unseen saints that we crush under our heels. Or let rot in the cracks of our broken world.

"You don't know hate. You were pure and beautiful on the inside. You're not a beast." I whispered. *"I'm sorry."*

Why Oh Why God am I grief-stricken over a bug at a time like this?! And why Oh Why God have you cut yourself off from *me!?*

I sat down in her bed and pinched my sides, considering what I was about to do and wondering what this means for my salvation?

"I don't wanna be a beast." I muttered. Choked up. *"I don't wanna be a beast."*

But I fear, free will or not, I have to endure it. I pressed my fist into my leg.

If I have to be a beast... I will be. Imagined or not, I must endure it. If it is so, then I am the beast that loves. Forbidden to hold it close, broken without it. I clenched my teeth.

The front door of the house opened and slammed shut then—it was so loud I felt it.

Mom.

I jumped up and ran over to the door, hand gripped on the handle, but hesitant to open it and look.

Imagined or not, I have to endure it, I reminded myself. I filled my chest with air and met her in the living room. When she saw me emerge from the hall she stood firm in her place and waited for me to approach her.

"We need to talk." She said from across the way. Firm. Desperate. As if her stone cold face was conjured up with all the bravery she could muster. Like she stood in the face of a dragon.

I burrowed past her. *"I don't want to talk."* Eyes burning. "I have to go."

With two fingers she pressed into my shoulder and pinned me to the wall.

"No—!" She whimpered. "Listen to me—" Her eyes poured into mine. Waxy. Broken. Terrified. She held up a finger. "Listen to me."

I tilted my head.

"Everything that happened—with us, last summer—and everything after that—I do not like it, okay?

"I never liked it. I—I never want to argue with you, o-or be mad at you. Or feel sad when you're gone because we got into a fight.

"—And know you're hurting the entire time."

I was cold.

"We get let down, we fight, but all of those things make us who we are. Believe me—even a bad situation can turn out to be good in the end."

She clasped her hands around my face, gentle, smooth as morning sun. Oh so maternal—like I always dreamed.

But I don't dream anymore. *Because of you.* I sucked in a shaky breath.

"I try my best with you. That's for real. I try my best with you. And on top of that, I'm trying to be a Good person.

"But with you... sometimes trying just isn't enough. You need more from me than a boy should. And your father is not around, and I know you need th—"

"OH MY GOD, I DON'T GIVE A SHIT ABOUT MY FATHER, I JUST NEEDED YOU!"

"You are precisely why we are in this predicament, mother! Not because my father's a crook! Not because I need too much from you! It's just **YOU.**

"You don't want to feel anything real because it scares you! It's too much! Your fear is so deep you can't look your sins in the face because it would make your fucking head explode! *You cower away from me like I'm made of the DARK!"*

Her face turned white. I went for the door.

"I KNOW WHO I AM!" She screamed with shredding conviction. "I know who I am! Even if I hate it, I know what I need to do in life!

"And I give every swing all I have. I have to. But—"

She sniffed.

"But I was born with broken arms.

"We're a family, Nunu. We're a family.

"I just want to fix all of this before the baby comes. Whatever it takes, Son, to make us better than before."

"I love you."

The phrase that I ached to hear every day. Always three words away... *always three words away.* To finally hear it,

And feel so empty... .

I choked.

"—I'd've been your knight in shining armor. Valiant at your side. Strong enough to lift not just you, not just the two of us, but all of us.

"I suffered for all of it. Only to die at your feet. Heart crushed in your fist.

"It kills me to know how I erased myself over you. Because you weren't worth it. You don't love *me.* You don't even know me.

"And worst of all, you don't know what love is. None of us in this family do. Love, for us, never collapses into truth.

"Everything I ever did, sleeping in car garages, leaving my body at night to find you, taking abuse, moving around, jumping off a fucking cliff!

"I did for you!

"And you... were just an idea...

"A faceless title that every child needs. You're not my mother. You're just Priscilla. You're just a teenage girl that got knocked up but a million fucking years have passed and you never learned how to be a fucking person!

"You don't like everything that has happened? Imagine how it feels on the other side?

"And what a fucking shame. That all of this tragedy could have brought us closer together. I was stupid to think surviving that cliff would make you finally cherish me.

"I'm your baby. Your number one. I know you don't—*want* me to be this.

"This isn't what *I want* to be.

"But nobody in this family ever wants to admit what they've done. You either get swept under the rug or die trying to crawl out from under it. You're just another casualty. But you're a part of this too.

"I'd rather suffer the seemingly timeless agony of a dead mother than suffer the waking life of being a monster who craves it from you!"

I opened the door and slammed it shut behind me. Leaving her there in the dark. Lonely and haunted.

Just like me.

I cried all the way to Leonel's apartment. Just sobbing ugly into my arm. Still committed to my decisions, marching miles into town, down the poorly lit streets, crying harder than I ever had before. Trying to get the last of it out of me so it wouldn't get in the way of things.

When I made it to those dilapidated stairs where he and I shared a tender moment together, I reimagined the scene in my mind.

One night I walked home late from a metaphysical store in Pasadena. I was fifteen. A witches' open circle had caught my attention and I attended in search of advice. On the outskirts of town I heard someone whistling at me in the dark.

It was him. Sitting alone at the foot of his stairs listening to music on his phone. It took me a second for his face to register—but when it did I was disarmed immediately. I even smiled. Played it cool. He was so much more handsome in person.

The knowledge that I liked boys took me by surprise like I had been attacked by a grizzly bear. They don't take kindly to guys like me in Woodrow. Guys who are... you know. And with my powers spiraling out of control I was already a known freak. People talked. Some hated me. Called me the devil.

Leonel wasn't one of those people. I guess that's what made him stand out so much. Because... I would have expected him to be. We weren't exactly friends but he was nice to me. He even added me on instagram and messaged me from time to time, saying that we should hang out but I was always too shy. I didn't want him to think I liked him too much, even though I was very curious about him. I'd comment on his shirtless pictures with fire emojis and play it off as friendly. Sometimes he'd flirt back in the way straight guys do.

"Alexander?" He asked, seeming unsure, but eager.

"Oh—" I smiled wider. I was delighted. "Leonel, hey, what's up?"

He pulled me into a sudden hug that made my loins fire up. "What are you doing here?"

"Uh—I'm walking back from a little mission I was on."

"Active ass fool." He joked, nudging me.

I hummed in a high pitch to disagree. Honest because I wanted him to be interested, and also to clear up any idea about gangs because I'm not about that life.

"Uh—No, no, uh—there's this group of witches or something, um, that uh, have these little meetings in Pasadena." I clasped my hand over the back of my neck and looked at my shoes.

"I have some—stuff going on at home and. . I wanted a little help."

He looked a little uneasy then. "You fuck with that?"

"No." I protested. I let go of my neck and shoved my hands in my pockets. "No—it's not like that. I kind of..." I wasn't sure how to say it without sounding crazy.

"I just have some weird stuff going on at home, I just wanted some advice on how to manage it." *"Or make it stop."* I added in a quick mutter.

He glanced around. "Hang out with me," nodding over to where he sat. "Have a cold one."

I put up a hand. "Oh, haha, no, I'm good, thanks. I'm, like, a clean-cut kinda guy. No judgement to you though, I mean, do what thou wilt."

"I respect that." He said, smile returning. "You smoke?"

Again, "No. Sorry if that makes me boring."

"Don't trip." He inched closer. "I got some Tampico inside. You want some of that?" He flashed his teeth. So perfect. So white. He was even more handsome up close. *I wished that I could stay.*

Then it began to drizzle. The concrete, orange in the light that came from his complex turned grey dot by dot in the building momentum of the storm that came in all of a sudden.

"Er—I'll pass on the juice. But, uh, I'm down to hang out for a while, sure. Let's do it."

"Nice."

The storm raged just a foot away from us. Loud and frigid. He and I sat under the canopy of the stairwell on the second to last step, leg to leg because it was so narrow. He pulled out his phone and we played twenty-one questions, dancing awkwardly around all the ones that were sexually charged. I answered a few but I think my lack of experience was obvious. I very much enjoyed myself. I was surprised to learn that his favorite color was turquoise and his idea of the perfect date is line dancing. When I told him my favorite color was white he said I was "different." And he laughed when I told him that my idea of the perfect first date was mushroom ravioli and a coca cola.

After a while we got bored of all the shallow details and began poking each other's brains about ourselves and our lives. He seemed really interested in everything I had to say, watching the storm intently like he was taking mental notes on all the details of my little world. I noticed he shied away from my questions about his family life but I didn't prod.

"So what's going on with you at home?" He asked, a bit brash, a bit shy, peeking at me from his peripheral.

I let out a breath and threw myself over my knees. "Where do I even start? Is that beer still on the table?"

He shot up. "Yeah!" "Actually, I got some tequila if you—wanna—" grinning, he saw the look on my face and stopped himself there.

I laughed. "I'm kidding!"

He settled back into the stair, chuckling like he was embarrassed by how excited he'd allowed himself to become.

Not long after, my smile fell. "My mother and I have just been fighting a lot. It really tears me up to shreds.

"I'm hardly home anymore, because of it, honestly. It's all too much. But when I am weird stuff happens around the house and..." I trailed off.

I saw the dog's lifeless body in my mind again. Lily, sprawled out on the vet's table with a white cloth covering her stitches. Her beautiful white Siberian fur was dry and lifeless. And her eyes, once blue and so full of tenderness, a dead thousand-yard stare.

Everyone was crying over her body. But not me. I just couldn't. I couldn't believe it was real.

He choked, hand on my thigh. Gentle squeeze. It yanked me out of the melancholy and relit the spark in my heavy chest.

"Oh—shit—I meant the brujaria stuff, my bad. I'm sorry."

I cringed. Sucking in a breath through my teeth.

"Fuck—Um. Yeah about that..." I filled my chest with air and pinched an eye shut. "Well, it is connected to my mom, I think. I mean it all started when she and I..." I muttered off again. I didn't wanna say it.

"Uh. Anyway. I started having these bad dreams that the world was ending and it was my fault somehow. I don't know what I did, exactly. You know dream logic. But I just knew, you know?

"The moon would turn red and crash into the earth while I stood there... waiting for it.

"It was just that for a while. Bad dreams. But then I started to notice all these little coincidences. I'd lie about something and it's suddenly not a lie. Like, the evidence to back it up would just happen—or like, if I was talking out of my ass, turns out my bullshit was right.

"Sometimes I get mad and the lights flicker or the TV just—shuts off suddenly.

"Or..." I glanced up from my shoes and looked to the storm.

I wished that I could stay.

"It's insidious how it happens. It conveniently starts raining when I'm in the mood for it. For better or for worse. Usually for worse.

"At first I thought, maybe, there was something following me. Messing with me. Something I couldn't see. But I've kind of been in denial this whole time that it *is* me. And just like my dreams... I don't know how I know. I just. Know."

He gulped.

"I don't know. I made a joke about the dog dying yesterday and—" I couldn't say it. I didn't wanna get myself worked up again. "You can fill in the blanks."

"The dog died?"

My silence confirmed the truth. He was speechless for a moment.

"That's really fucked up." He blurted, chugging the last of his fourth can with his eyes open.

"Is it true?"

I shifted a little. Shoulders growing tense again. And then sighed, letting all that stress go. I looked him in the eyes and smiled. I wanted to kiss him and tell him thank you. It was turning out to be a better night.

"That is man's greatest suspense, isn't it? Whether or not any of it is true?" I said. Trying to be flirty by waxing philosophical.

He was muddled. I elaborated further, nudging him with my leg. "God and The Devil and all that jazz."

"I believe in God." He said defensively.

"So do I."

He stirred. Perhaps too tipsy for such a bizarre conversation. Then he surprised me with a confession. Like me, what he said was true. And hurtful. He stared at the steps and said,

"One time I was praying... asking God why I was born in this place, at this time, in this family, and all that. I was high as fuck. Maybe I was tripping. But I *felt* him listening to me. This—sudden silence was with me. And I know it was God. Like... really him. You'd think I'd've been happy but. . .

"Is it fucked up that I was scared?"

He went quiet. So did I. Then, he whispered in my ear.

"I don't know. It's like... seeing all the stars at night. Have you ever seen all the stars at night? Like, out in the country?"

"No. But I've seen pictures. I can only imagine how beautiful."

"It's sublime." He said.

I was surprised.

He smiled coyly and kinda shrugged. "You gotta pay attention in class to play varsity."

"So then you do understand?"

He was even closer. "What?"

"That is the sublime. That feeling. When something is so grand it's uncanny. You said it scared you... But I bet you've prayed every night since then. Just feel it again."

"I do." He shuttered. "How did you know that?"

I cracked a wry smile despite myself. What I was about to say was sick.

"Because it happens to me too. Just not with..." I frowned. "Just not with God. With something else inside of me.

"You said yours is a sudden silence? Mines is like the sun peeking over the horizon just before dawn."

"That's good right?"

My fists clenched. He reached for my hand with his pinky, palm still on my leg.

"No. The sky just keeps getting darker and darker every time I feel it. The stars disappear. But the sun never goes away. It's just a light... that illuminates nothing. A paradox.

"A midnight sun."

Thunder rolled. The wind blew so hard it sent the screen door flying open only for it to slam shut right after. I watched his porch light turn on. A moment later two fingers spread open the blinds and there were his peeking eyes. Then the door opened.

"Jacob?" Leonel called, hand shielding his face from the high winds. I stood just out of the light, in the middle of the road and stared at him.

He saw me. But from his point of view, he saw Something.

"Jacob! Is that you?"

He stood there in his boxer shorts and a tank top. He framed his vision with his palms in an attempt to narrow his focus on my silhouette. A girl in her underwear and t-shirt three sizes too large stepped past him to see what all the commotion was about. I curled my fingers and cast Ref's sigil on the wall of the alley, projecting his shadow across it in a full sprint. The pair jumped when they saw it contort on the wall—Leonel yanked himself by the shorts.

"The fuck was that!?" The two scurried inside and slammed the door shut.

I waved my hands and waited for them to come back outside. It was only Leonel with a bat and a pair of sweatpants, his phone clutched in his hand. Girlfriend on speaker.

He ran down the steps and into the foot of the alley. "Hey who the fuck is out here!?" He screamed, trying to sound threatening. I threw Ref's spirit into a pile of broken-down palettes by the transformer enclosure. He rattled around in the mess. Leonel got closer, ready to swing. Terrified.

I tackled him from the side—jumping out of the dark and started punching him in the face over and over again. I hit him so hard I felt my hands go numb from the shock. His girlfriend screamed on the phone.

So noisy. I kicked it into the fence and the screen cracked. I climbed on top of him and hit him again and again, and then three more times.

I stopped to take a break, rising and panting like a dog. He tried to get up, limp—I pressed him into the concrete with my foot.

"Are you the—" He coughed. "Are you the—?"

I punched him in the face again. Blood spattered on the floor next to him. His bottom lip was ruined. He hissed like it was a power up before he leapt up and tackled me into the floor, grunting and cursing at me.

Leonel pinned my wrist into the ground. I felt the little bits of gravel and glass scrape up my hand all over as I struggled against his grip. He punched me. He punched me again. In the whiplash I saw The Wayback standing at the end of the alley, hand over his mouth like he was giggling. With my free hand I grabbed his face and pressed my thumb into his eye. He only let it happen a second before screaming and throwing himself off of me.

"STOP—" He sobbed, hands flung up in desperate surrender. I sighed, swallowed the pain all over my body, and picked up his bat. The metal scraped against the concrete like nails on a chalkboard. I swung it over my shoulder and got closer.

"Alexander—!?" He scurried until his back was against the metal cage.

I swung the bat behind me. He screamed again. *"Why are you doing this!?"*

I threw and it missed his head by an inch. **CRASH!** It slammed into the transformer and caused it to spark and flash.

I grabbed him by the chain around his neck and yanked him close, the cold metal coiling in my fist until my knuckles were bare. I twisted, harder until I felt it bite against the flesh of his neck. And then I drew him close—so close I could taste the fear in the air between us. His breath hitched when our eyes locked in some macabre embrace.

For a few seconds, it was just he and I. Existence fell away—the sounds, the wind, even the hammering of our hearts. His eyes, frantic at first, faltered—turned to stone—caught by something in mine he could not comprehend. Something older that peered out through me.

And in that terrible stillness, he saw it.

His pupils shrank to pinpricks. His face blanched as if he'd looked upon some unspeakable thing—a glimpse beyond the veil, maybe, or the reflection of his own soul stripped down to nothing. His mouth parted like he wanted to speak, but no sound came out, only a ragged breath.

He trembled in my grip, his whole body sagging as though whatever he saw drained the strength right out of him.

What he saw, I did not know. I only felt the tremor run through him— the way his pulse thundered beneath my fingers, the way his breath turned shallow and broken.

Then, everything came back. I hurled him down onto the grass.

"Are you The Devil?" He wheezed, quivering and broken. I stood over him.

"I am your greatest fear, because it is in your very genes to fear what you do not know. I am the beast that reaches for your hand.

I am the Midnight Sun.   "

The wind howled in the revelation. And just as I desired, he wept at the sight of it. I pointed an angry, spiteful finger at him. So that the stars should turn into bullets and strike him all at once.

*"You deserve this! You hear me!? You—**deserve** this!"*

I brought my wrists together, fingers bent in crooked arcs, as if shaping some ancient curse kept in the marrow of my bones, and twisted. *Hands trembling, charged bright and fervent with intent, I strike down my greatest enemy.*

And in my head I had a vision. I saw my true enemy. I saw my mother's face. A swift, deliberate motion, I slashed the air toward Leonel— to sever him from grace completely—and cast it.

He coughed and took in a wheezy breath. *"Alexander—I'm sorry—"* was the last thing he said before his eyes rolled back. The rage spun into shock when his body went limp and cold before me.

The Wayback snickered behind his palm—squealing and shaking like a little kid.

Slowly, I turned around to face him, breathing heavily, with my bloody hands out.

"Dear, God.... What have I done. . ?"

"I'm not God." He snarled.

"Then there is nothing more to say." I uttered.

I didn't even have the guts to make sure Leonel was still alive. I just ran away and left him there in the potholes and the trash. The Wayback cackled into the night. For once, not in the voice of little children, but like The Devil. Deep, malevolent, and satisfied—that he saw it.

That he saw what's really in me.

Every dog on the block heard it—barking, shrieking, crying out—howling in alarm. I ran like a man fleeing the gates of Hell.

I ran and ran and ran until I fell over on the sidewalk from exhaustion. My face hit the ground. Hard. Someone heard and shuffled over from across the street.

"Are you dead?" A voice asked, high and screechy, almost childlike but obviously aged. I was poked at by what I assumed was a twig.

I didn't move at first—not enough strength. I rolled over with everything I had left and moaned in agony.

"Holy shit." He said, a little antsy. "Holy shit—" He lifted me up and tucked himself under my shoulder to hold me up. *You're Alexander Husucker!"*

I struggled to keep my eyes open—beneath me a boy I had not ever met in my entire life waded us toward a black metal gate that seemed vaguely familiar. He had hair just like Dante but he was incredibly short. Shorter than me, even. A small munchkin of a man. I struggled against him but I was too weak to fight him off.

"H—How do you know me?" I said in a drawn-out slur.

"I'm Twinkle's best friend, Johnny. Haven't you heard of me?"

Tyler's namesake was enough security that I felt safe enough to succumb to the shock. I passed out on his friends back.

Chapter Twelve

I was gone just a moment. But I saw something. Something lost when I returned to invasive sensations. To clamor, hands and frantic voices. I kept my eyes closed, too weak to fight off the heaviness of a thousand sleepless nights and the pallor of my wounded body. I wanted to peek—to see where exactly I was being taken—but I think I had just shut down completely. Behind the static of my closed eyes I saw this red, throbbing, light that pulsed in tandem with a clinical headache. And ah, there it was! I was seeing it again! So intense I could feel it in my sinuses and in my ears.

I'd liken it to the white light people who return from death claim to see. It drew me in closer. But my flesh refused to give. The noise beyond me kept my attention firm on the material world. The loudest thing was the pounding of boots and the squeak of wet sneakers on hard-wood stairs, loud thumps that bounced off the walls of a narrow hallway. And the worst feeling ... Four hands... four hands... two of them too grabby and too small, both pairs gripping me tight and lugging me up the stairs.

I was afraid. In all the upheaval I imagined two goblins dragging me into hell, goblins with twisted faces and sharp noses. Yellow eyes and sharp teeth. *Is that where the red light is taking me?* I started to writhe in the grip of these four hands—then, one voice, *Tyler's voice,* said to me through a strain,

"It's okay—It's okay—"

The goblins went away.

"Open the door!"

More thumps, the squeak of a rusty hinge, and then... more bickering. Words I didn't catch.

So dizzy. . .

The other hands let go, and Tyler lifted me in his arms before gently setting me against the foot of his bed. I held onto consciousness with all I had and listened as best as I could. His fingers coiled around my shoulders and he squeezed tight, a little shake, and I snapped to attention like he'd run smelling salts under my nose.

His face fell into view from a nasty dark fuzz. Like all of reality had seeped in through needlepoints.

Tyler... Tyler... Oh no Tyler... I shot forward to get away, but he steadied me with both hands and mournful eyes.

I noticed a boy standing anxiously behind him, shoulders tense, in a leather pilots' jacket two-sizes too big and a bright ginger afro. His fists were balled under the cuffs. His face was flushed red over his freckles.

Tyler brought me back to his with a waxy shift of the eyes. "Alexander?" He urged.

"Alexander??" My name again, though less a name and more of a command to speak on the second one.

I brought out a shaky, bloody hand and beheld it.

"A-l-l-lexander." Tyler exhaled sharply, looking me up and down in horror. "Wh..."

"I got into a fight." Voice grim.

"You don't look like you got into a fight..." He was staring at my hands again.

"Did you call the police?" I asked, fear seeping in a little. I imagined myself surrounded by police, guns blazing.

Their eyes popped like I'd confirmed their theories to be true.

The ginger boy let out a distressed sigh. *"Maybe we should call the police..."*

"NO!" Tyler shouted across the room, torn to pieces.

"I-I called Katie..." He said carefully, eyes everywhere else my body but my eyes now.

"So you *did* call the police." I spat darkly. Unsure what about all of this was so funny.

"Alexander!" He hissed through a breath, not angry, just distressed. "She's not coming. I need you to tell me everything. Please. Please, Alexander, Please I need you to tell me what you did. Who else is hurt?"

I saw Leonel's name written in red across a black plane. But I did not speak it. Tyler has no idea who he is.

In a daze, I told him everything. And I started with my birthday. And then Halloween night. And The Empty. And then about The Wayback and how he's tortured me. About what happened to Jonah. And last, about Leonel. Who he was to me and what I did to him.

The pair sat and listened as another starless sky turned above us.

They were deeply afraid of me afterward. Both for different reasons. Johnny was afraid that they were harboring a murderer and chewed his nails down so much the tips of his fingers turned pink. And Tyler was afraid that I had lost my head.

I told him that he was exactly right.

When there was, truly, nothing else left to say, Tyler sighed like he needed a drink and threw himself right beside me at the foot of his bed.

The room was quiet for about as long as I'd spoken. In the quiet, I thought of nothing. I just stared at the carpet and recalled the last time I was here.

He asked Johnny to leave and took me into the bathroom to help me get cleaned up. Before Johnny left, he pulled Tyler in and asked him,

"Is it safe? To be left alone with him—?" cutting his sentence short when he saw the raw look in my eye.

I stripped down to my boxers and sat on the toilet while Tyler took cotton balls damp with peroxide to my skin. It stung for a little while, but he was delicate. Surgical. By the end of it he'd wasted the entire bag and half a roll of toilet paper. Turned out I wasn't as dinged up as I thought. Most of the blood *was* Leonels.

He questioned me the entire time. Not lecturing, not prodding—just dialogue. And dialogue invites engagement. I couldn't help but answer everything in horrific detail. To my surprise he managed to stomach it.

But every time I said The Wayback's name... he looked over his shoulder like there was something standing behind him he couldn't see.

I didn't feel anything there. But maybe that's because I was too in my head to really notice.

"What else have I caused?" I whispered, lurching into myself. He stood up and pressed my head into his side in an awkward hug.

He bent down to his knees and looked me in the eyes,

"It hurts me, really, to see you like this after all this time.

"I've been so caught up with work. Last I hear you're locked in your house and you won't speak to anyone... And now..."

"When does this end?" I cried, one hand covering the whole of my face.

Tyler, innocent, said to me, "It ends with you. If you chose it. And keep choosing it every day until it sticks. And it won't be worth it right away, and you'll tell yourself you're bad and you don't deserve it the entire time, but I promise you, it ends with you. **You** become what **you** choose to be."

I broke our gaze and dragged my hands down my face after I wiped my tears away.

"Are you mad at me?" I asked, tone flat despite feeling so desperate on the inside.

He scoffed. Bewildered. But he knew that the question came from a hard place. He answered truthfully.

"I'm not mad at you, Alex. I've been low, too, so, I get it. Kind of. I'm not happy about it, but I understand. We're only humans just... trying to cope. Sometimes we just snap. Hurt people hurt people."

A lump had formed in my throat. *"I'm not human."* I croaked.

He frowned. "You have to stop believing stuff like that. You're not a monster. I know this isn't what you want to be. This isn't who you are."

I pinched my eyes shut and crushed my tears. He stood.

"You can stay here tonight."

He squeezed my shoulder before he frowned and left me alone to get dressed, closing the door behind him.

I sat there broken and imagined Jonah sitting on the floor where he was, those pensive eyes I missed so much tearing me to shreds.

He put his hand on my knee and frowned too.

While I dreamt, a cherub emerged from the ceiling in the form of an infant, illuminated by a halo of neon blue light. His descent was like that of a feather. Soft, slow, and mathematically divine.

It stopped inches from my face, sniffing not at my body but something else. Something wretched inside me. He wept at the sight of it, tears fallen silent and gleaming in the middle of the night. He passed his holy judgement onto this wretchedness, saying,

"Your ideas will cost you everything."

A heat flash woke me up and the angel was gone. But the sound of his whispers lingered in the hall. Frail, woeful, and rehearsed—like the hymns of a funeral procession.

I sat up, hot and sweaty, bands of hair slicked to my face and ears, and slowly lowered my head in grief. The air danced in an unseen number of presences. All far older than numbers could date. Their bodies drank all of the light. Devoured it like a bottomless pit's unquenchable thirst. Not one photon to spare.

I wasn't afraid. They've been around long before I have. If anything, I'm their guest. But there was one there amongst them. Something wicked and uninvited that watched me from the crowd. I did not know where, exactly. I could feel him everywhere.

When my feet touched the carpet I could feel gravity dragging me down in ways it never had before. My movements weren't as swift. My bones, no longer as dense. The difference was quite a shock. And worst of all, my spine ached from the middle. As I stepped forward I felt something under my gut kick and squirm. I moaned like a startled lamb—and clasped my hand over my mouth with a sharp gasp.

I ran to the bathroom and flicked the switch. *FLICK. FLICK. FLICK.* No matter what it wouldn't work.

A final one just in case the power returned. *FLICK.*

Stressed, I ran the faucet and brought my lips to the running water and drank to stop the lightheadedness from settling in further. *Cold, forgiving, water.* I ran my hands under the stream and rinsed my face.

When I peered into the mirror a horror awaited me. My mother's reflection stared back at me. And behind her stood a man made of red smoke, with long black claws pointed at her.

It was clear to me then that I was that man of smoke. That wretched thing inside of her. And I was not a man. I don't know what I was, but it was apparent to the both of us that I wasn't human, and I wasn't Good, either.

We locked eyes through the glass, hers wide and tearful suddenly. She clutched the edges of the sink so hard I saw the veins in her hands. I noticed that everything about her seemed... off. Her hair was dyed jet-black. Her face was softer—younger. And her body was much less developed. Her arms were all skinny and her shoulders were dainty and defined like a ballerina. And that hummingbird tattoo on her arm that she's had as long as I can remember wasn't there anymore. None of her tattoos, in fact.

I waved my hand and commanded her to turn around and face me with a voice modular and broken, like that of some evil analog machine.

In her eyes I saw greater pain. A lifetime marred by darkness and ruin well into her years. Faces of people who shape her in one way or another. People she would love and lose. I raised my hand and pointed a finger at her, talon aimed right at her navel.

"It ends with me." I said. Both accusing and affirmative.

Hell flames engulfed me in a sudden blaze. Everything about me and my crooked ways to be eviscerated by the flames of Saint Michael's sword. I howled from the deepest pit of existence, hand above my head as if begging God to watch me as I sang a swan song that tore out of me in one final act of love.

Priscilla buried herself in the corner with her arms clutched over her head, to tune out the sound of my screams, for she could not endure it.

"What was that?" Tyler groaned. Too exhausted to sound urgent. His voice stirred me to consciousness. I wasn't sure what sound he referred to. I sat at the foot of his bed, sore and beat. Eyes heavy, I sat there staring blindly. *What time is it?* He thought.

"It's Midnight."

He turned to me, half-conscious on his belly, and slapped a hand on my head like I was a snooze-button.

"Did I wake you up?" He yawned.

"I wasn't asleep."

He moved his hand from my head to my shoulder, and tried to tug at me so I would face him. But I stiffened. I did not want to look away from the dancing lights on his wall. They called to me, *dance, keep dancing,* but I did not wish to join them. Only watch as I unmake.

Tyler seemed not to notice them. *"Alexander..."* he whined with his face in his pillow.

"Go back to sleep." I commanded in a whisper and wave of the finger. And he fell into a silent slumber. I looked at him from the corner of my eye and then I left.

The Santa Ana winds had passed for the night. Another insidious coincidence. But one that I endorsed. *I hate the wind.* The night was still as it was silent. I stepped out of darkness into more darkness.

I was headed 'home', though I really, truly, did not want to return. But I had nowhere else to go. To keep myself from walking with shame, I listened to the crunch of gravel under my heel and pictured myself walking alone on the moon.

"What I would give to speak to you on a night like this." I said into the air, eyes lingering on the empty spot next to me.

More silence.

"I don't have anything *to* give, actually. But I'm glad, in a way, I guess. Maybe it's better that you don't have to be here for any of this. I wonder what you would think of me now."

Nothing.

I continued down Huntington Drive, feeling a different kind of light. Not happiness—oh no, definitely not that—but a brief release from the constant, dragging weight of my pain. Despite all that has happened, I walked briskly, like someone with nothing to lose. And I guess, through a breath, I realized all the things I feared would happen already had. At least that's over now. Behind my human face, I smiled—just a crack. Not with joy, but with ill temper.

click click. The sidewalk stretched far out into the distance. So far that I could not see all the way to the end. Just blurry lights into black. *click click.*

click click.

click click.

click click.

click click.

click click.

click—

click. . .

click—

At the last second I decided to take the Shelley Street alley and walk home from there. I guess I was looking for more trouble. Maybe even a thrill to wake me up inside. I glanced at sketchy cars and the silhouettes of men lamed by society as I crept.

None of them saw me. It was like I wasn't there at all.

The mouth of the alley is right across the street from the house, between the 7-Eleven and the evangelical church. There I noticed that the front door of my Nanna's was wide open, and there she sat on the porch pinching her sides—wondering if she was living in a nightmare.

I approached her.

The metal clang of the gate interrupted her prayer—her eyes flew to mine. She glowered at me. In an instant she stood up and into a lecture. On the porch she towered over me. I stood at the foot of the steps.

"Where'd you run off to, dammit!?"

I rudely curled my lip and glanced past her. She was the only thing between me and the front door, so I had no choice but to answer. I made sure to keep my hands tucked behind my back—so she wouldn't see the blood on my cuffs.

"I was at Leonel's."

"Who the hell is that?"

I shrank. She let out a sigh that cracked halfway through and turned into a sob. She covered her mouth with a fist and started blinking to keep the tears from breaking.

I didn't know how to react.

I asked, simply, "What is the matter now?"

She peeked at me, horrified. Starting to rock in place. I was beginning to worry—and cursed myself for having the desire for thrills in the alley.

"Well?" I urged.

Her face twisted from horror to anger. She pointed at me and screamed, *"What have you done!?"*

My stomach turned.

She barged down the steps toward me, *"I know what you said to your mother before you left!"* She accused through her teeth.

Oh no. My head started to spin—something in me began putting the pieces together before she even had the chance to tell me the rest.

"What happened?" I asked—breath sharp. Irene fanned her eyes and tried to speak, but she could not hold her composure. She shed three tears despite herself.

"You—!" She hicced, still pointing, *"You have the **Devil** in you, Nunu!"* She seemed almost shattered to say it. Like it was true, and she didn't hate me for it—she mourned.

*"You have the **Devil** in you!"*

I met her face to face, and looked her in the eyes as I asked again, shaking.

"Where is my mother?"

She pinched her eyes shut and hid her face behind her hair. I grabbed her by the arms and screamed, **"WHERE IS MY MOTHER!?"**

She burst into tears—completely utterly unreachable. *"You better pray that she makes it through the night! Because if I have to choose between her or the baby—God help me, I have to save the baby! I have to!"*

My chest tightened—I ran into the house, **"MOM!?" "MOM!?"**

I slammed to a stop when I saw that the tile where I had last seen her was stained with streaks of poorly mopped blood. Eyes wide in horror, I knew with certainty that this's got nothing to do with the devil.

It's me.

Me!

I ran as fast as I could.

But I hadn't a lick of strength to carry on.

I hadn't even made it half-way there by the time I had to stop running.

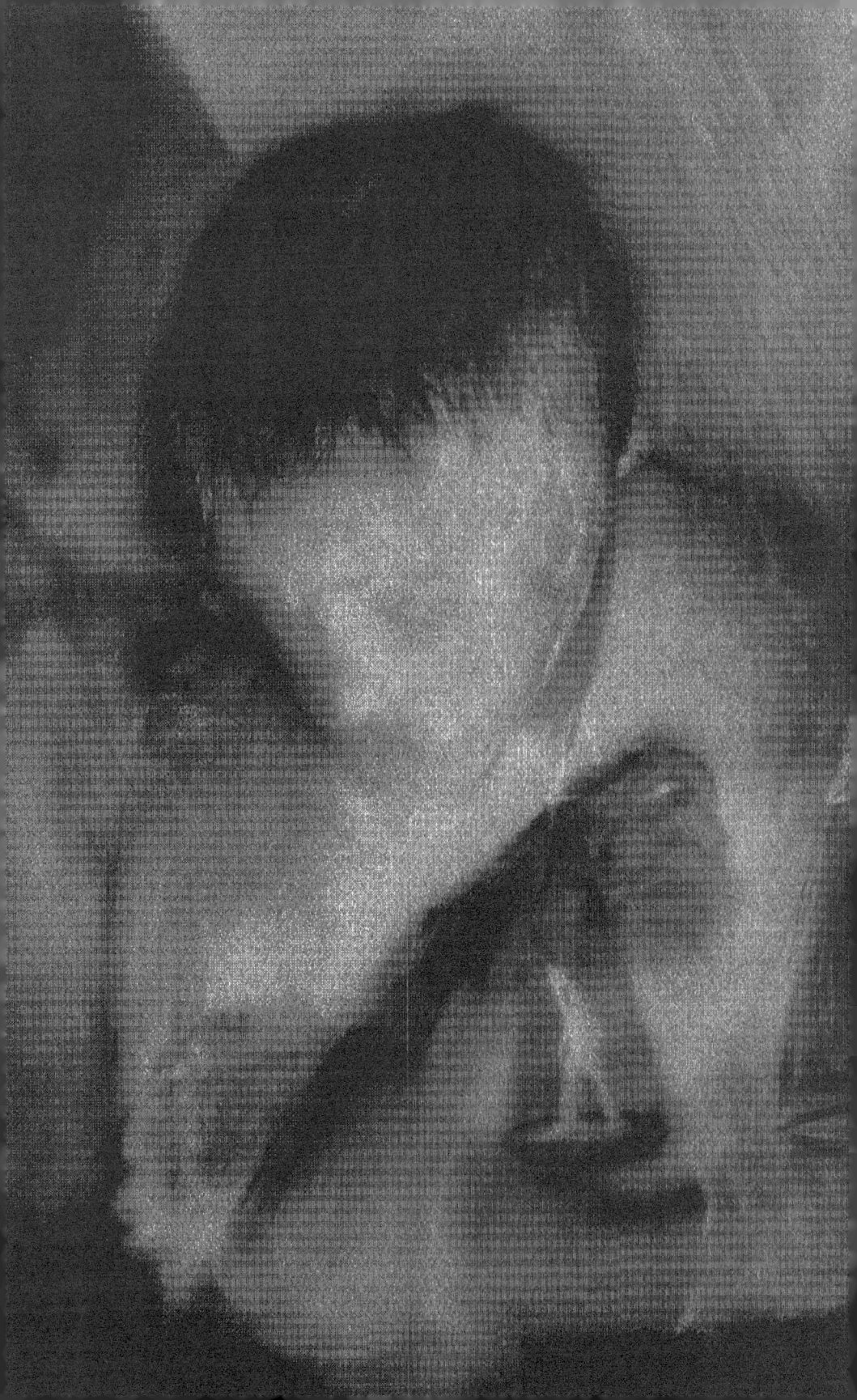

I ran all the way down Morant Boulevard onto Main Street,

And from there I walked......

And walked.....

And walked....

All the way down that same sidewalk.....

Until I reached San Gabriel Medical Center on Las Tunas Drive.

It took me two hours to get there on foot.

The only light in the room came from the patient monitor. Her face, frozen in agony, seemed to glow in the dark. Gently, I placed my hand atop her head and closed my eyes—trying to keep it together. I held my breath for a while, and then let go.

Tormented with guilt, I leaned over and pressed my forehead into hers, whispering,

"I hope you can forgive what I've done."

I stood there for a while. *I have absolutely nothing left.* Just the grisly reminder of what I'd said. And what a fucking tragedy—How deeply sorry I am for those words which struck her down, and how in my heart, I still mean it.

I threw myself into the blunt metal chair tucked behind the door, arms folded, slouching, and forcing myself to count every dreadful beat of her unborn child's heart through the cardiograph. And what an awful sound it is. Like a metronome ticking incessantly. Counting down the seconds until the doctors are forced to choose between *her* or *the baby!*

Irene made her priorities clear as crystal. I rocked back in fourth with my thumb in my teeth as the gravity of the situation choked me.

An hour of sound and nothing else passed. The suspense was excruciating. My eyes burned, but I kept them open. Being here, having to endure it, was my penance. I was whittled down to a toothpick by the hateful voice in my head that told me this is what I deserve.

But not her—Even if I think she's the worst mother ever—Even though she tore me apart atom by atom—She doesn't deserve this.

The monitor's pale light lit up every fragile detail of her face—I looked at the scar on her forehead and shed a single tear.

A wretched fever of sonder possessed me. I recalled the story of how she got that scar. I remembered it clearly—vividly—as if I was there to experience it with her.

She was around six or seven, sometime in the late eighties, playing a game with her father and hiding under the kitchen table. Happy, giggling, innocent. Irene burst in, calling for her, and startled her so badly she jumped up—smacking her head against the underside of the table hard enough to split the skin right open. My eyes began to water. I imagined her cries. I imagined her in her father's arms. Her father who died tragically of an overdose that same year.

And even though he was gone, and her smile stopped meeting her eyes, she still sang George Michael for the people in town and clung to Irene's legs just as she had before saying, *"I love you, I love you,"* over and over again. Only this time marred by the idea that one day Irene, too, would leave her forever.

She stopped telling people goodbye and insisted on saying *"See you later,"* instead, because goodbye was the last thing she told her father and it was, indeed, a goodbye.

Maybe she wished she had told him *see you later* instead. Maybe she thought she might've caused it.

A superstition she passed onto me and my brothers. I remember when I was a child and she sat me down before school, on her knees, at my level, and said to me,

"My baby, never tell anyone goodbye. Always say see you later."

I never tell anyone goodbye. Just as she told me to. I pinched my eyes shut to crush the tears.

The cardiograph throbbed with relentless rhythm:

WOMWOMWOMWOMWOMWOMWOMWOMWOMWOM

Its mechanical breath clawed away at my heart, razor blades against glass. From the mouth of the machine a strip of graph paper spilled out in slow procession, charting the infant's tiny heartbeat in looping peaks and valleys.

I stared at the spool in agony, not wishing it any harm, but definitely holding a preference.

WOMWOMWOMWOM—I wanted to plug my ears and drown out the sound. But I didn't. I just whispered to myself again,

"Alexander Hunsucker, you deserve this."

Even unconscious, she looked tortured. Maybe it's the existentialist in me, but as she lay there, hooked to wires, tubes, and machines—still as a body already gone, I didn't see her as my mother anymore. She was just Priscilla.

A woman born into this world with broken arms. Who's mortal, fallible, and trying her hardest.

Even if that is to no avail. Even if it's not enough.

And in that I saw she and I weren't so different in the grand scheme of everything.

Oh God. I have been a fool.

My fingers stirred in my clenched fist.

"Mom..." "Mom!" "Please wake up..."

WOMWOMWOMWOMWOMWOMWOMWOMWOMWOM

"You have to..."

WOMWOMWOMWOMWOMWOMWOMWOMWOMWOM

"I didn't want this. Certainly not at all. I always just wanted you. It was always you. It was my mistake, tethering my life to you. Every choice I had ever made, I made because of you.

"You never asked that of me. I know it. But... you never needed to. You were the woman who was supposed to save me. Instead, I let you destroy me. I'm not blaming you for all my struggles, but they are born of the choices you've made, and worst of all, the choices you never had it in you to make.

"Every bad stream in my life flowed from your river. Everything is askew. This wasn't my fault, but now I stand before it as if I'm the one who must answer for it.

"I didn't alienate me. I didn't neglect and abuse me. I didn't push my head into a doorframe and throw myself out into the streets at two in the morning. I'm not gonna stand here and tell you every horrible thing this family has done to me, I just hoped at some point you would reflect.

"Just as I have. Just as I always do.

"I do love you mother. That is true. The only thing I know to be true. I love you and you failed me.

"You've never been the woman that I needed you to be. I hoped that one day you would see. And maybe you'd even understand. And we'd be closer. And my love wouldn't have to collapse into scary monsters a n d friendly ghosts.

"It could become a life with you.

"I chased you for years... dreamt of us, a family again, all my youth... and when I thought I had finally reached you, it took three months for you to unravel on me.

"And things just got worse and worse. And then you let Adriana and Irene throw me out into the streets, and I was homeless and I tried to—!" I winced. Quiet for a moment. Crumbling. Fists shaking.

WOMWOMWOMWOMWOMWOMWOMWOMWOMWOM

"You cried and plead I return. And you promised me that you'd never hurt me again. Your words were not hollow then, I know it. I know you never wanted to cause me pain. But you did. You caused a fervid pain within me. You broke me and broke me again and just kept on doing it until there was nothing left.

"You killed your son. You killed me.

"In every moment. In every choice. In every word.

"I've been crying alone at night for a long time. And I cry harder because you're not here.

"I miss you. I miss your gaze. Even now, I hope that one day you could hold me when I'm out of the race.

"But this isn't looking good, mommy. This isn't... looking good.

"Love, for us, is just... collapsing.

"I dream of all we could have had. Even though it wasn't much. You were enough for me.

"I don't want you to feel pain. I don't want you to die. And I don't want you to think that I hate you. I don't hate you.

"But you've hurt me so badly, I'm barely hanging on.

"I had always believed you could make the right choices. If you leave... I'll never get to see if I was right about that. . .

"Mommy... Mommy, I'm scared. What if I lose you? What will become of me when this night passes? Could courtesy and valor reside in me as it once had when I was young? Or has that, like all hope, vanished completely?"

I began to weep. I ran over to her bedside and got down on my knees in prayer, begging God to hear me, just this once even if it had to mean never again.

1. *Spare her, Oh God, for the waters have come up to her neck.*
2. *I come before you, worn and thin, crying out for help.*
3. *We are afflicted with hatred in our hearts.*
4. *My eyes search endlessly for some kind of grace, but it is to no avail.*
5. *I am immobilized.*
6. *You, God, know our folly; our pain is not hidden from you.*
7. *My deepest shame is not hidden from you. I say again, father, I am immobilized.*
8. *Let my tongue not wag in vain.*
9. *Let not my mother suffer on account of me.*
10. *Let my words mar me alone. Make me their vessel, burn me hollow if you must.*
11. *Do not sentence her to death because of my mistakes.*
12. *Rescue her from my darkness which hath come upon her, my Lord.*
13. *For she is my maker. My deepest wound. My greater pain.*
14. *Take my power from my hands. Take away my very name. Take my life if you must, but not hers.*
15. *If I was ever your child, God, then I ask you—let mine not be the voice that silences hers forever.*
16. *In the shadow of her sorrow, at grief so deep, I would remain forever to buy her another chance.*
17. *If it is true, if I am darkness, strike me down where I stand.*
18. *I don't want to be a beast. I will not be a prophet if the cost is my mother   and my heart.*
19. *She is my first love, she is my first heartbreak. She is my mother of sighs.*
20. *And I am The. . .*

WOMWOMWOMWOMWOMWOMWOMWOMWOMWOM—